MW00610120

THE BOOK OF ISAIAH

THE BOOK OF ISAIAH

A NEW TRANSLATION WITH INTERPRETIVE KEYS FROM THE BOOK OF MORMON

AVRAHAM GILEADI

Deseret Book Company
Salt Lake City, Utah

©1988 Avraham Gileadi

All rights reserved. No part of this book may be reproduced in any form or by any means without permission in writing from the publisher, Deseret Book Company, P.O. Box 30178, Salt Lake City, Utah 84130.

Deseret Book is a registered trademark of Deseret Book Company.

First printing in paperbound edition, September 1989

Library of Congress Cataloging-in-Publication Data

Bible. O.T. Isaiah. English. Gileadi. 1988.
   The Book of Isaiah.

   Bibliography: p.
   Includes index.
   1. Bible.   O.T. Isaiah — Criticism, interpretation,
etc. I. Gileadi, Avraham. II. Title.
BS1513.G55   1988   224'.1052   88-3716
ISBN 0-87579-076-3 (hardbound ed.)
ISBN 0-87579-279-0 (paperbound ed.)

Printed in the United States of America

10   9   8   7   6   5   4

CONTENTS

FOREWORD

Ellis T. Rasmussen
Dean Emeritus, Religious Instruction
Brigham Young University

Avraham Gileadi here gives us a straightforward, clear, and beautifully phrased translation of the book of Isaiah with an interpretive introduction that shows uncommon knowledge and insight into that masterwork of Hebrew prophecy. The Latter-day Saint community urgently needs a work of this high caliber: it combines in a single volume the means for understanding Isaiah.

Some have observed, anciently and in our day, that Isaiah's poetic prophecy is not easy to understand. Nephi said that Isaiah spoke many things that were hard for many of his people to understand (2 Nephi 25:1)—and Nephi's people still spoke the language Isaiah spoke! In New Testament times a missionary asked someone who was reading Isaiah whether he understood it, and he responded, "How can I, except some man should guide me?" (Acts 8:27-31). I think this response is typical. Avraham Gileadi provides such a penetrating study and commentary to guide the reader through many of the more difficult parts of Isaiah's prophecies with relative ease.

Gileadi has called Isaiah an apocalyptic book, and this is so in two related ways: it pertains to events of the end time and to the ultimate purposes of God; and it brings hidden things to light, things kept from the world at large. But an apocalyptic book is not easily understood. Gileadi has turned to the Book of Mormon to discover a context for Isaiah that is thoroughly Latter-day Saint. He has brought Isaiah's writings to a level of understanding to which each of us can relate.

Jesus himself calls Isaiah's words "great" and tells the people to search them diligently (3 Nephi 23:1). And Moroni, writing some appendices to his father's book, echoes, "Search the prophecies of Isaiah" (Mormon 8:23). New Testament writers quote Isaiah more than seventy times, far more than all the other prophets combined.

Our own dispensation was opened with a recitation of the eleventh chapter of Isaiah by an angel, with the promise that the prophecy was about to be fulfilled (Joseph Smith–History 1:40). We can dismiss the relevance of Isaiah's message to our people only to our hurt. We face the challenge of understanding Isaiah as an integral part of our heritage and obligation.

Fortunately, Isaiah can be understood. Philip, an early missionary, joined an Ethiopian in his chariot and explained the significance of Isaiah 53 as they traveled together. As a result, when they came to a suitable place of water, the Ethiopian asked to be baptized (Acts 8:26–38). Nephi asserted that the Jews understood Isaiah, as do those "taught after the manner of the things of the Jews" (2 Nephi 25:5). He also said the words of Isaiah "are plain unto those that are filled with the spirit of prophecy" (2 Nephi 25:4). Probably not many readers have either a Jewish background or an education in the manner of prophesying in the Old Testament; and perhaps not many who could have the gift of prophecy, a gift of the Holy Ghost, really exercise it. But help from someone like Philip, who had one or more of those tools of understanding, is available.

Gileadi has a better set of intellectual and spiritual tools than most other scriptural scholars I know. He possesses a background gained through Judaic studies in Israel, religious and scholarly pursuits at Brigham Young University, and graduate work in biblical languages and literature with noted conservative biblical scholars at the Toronto School of Theology. These educational opportunities have enabled him, over many years of intense study and research, to develop and sharpen his talents and exercise his spiritual intuition in unfolding prophetic literature. Although the peculiarities in literary idiom and structure in the prophetic genre are not readily understood by every reader, or indeed by every scholar, Gileadi has attained a fine balance of inspiration and intellect in interpreting and translating Isaiah.

I consider his contribution helpful in several ways. First, the translation is in modern language, easily comprehensible, poetically written. Because it is "after the manner of our language, that [we] might come to understanding" (D&C 1:24), we more readily grasp its message. Second, the translation is true to the Hebrew. It faithfully abides by the strictures of the translating process, putting the reader at ease about meanings and concepts. Third, the interpretive keys are well-founded, originating in the Book of Mormon, and considerably expanded by discoveries made when applying these keys during years of study. Finally, the interpretive keys approach the book of Isaiah as a whole; they interrelate and correlate all parts in order to clarify any one part of Isaiah's message. These aspects of Gileadi's work make his a unique and powerful contribution.

The genius of the Hebrew manner of prophesying that is here set out is that the prophets, in communicating truths, speak to peoples of many time periods. Nephi was able to liken Isaiah's scriptures to his own people for their "profit and learning" (1 Nephi 19:23). He also asserted that they could be likened to "all the house of Israel" (2 Nephi 6:5). Again, he said to his readers, "Ye may liken them unto you and unto all men" (2 Nephi 11:8). Gileadi likens or applies the teachings of Isaiah to us in the latter days, and in so doing gives us an interpretation that is certainly justified both linguistically and doctrinally. His may not be the only interpretation possible, and he himself maintains that there exist many levels for interpreting Isaiah's prophecies. But in relating them to us, he has focused on the one context that most enables us to apply Isaiah's prophecies to ourselves. He has discovered structures and literary patterns that point to the latter days as the main thrust of Isaiah's message. This, in my opinion, is the greatest merit of his work.

As we "seek learning, even by study and also by faith" (D&C 88:118), we, by our own intelligence, as enlightened by the Holy Spirit, can determine what is good and true. All men have this capacity. The testimonials of many readers since the first, smaller edition of this work have been significant. Professor R. K. Harrison of Wycliffe College in Toronto commends Gileadi's translation as one that "reflects closely the nuances of Isaiah's thought" and recognizes his discovery of "parallelisms of entire groups of chapters and subjects" that by their structure present dramatic evidence of the unity of the book of Isaiah—while the trend of many scholars has been to show that it is made up of fragments from many authors. Harrison goes so far as to say that Gileadi's work "will render obsolete almost all the speculations of Isaiah scholars over the last one hundred years" of the popular *higher criticism* of the Bible.

Hugh Nibley considers Gileadi "the only Latter-day Saint scholar I know of who is thoroughly prepared to enter into serious and

proper study and teaching of the works of Isaiah.'' He says further
of the work:

> It gives the reader a sense of intimacy with Isaiah which is
> unique. The discussions are stimulating and thought-provoking.
> The work . . . is not controversial and inspires reflection rather
> than contention. Above all it leads the reader into a spiritual state
> of mind that brings Isaiah to life.

Professor David Noel Freedman of the University of Michigan
finds Avraham Gileadi's work on the literary unity, message,
and intent of the book of Isaiah impressive and regards him as
''eminently qualified'' and ''far in advance of others'' in the work
of analyzing Isaiah. He believes ''Dr. Gileadi has achieved or will
achieve a major breakthrough in the investigation of a book of such
complexity as the book of Isaiah.''

A literary critic, Arthur Henry King, president of the LDS
London Temple, commends Gileadi's ''sense of style'' and his ''right
totality'' in the new English rendition of Isaiah's prophecies by this
''fastidiously and meticulously careful scholar.'' He concludes:

> It is my testimony that this man has been brought forward
> and trained in a time to help those inside the Church into Isaiah,
> and those outside the Church, Jew and Gentile, through Isaiah
> into the Church.

Professor Peter C. Craigie, prominent Old Testament scholar
and formerly academic vice-president of the University of Calgary,
finds Gileadi's study ''an original and creative approach to old problems.'' Professor Ronald Youngblood of Bethel Theological Seminary
thinks ''Dr. Gileadi has clearly demonstrated his mastery of the book
of Isaiah and of the scholarly literature dealing with it.''

Professor F. D. Wasden of Educational Administration at
Brigham Young University, who enrolled in a class on Isaiah taught
by Gileadi, says:

> Seldom have I been so stimulated by gospel study as in this
> class. What a pleasure it has been to be confronted with an
> experience which develops testimony and scholarship at the same
> instant and to recognize that they are not mutually exclusive
> attributes. Brother Gileadi is a genuine individual as well as a

superb teacher. He shows concern for the spiritual welfare of each class member. . . . Perhaps the most significant element to be mentioned is the overriding assurance that the mentor is motivated to excellence by a firm and ever present testimony of the gospel.

My own observations over the years that I have been associated with Avraham Gileadi, in producing explanatory footnotes in the LDS edition of the Bible, and in researching the Hebrew antecedents and renditions of Hebrew idioms in the Book of Mormon, lead me to conclude that much of the teamwork we accomplished in that area would have been inadequate, if not impossible, were it not for his valuable and sensitive contributions. This latest work of his, the translation of Isaiah with interpretive keys, is undoubtedly his greatest contribution thus far to our scholars and students, our Saints and converts. It is my testimony that the reading of this work in the spirit of inquiry will be a rewarding intellectual and spiritual experience, and very likely your search of Isaiah, admonished by Jesus, will have at last begun.

PREFACE

I was born in the Netherlands during World War II. In the course of the war, my father, who served in the Dutch resistance, helped a New Zealand pilot escape to Britain. After the war, many emigrated from wartorn Europe to new lands of opportunity. Although my father prospered, idealism led him to emigrate to New Zealand. There I grew up, participating in my teens in a successful rock and jazz group. Haunted by my spiritual childhood in the Netherlands, however, I broke with that subculture, seeking again my roots as a Catholic.

I underwent a period of introspection, such as the literature of the Catholic church encourages, reevaluating my priorities and internalizing spiritual principles. Becoming religiously active and involved, I yet sensed a lack of spiritual fulfillment. Soon, Israel's history in the Old Testament became the focus of my attention. Recognizing what I believed to be a partial fulfillment of prophecy in the modern state of Israel, I felt a desire to participate in it. In 1968, in a second, radical break with the past, I left New Zealand to settle in Israel.

Life in Israel soon involved me deeply in the Old Testament and in its religious offspring, Judaism. Judaism attracted me because of the unique manner in which the Jews view the Law and the Prophets. Among the Jews, I felt a depth of understanding that as a Gentile, I had not hitherto known. While the analytical manner of the Jews was to me highly unusual, I could not fault it. It penetrated the words of scripture in such a way as to bring out an entirely new context that lay behind the words. I began to understand the New Testament differently also. I saw in Jesus' parables of the two sons broad allusions to the two houses of Israel, Judah and Joseph. I recognized in Paul's early years as a Christian the Nazirite vow. I, too, took the vow.

While still in New Zealand, I had determined, simply by studying a map of Israel, to which place I would go to live in Israel. On reaching Israel, I took an intensive course in Hebrew and began to study Judaism. When opportunity arose, I located at Jezreel, the place I had determined. This place turned out to be an agricultural settlement, unique in Israel, for Jewish immigrants from South Africa, Australia, and New Zealand. I had worked there a year when, on visiting the library, the librarian handed me the Book of Mormon and suggested I read it. I declined. At her insistence (her words were, "This is for you; you must read this!"), I took the book to be polite. I read it out of curiosity.

The Book of Mormon at once filled many gaps in the picture I had formed in my mind from reading the Old and the New Testaments. Many times I experienced a sense of spiritual joy, which, I soon realized, was the influence of the Holy Ghost. Although the Book of Mormon contained new ideas, things I had not imagined (such as Zion on the American continent), still I knew the book was true. The things with which I had difficulty I resolved by praying and fasting. I was determined, above all, to be baptized into The Church of Jesus Christ of Latter-day Saints.

To my dismay, although I pursued every possible avenue, I could find no sign of the Church in Israel. When all proved fruitless, I prayed about what course to follow. It then dawned on me that I must continue to *study the manner of the Jews* until the Lord would permit me to be baptized. Thereafter, I studied Hebrew even more earnestly. I took instruction in Judaism from several rabbis. Taking this new, though paradoxical course, I felt at peace, conscious of being wholly in accord with God's will. I saw the law of Moses as a necessary schoolmaster to the fulness of the gospel I would some-day embrace. My studies took me to an orthodox religious kibbutz, at which time I was formally received into the Jewish faith. I became an Israeli citizen. I truly felt with Ruth: "Thy people shall be my people, and thy God my God" (Ruth 1:16). The climax of my life as an orthodox Jew came when I studied at a rabbinic school in Jerusalem. My closest friends were orthodox Jews who nonetheless believed, as I did, that Jesus is the Messiah.

When I had thus fully absorbed the principle behind the Jewish manner of studying the scriptures, I discovered the LDS church. I met brethren evidently imbued with the Spirit of God—they stood out from all other people I had met. There followed some weeks of intense questioning by me, rather than the regular missionary discussions. The day I was baptized I left rabbinic school—one of the most memorable experiences of my life—and entered an entirely new phase. Although I was now a member of the Church, fulfilled spiritually in a way I had not hitherto known, I would nonetheless carry with me the manner of the Jews.

In 1973, visiting the United States for the purpose of receiving my temple endowment, I stayed to study at Brigham Young University. I grew acquainted with men such as Ellis Rasmussen, Hugh Nibley, and Arthur Henry King, men who became longtime mentors and friends. I met my wife, Cathy Sweet, an American Jewish convert to the Church; we pursued degrees at Brigham Young University. Here I was hired to produce footnotes clarifying translation problems in the Old Testament for the Latter-day Saint edition of the Bible; in addition, I worked on the Hebrew translation of LDS texts.

For my master's thesis I set myself the challenge of making Isaiah intelligible in English, yet true to the Hebrew. I completed a partial translation of Isaiah (chapters 1–29), satisfied it could be done. I finished this new translation of Isaiah during my Ph.D. program, working from the Hebrew Masoretic Text and comparing the Dead Sea Scroll of Isaiah and Septuagint Version. I used the best dictionaries and lexicons available. Although I was fluent in Hebrew (I had by now also taught Hebrew at BYU for a number of years), I nonetheless used lexical tools constantly in order to catch every nuance of meaning in the original language. As part of this process, I compared closely twelve of the most authoritative versions of the Bible. After completing my doctoral studies, I published my translation of Isaiah under the title *The Apocalyptic Book of Isaiah*. That book sold five thousand copies and has received favorable reviews both in and out of the Church.

My approach in *The Apocalyptic Book of Isaiah* was to write a short interpretive key that would suit equally the Latter-day Saint and non-Latter-day Saint reader. That approach was not my own. My doctoral chairman, Hugh Nibley, had earlier challenged me to interpret Isaiah according to the way the supporting scriptures— the Book of Mormon and the Doctrine and Covenants—interpret Isaiah, but to do this entirely from internal literary evidence. Now, my learning in the manner of the Jews would be put to the test: Isaiah is the most difficult book in the Bible.

At this point, I sought out and studied under Professor R. K. Harrison of Toronto, Canada, a renowned Old Testament scholar noted for his conservative theological position. He introduced me to a major literary structure of Isaiah, which I analyzed as part of my doctoral dissertation. In the course of my analysis, I became aware more than ever of the complexity and sophistication of the book of Isaiah. Indeed, without my training in the manner of the Jews, as well as my knowledge of the gospel, I would have made little progress in literary analysis. The literary tools the Jews use are not had in Christian universities, nor do the Jews possess the insights the Book of Mormon and Doctrine and Covenants provide.

Since then, over the course of the years I have devoted to studying Isaiah, I have discovered many literary features, each of which helps explain Isaiah's theological message. During this time, I formulated a holistic methodology I find equally effective in the book of Isaiah, the Book of Mormon, and other scriptural texts. This methodology consists of, first, structural analysis, which examines blocks of material, such as chapters, groups of chapters, and overarching ideas, as well as forms of speech, poems, chiasms, and parallelisms; second, typological analysis, which examines patterns, types, cycles, phenomena, and contexts; and third, rhetorical analysis, which examines language, definitions, terms, motifs, code names, linking ideas, and imagery. This three-fold method, which lends itself naturally to the study of the scriptures, incorporates the manner of the Jews without limiting itself to it. It forms the approach of the Introduction in this book.

My commitment to the book of Isaiah results not merely from seeing the fruits of applying this literary methodology but from the realization that Isaiah's message concerns every Latter-day Saint. The fact that the average Latter-day Saint has little awareness of this message leads me to conclude that the best good I can now achieve is to share what I have learned. I leave it to the reader to judge its worth.

Acknowledgments

While part of this work consists of my translation of Isaiah, previously published as *The Apocalyptic Book of Isaiah* (Provo, Utah: Hebraeus Press, 1982), the Introduction consists largely of newly written material. This new material is based on a talk first published as "Isaiah: Four Latter-day Keys to an Ancient Book," in *Isaiah and the Prophets*, edited by Monte S. Nyman (Provo, Utah: Brigham Young University Religious Studies Series, 1984), which I use with permission; on material recorded on audiocassettes as *Book of Mormon Keys to Understanding Isaiah* (Salt Lake City: Covenant Recordings, 1986); on material recorded on the video series *The Message of Isaiah* (Orem, Utah: Media America, 1986); and on the "Apocalyptic Key" in the first edition of the translation.

Producing this book required much support from friends and colleagues, who rendered counsel and advice, material help, and other expertise equal to the complexities of publishing such a technical piece. Working closely with them has been a warm and rewarding experience, creating moments of joy and building lasting affections and mutual respect. Just as a need would arise in this or that aspect of the work, someone would be there to provide the help or counsel required. Long before the project was completed, I felt that it was no longer my own. My appreciation for all who have assisted goes far beyond what they contributed. I have learned to love them for what they are.

Among the many I would like to thank are Don E. Norton and John D. Wolverton, who edited the early stages of the manuscript; Robin Mason and MaryJan Gay, who typed and corrected subsequent drafts; Arthur Henry King, who gave advice on composing the Introduction; Linda Hunter Adams, Dennis J. Packard, and my wife, Cathy, who made helpful editorial suggestions; Ellis T. Rasmussen, who wrote the Foreword and provided counsel on doctrinal aspects; Linda Hunter Adams and Karl F. Batdorff of the College of Humanities Publications Center, Brigham Young University, who checked sources and typeset the book; Patricia Stokes, Shirley Warren, and Deborah Allen, who proofread; Philip W. White, who did the pasteups; Melvin R. Smith and Lisa Roper, who computerized the translation and compiled the Index of Terms; the Keter Foundation (P.O. Box 1312, Provo, Utah, 84603), a nonprofit corporation that supports the preparing and publishing of select Latter-day Saint books; Howard A. Christy and Louise Williams of Brigham Young University Scholarly Publications, which provided editorial and administrative support; Richard L. Erickson, who designed the book, and Suzanne Brady, who managed the project, both of Deseret Book.

INTRODUCTION:
INTERPRETIVE KEYS

Isaiah's message vitally concerns all the Lord's people, including the Latter-day Saints. The Book of Mormon urges us to study Isaiah and also gives four keys for doing so. I call them keys to a *sealed book*, because without them Isaiah's writings, in effect, remain sealed—almost impossible for anyone to understand. I draw this analogy with a sealed book deliberately, because sealed books are supposed to reveal the events of the last days. When we apply these Book of Mormon keys to Isaiah, there unfolds from his writings just such a vision. This vision makes Isaiah's writings the guidebook they are meant to be—a consolation in troubled times for all who understand them.

The four Book of Mormon keys settle once and for all the question we often ask ourselves: Can anyone understand Isaiah? I answer a resounding yes! By this I do not mean that we will comprehend Isaiah's words unreservedly, that Isaiah will hold no surprises for us. I do mean emphatically, however, that we will comprehend Isaiah's message for our time, that we will understand many details of the picture he presents. This message and picture, and the means by which Isaiah communicates them, may nonetheless vary from what we might suppose. Our past experience with Isaiah has disappointed us—we have read his words but have not understood them. When we apply the Book of Mormon keys, we should expect something different from what we experienced before.

Nephi introduces two keys and so does Jesus. Both quote from Isaiah at length before they introduce them. Nephi's keys I call the *spirit of prophecy* and the *letter of prophecy*. These are analogous to the spirit and the letter of the law—they complement one another. Jesus' keys consist of *searching* the text and studying *types*. Types means that what has happened in the past will recur: Israel's

1

history repeats itself in the last days. To convey his message, Isaiah employs biblical types in a well-defined, prefigured pattern.

Applying these four keys reveals how proximately we live to the time Isaiah's prophecies will see fulfillment. Today we clearly discern many parts of the picture Isaiah presents, so near are we to the time. Much of that picture deals with political and spiritual realities existing in our world. Much of it condemns evil practices among the Lord's people. But amid so much that is condemnatory in tone, we always sense that Isaiah holds out hope for those who repent. His book serves as a call to such repentance. Some qualify for salvation who, influenced by Isaiah's message, recognize their error and renew their faith. With his promise of a glorious salvation on earth—unequaled by any of Israel's other prophets—Isaiah balances his harsh indictments.

I make no apology that Isaiah's prophecies address us. If in the course of applying the four Book of Mormon keys we discover that Isaiah has seen our day and describes it perfectly, that, to me, would be all the more cause for us to familiarize ourselves with his words. There must be a good reason why we are told that the prophecies of Isaiah are important for us to know. One reason may be that those who understand Isaiah will be spared the agony of learning too late the need for us all to repent and to obtain the Lord's Spirit.

In using these keys for understanding Isaiah, I try to apply the challenge of Isaiah's message to myself. The more I comprehend it, the more it causes me to sharpen my thinking, to see myself clearly. If I can relate to all the censuring things Isaiah writes, changing my way of life accordingly, then perhaps I will qualify for the promises he holds out. Without doing that I might act presumptuously; I might neglect some pertinent aspect of what Isaiah says. I am certain Isaiah did not intend us to read his words selectively—noting some things while overlooking the rest, applying to ourselves what appeals, relegating to others what does not.

From the time I was in rabbinic school, when I began to understand Isaiah, his message has increasingly become a part of me. After many years of studying Isaiah, I am conscious of the immensity of this prophet's burden. Yet, what I have learned is not for me alone, but for all men, especially the Lord's people. The time approaches that we must understand Isaiah or be swept away by the events of the last days. The book of Isaiah is a handbook for our time, a gift from God, not for us to reject but to receive with joy.

Spirit of Prophecy

In 2 Nephi 25:1, Nephi says, "Isaiah spake many things which were hard for many of my people to understand; for they know not concerning the manner of prophesying among the Jews." Nephi adds that he did not teach his people many things concerning the manner of prophesying among the Jews, because their works were "works of darkness," their doings "abominations" (2 Nephi 25:2). Nephi's comments reflect the inscrutable nature of Isaiah's prophecies. Isaiah hid the meaning of his words from the wicked, using the Jewish manner. His subtlety in doing so was equal to that of the wicked of his people (compare Jacob 4:14). Those who had ears to hear would nonetheless understand his words; Isaiah did not write them in vain. Nephi then gives the first key: "Because the words of Isaiah are not plain unto you, nevertheless they are plain unto all those that are filled with the spirit of prophecy" (2 Nephi 25:4). The spirit of prophecy—specifically, being filled with the spirit of prophecy—makes Isaiah's words *plain* to the reader or listener. When we possess the power of this spirit, it aids us in understanding Isaiah's words.

But what is the spirit of prophecy? The angel speaking in Revelation 19:10 equates the spirit of prophecy with the testimony of Jesus. Having a testimony that Jesus is the Christ, that he atoned for the sins of mankind, comes, of course, by the Holy Ghost. Only the Holy Ghost can reveal this to the hearts and minds of men so they will know that it is true. Thus it is with the spirit or operation of prophecy. According to Peter, "prophecy came not in old time by the will of man: but holy men of God spake as they were moved by the Holy Ghost" (2 Peter 1:21). Paul, too, notes that "the things of God knoweth no man, but the Spirit of God" (1 Corinthians 2:11). In other words, we cannot truly understand the revelations the Lord gave through the prophets except by that same Spirit which gave the prophets utterance. That, of course, makes good sense.

Nephi emphasizes that the words of Isaiah are "not plain" to men, but they become plain when understood through the spirit of prophecy: the Holy Ghost. Nephi then contrasts Isaiah's words with his own words, which *are* plain (see 2 Nephi 25:4). Nephi says his soul delights in plainness, and he himself speaks in plainness. Indeed, despite the presence throughout the Book of Mormon of

Hebrew substructures, its plain style is its single most obvious feature. As far as Isaiah is concerned, however, his words cannot become plain, according to Nephi, except through the spirit of prophecy. To understand Isaiah, we must possess this spirit.

But possessing the spirit of prophecy, or the gift of prophecy, depends on personal worthiness: when we continually exercise faith and repentance, when we receive baptism by one having authority and take upon ourselves the name of Christ, renewing this covenant often, bearing this identity valiantly before the world, we qualify for the gift of the Holy Ghost. We then equip ourselves to understand Isaiah. The first key, therefore, depends on how we relate to God. We qualify for the gift of the Holy Ghost, and it fills our souls, when we show ourselves righteous by God's standards, when we live his law. There is no getting around this key. We see its first importance, because without it we cannot become enlightened— we cannot understand Isaiah plainly. Built into this key is a vertical dimension (how we relate to God) that guarantees our understanding or ensures our lack of it, depending on our worthiness.

Letter of Prophecy

Nephi gives the second key in 2 Nephi 25:5 when he says, "My soul delighteth in the words of Isaiah, for I came out from Jerusalem, and mine eyes hath beheld the things of the Jews, and I know that the Jews do understand the things of the prophets, and there is none other people that understand the things which were spoken unto the Jews like unto them, save it be that they are taught after the manner of the things of the Jews." A key idea here is to be *taught*, just as in the first key it was having things made *plain*. In connection with this idea, Nephi again speaks of a "manner" of the Jews (compare "manner" of prophesying, v. 1). In order to understand the things of the prophets, a person must learn the peculiar manner in which the Jews use words. In Hebrew, the term *things (děbārîm)* also means "words" (*děbārîm*). The things spoken to the Jews thus constitute the words of the prophets.

The Jews still teach the prophets' manner of using words in the rabbinic schools of today. In these schools, the Jews rely on interpretive devices such as types and shadows, allegorical language, literary patterns, underlying structures, parallelisms, double meanings, key words, code names, and other mechanical tools. Their

4

approach is entirely analytical. In their oversized books, a small square in the center of each page encloses the single verse or passage being studied. Filling up what is by far the greater part of the page (in fine print, completely surrounding the square) appear large columns of the best-known rabbinic commentaries on the verse or passage in the center. I recall spending an entire month of my time in rabbinic school debating just one such verse, exploring it from every angle, studying all its potentialities, its varied ramifications, its several levels of applicability, its definable limitations, and so forth, until we (the group of students around the table, with the rabbi at the head) had wholly assimilated that passage.

To me, this constituted a new approach. That kind of perseverance, although difficult and at times vexing, brought home to me a most important dimension in studying the scriptures: the *letter of prophecy*. The Jews, exclusively, use this approach. But with it comes a unique point of view, an analytical mind-set. It allows for great flexibility as far as interpreting any given scripture is concerned. It recognizes the broad applicability of the word of God. Yet such analysis ensures that whatever interpretation I arrive at must be verifiable within the limits of the analysis. It contains internal checks; it safeguards me from misinterpreting the scripture.

This is a far cry from the dogmatic, superficial approach that assigns a single interpretation to every scripture, thereby denying a number of other intended levels of meaning. It consists of the opposite of proof texting, which first accepts a doctrine and then seeks support for it by drawing on passages of scripture of perhaps entirely different contexts. The Jewish method is essentially open-minded. It seeks to elicit meanings from the scripture itself, not to impose or read doctrinal presuppositions into it. It lets the scripture speak. We may wrest the sacred text only to our condemnation. The Jewish manner eschews such a practice.

Thus, Nephi says, "There is none other people that understand the things which were spoken unto the Jews like unto them, save it be that they are taught after the manner of the things of the Jews" (2 Nephi 25:5). We cannot obtain this key to Isaiah from any other source. We must learn it from the Jews themselves. Yet, the Jews do not advertise or disseminate among others their method of interpreting the prophets. The very language, script, and contents of their books are unique to themselves. The Jews hand down this methodology orally in the rabbinic schools. Here, the types and shadows, and all else are transmitted individually from teacher to students. As a number of Latter-day Saints who have studied with a Jewish teacher testify, this experience opens up a new dimension in the study of scripture. In noting this, I do not advocate that all of us take this course, merely that we give credence to Nephi's words. The manner of the Jews deserves our recognition.

I call the second key the *letter of prophecy*, because the analytical approach to every word and letter originates in the ancient schools of the Hebrew prophets. In addition to learning how to obtain the spirit of prophecy, the prophets' disciples learned various oral and literary forms—the mechanics of prophesying. They considered this essential for communicating their message in their day. Nothing the ancient prophets wrote or spoke lacked a particular form or structure. They scrupulously observed ancient Near Eastern scribal custom. The Hebrews were not alone in this. Throughout the ancient Near East, once a literary practice became established, it was carefully maintained. With the passing of time, tradition would modify it but never discard it. These literary dimensions permeate Isaiah's writings.

When we recognize the several layers of meaning of their prophecies, we gain an appreciation for what the Hebrew prophets learned, how much they communicate in so few words. Isaiah not only followed the oral tradition of such prophets as Elijah and Elisha but also benefited from the innovative literary tradition of Amos and Hosea. Legend claims that Isaiah was of royal lineage, reared in the scribal tradition at the court of the king. This would explain much of his literary expertise. Isaiah, however, far excels all the prophets in his style and methodology. We must assume, therefore, that he internalized so well the literary manner of the Jews, together with the theology of his prophet predecessors, as to outclass them all. His work, as a result, is a classic. In one sense, it serves as a standard by which we measure other scriptures.

The Jews, in their quest to analyze intellectually the literary message of the prophets, nonetheless tend to exclude the *spirit of prophecy*. We only feel this, however, having experienced beforehand the spirit of prophecy—the Holy Ghost. In our day, these complementary dimensions of interpreting scripture largely exist separately. The Jewish approach is in the main analytical and horizontal. The Jews study carefully the words of the prophets. They analyze even each letter and the significance of that letter according to the Hebrew alphabet. Every letter possesses a numerical value. The word *serpent* (*nāḥāš*), for example, equates numerically with the word *messiah* (*māšiaḥ*). Thus, the word *serpent* also serves as a symbol for *messiah*. This symbolism we see in the brazen serpent Moses lifts up in the wilderness and perhaps in the Mesoamerican emphasis on the serpent figure.

Analyzing the words of the prophets with such detail requires effort and takes time. The Latter-day Saints, unfortunately, know little of such analysis. In reading the scriptures, we emphasize the *spirit of prophecy*. But we know that the Spirit of the Lord tends to increase in proportion to the amount of intelligence we seek and the degree of diligence we apply to the scriptures—studying them out in our minds, making connections with what we have learned, assimilating their message, putting them into practice. Such study generates in us a positive spiritual climate. It paves the way for the influence of the Holy Ghost. Both dimensions, the vertical and the horizontal, are essential to understanding Isaiah. We must accustom ourselves to that fact. If we do not, we will miss out on something very important.

Nephi relates the second key, the letter of prophecy, to the locale of Jerusalem. He says, "I, of myself, have dwelt at Jerusalem, wherefore I know concerning the regions round about" (2 Nephi 25:6). Modern scholars singularly realize that ancient Israel did not live in a vacuum. Israel, in the ancient world, participated in a Semitic culture, much the same as America forms a part of Western culture in the world today. When Nephi claims to know concerning the regions round about, he certainly means that there exist cultures and literatures with which he is familiar. The Book of Mormon confirms this meaning. Nephi and his descendants use many biblical and ancient Near Eastern literary patterns to communicate their message. Such knowledge helps Nephi to understand Isaiah better, because every structure that shapes a scripture possesses its own, self-contained message over and above the written text. The Hebrew prophets draw on all known literary devices as vehicles to convey information. They incorporate them into their writings to enhance and enrich their meaning.

Governing Structures

We find when we examine the book of Isaiah that Isaiah employs and transforms the literary patterns of many ancient Near Eastern peoples. The Egyptians, for example, long before Isaiah's time, wove narrative stories around a certain literary structure. The story of Sinuhe forms a classic model.[1] The hero of the story, who is of royal origin, finds himself in trouble, political or otherwise, in his homeland. He is exiled from his country—forced to flee for his life. Making his way among a foreign people and culture, he comes to understand himself. When he attains this self-awareness—realizing who he is, what he must do with his life—there arises in him a desire to return to his homeland. Oddly enough, at that point those in authority welcome him back, escort him home with much fanfare, and restore him to a high position.

This, of course, is also the story of Israel, and Isaiah frames his entire book around it as a literary pattern. In the first part of the book of Isaiah (chaps. 1–39), Israel finds herself in trouble in her homeland. Because of her rebellion and apostasy, the Lord exiles her into the world at large, where she interacts with people and events (chaps. 40–54). At some point, when Israel repents of her follies and comes to herself—realizing her true identity, renewing her allegiance to the Lord—she returns home in a glorious home-coming, a great and marvelous event (chaps. 55–66).

Fittingly, Jacob, father of the nation Israel, typifies this structure. Jacob flees from Esau into the land of Haran. There he interacts with people; acquires wives, children, flocks, and herds; and attains considerable stature. At that point the Lord summons him back to the land of Canaan, where he dwells in strength as one of Israel's patriarchs. Going even further back, we note that this pattern reflects the story of man himself. God casts Adam out of paradise, and out of his presence, into a dreary world. There Adam makes his way, comes to himself, realizes who he is and what his destiny is to be. Then begins his struggle to return home. If he succeeds in returning to his Heavenly Father, he assumes great glory: Adam attains to a state far more splendid than he enjoyed formerly. Each one of us resonates with this cycle, or hero journey, as a paradigm of man himself.

Isaiah uses this literary pattern to great effect. It both reveals and conceals his message. Isaiah's structuring of his book according

---

[1] See the stories of Sinuhe, the Two Brothers, and the Foredoomed Prince in Adolf Erman, *The Ancient Egyptians* (New York: Harper and Row, 1966); Alan H. Gardiner, *Hieratic Papyri*, 3d Series (London: British Museum, 1935); John A. Wilson, trans., "Story of Si-nuhe," in *Ancient Near Eastern Texts*, ed. J. B. Pritchard (Princeton: Princeton University, 1969), 18–22.

to this pattern has proved a great stumbling block to scholars. Most view the different historical settings of the book—Israel before, during, and after the exile—as grounds for dividing the book's authorship. To account for these diverse, sustained historical settings, scholars allege that the book must have had at least three authors. A misunderstanding of a literary structure has caused scholars to pursue a mistaken course, not believing that Isaiah saw the time of exile and beyond. There exists a broad governing pattern to Israel's history. The themes of *trouble at home, exile abroad,* and *happy homecoming* reflect a divine plan for the Lord's people and for the world. It foresees the end from the beginning.

An important complementary idea with which Isaiah permeates his book consists of the progression of thought from nationalism to universalism to individualism. A national Israel apostatizes and is exiled. A universal Israel reawakens to her national identity. Individuals who repent return home from their scattered condition to resume this identity. Isaiah's literary structure thus contains another dimension. Notwithstanding her dramatic transformation, Israel preserves her identity through the ordeal. In many respects this preservation parallels the transformation of larva to pupa to butterfly that preserves the identity of the specimen (compare 41:14–15).

The basic plot of this literary pattern tells us that Israel's history does not end when she goes into exile. It resumes when Israel returns home—all part of a divinely ordained plan. According to this structure, the Lord foreordained Israel's exile: it forms an integral part of his saving plan for the world. When Israel goes into exile, the intermingling of her blood with the nations of the world gives all peoples a claim to Israel's unique heritage. In keeping with the Lord's blessing of Abraham, all nations would now be blessed because they themselves share the lineage of Israel. We know that in the Lord's plan there exists no salvation outside of Israel; the world can be reconciled to God only by being received into the house of Israel. The world's Savior is himself Israel's King. In Isaiah's structure, Israel's homecoming consists of the righteous of the nations returning to their God. Upon this, they receive a literal and glorious inheritance in the promised land.

Isaiah employs several other major Near Eastern literary patterns. He transforms a four-fold sructure we find in the Ugaritic myth of Baal and Anath. His structure consists of the four major prophetic themes: *apostasy, judgment, restoration,* and *salvation.* These parallel the themes of threat, war, victory, and feast that appear in the course of several cycles in the Baal myth. The myth's themes themselves also appear frequently in the book of Isaiah, where they lend insight into Isaiah's literary method.[2] Their transformation into Israel's apostasy, judgment, restoration, and salvation, however, predominates. Isaiah's message is foremost theological; his literary patterning serves a prophetic purpose.

One cycle of these themes encompasses the entire book of Isaiah. Its content as a whole deals with Israel's apostasy (chaps. 1–9), judgment (chaps. 10–34), restoration (chaps. 35–59), and salvation (chaps. 60–66). Forming a second overarching structure, these themes transcend the narrow focus we have when we read the text. Such patterning lifts individual prophecies off their historical base, and makes them part of and subservient to the book's wider message. This broad message is that Israel's literal existence does not cease with her apostasy and judgment, as might at first appear. It continues with Israel's restoration—according to a predetermined plan—until all the earth's righteous are saved and participate with her in a glorious new age. The nature of this cycle suggests, additionally, that its themes are a pattern of Israel's history in general: this cycle could manifest itself anciently, in Nephite times, or in the last days.

The subject of the four themes changes. Israel forms the subject of apostasy in chapters 1–9. Israel has alienated herself from the Lord, bringing retribution on herself (see 1:2–4). The Lord uses the king of Assyria to execute his judgment on Israel in chapters 10–34. Israel becomes the object of the Lord's anger, as the Lord commissions this tyrant to punish his people (see 10:5–6). The subject of a literal restoration in chapters 35–59, Israel's land and people experience rejuvenation (see 35:1–10). A righteous king rules (see Hezekiah, chaps. 36–38), and Israel looks forward to the coming of the Lord (see 40:3–5, 9–11). Finally, in chapters 60–66, the Lord comes to save his people. He comes as Redeemer to Zion (see 59:20), and a new era of salvation begins (see 60:1–22). Localized instances

---

[2] See William R. Millar, *Isaiah 24–27 and the Origin of Apocalyptic* (Missoula, Mont.: Scholars Press, 1976). Millar's study, although useful in pointing out the mythic cycle in Isaiah 24–27, unfortunately flounders amid historical presuppositions and fails to note the incidence of mythical patterns throughout the book of Isaiah as well as their transformation into Hebrew prophetic forms.

of these four themes appear throughout Isaiah,[3] signifying that this cycle occurs universally as a spiritual phenomenon as well as schematically to depict Israel's history.

A third such governing structure in the book of Isaiah consists of the associated ideas of *destruction or judgment of the wicked* (chaps. 1–36) and *deliverance or establishment of the righteous* (chaps. 40–66) at *the presence or accession to the throne of a righteous Davidic king* (chaps. 37–39). Like the cycle of apostasy, judgment, restoration, and salvation, this pattern occurs in many individual, localized instances. Virtually every time Isaiah mentions *Zion*, these ideas come together. In most of these localized instances of the pattern, the Davidic king appears under a pseudonym, such as the key words *ensign, staff, hand* of the Lord, *arm* of the Lord, and *righteousness*. I deal with these terms in the following discussion.

I call the association of ideas in this pattern Zion ideology. It originates in the idea of Zion as a safe place by virtue of the righteousness of her king, a loyal vassal or servant of the Lord. Because the Davidic covenant follows the pattern of the ancient Near Eastern covenant of grant made between a suzerain (overlord) king and one of his vassal kings,[4] the suzerain (in Israel's case, the Lord) protects the people of the vassal, so long as the vassal remains loyal to the suzerain.[5] In the days of King Hezekiah, an Assyrian army of 185,000 men surrounded Jerusalem, demanding its surrender. Because of Hezekiah's righteousness, and because the people were loyal to Hezekiah, the Lord smote the Assyrian horde with a plague, so that in one night all died (see Isaiah 37:33–36; 38:2–6).

This event was unique in Israel's history, one that saw the Lord's word fulfilled when put to the test. It established an important precedent that Isaiah must have deeply felt and pondered. Upon it

---

[3] See, for example, apostasy (1:20–23); judgment (1:24); restoration (1:25–26); salvation (1:27); apostasy (1:28–29); judgment (1:30–31); restoration (2:2–3); salvation (2:4–5); apostasy (57:11); judgment (57:12–13a); restoration (57:13b–14); salvation (57:15); apostasy (57:16–17a); judgment (57:17b); restoration (57:18); salvation (57:19).

[4] See Moshe Weinfeld, "The Covenant of Grant in the Old Testament and in the Ancient Near East," *Journal of the American Oriental Society* 90 (1970): 184–203; "Berîth," in G. Johannes Botterweck and Helmer Ringgren, eds., *Theological Dictionary of the Old Testament* (Grand Rapids, Mich.: Eerdmans, 1977), 2:253–79.

[5] See my essay, "The Davidic Covenant: A Theological Basis for Corporate Protection," in Avraham Gileadi, ed., *Israel's Apostasy and Restoration* (Grand Rapids, Mich.: Baker Book House, 1988), 157–63.

Isaiah builds a prophecy of the future. In so doing, he not only duplicates it in many localized instances in his writings but patterns his entire book after it. In Isaiah's structuring of his book according to the pattern of Zion ideology, that historical event forms the centerpiece.

The significance of this third governing structure is that temporal salvation (divine protection in the face of a mortal threat) occurs corporately for Israel as a universal, ongoing principle because of the Davidic covenant and its protection clause. A righteous Davidic king, a vassal of the Lord, will again stand as a proxy for Israel's temporal salvation when the Lord sees fit to restore a righteous descendant of David to this role. Without it, Israel can obtain divine protection only under the terms of the Sinai covenant. Then all Israel, to a man, would have to be righteous before the Lord. In that case, corporate Israel assumes the role of the Lord's vassal (as she did at Sinai), and the Lord requires the loyalty of the entire people. Isaiah cites both frameworks of divine protection—the Sinaitic and Davidic covenants—as ways the Lord uses to destroy the armies of Assyria, Israel's chief enemy. One of them only, however, forms an overarching idea, the one founded on the Davidic covenant.

Isaiah thus lets us know that divine protection because of a righteous Davidic king forms an important part of the Lord's plan for his people Israel. While this idea may surprise us, we cannot deny that it appears central to Isaiah's message. Nor, obviously, is it for us to counsel the Lord in the matter. The Jewish expectation of a messiah matches precisely this Davidic role in Israel's temporal salvation. The Jews further expect of their messiah that, as the Lord's vassal, he will restore the political kingdom of God on the earth, rebuild the Lord's temple in Jerusalem, and bring back the lost tribes of Israel. All these comprise aspects of restoration that the prophets predict will precede the Lord's coming to the earth in power. Jews today do not regard the task of redeeming Israel from her sins as a messianic role. One reason is that the Lord God himself, according to Isaiah and other prophets, ordains the forgiveness of sins. The Jews do not perceive the Lord to be a Man come forth to work out this redemption on the earth.

The Davidic king's role of proxy for Israel's temporal salvation forms a key idea in the book of Isaiah. It parallels Christ's role of proxy for Israel's spiritual salvation. Isaiah nonetheless keeps these two ideas fundamentally apart—with one exception. Christ's role of proxy for Israel's spiritual salvation possesses a type in the Davidic king's role of proxy for Israel's temporal salvation. In the Old Testament, the idea of a human proxy for securing national salvation resides alone in the Davidic king. Therefore, Christ himself must be a son of David. He is not identical, however, with the Davidic king, although the latter must also come of the lineage of David. For that reason, the Jews do not connect the two. The Davidic king serves as the Lord's vassal, as David and his ruling descendants did anciently. The suzerain–vassal paradigm best expresses their relationship. Their roles remain quite distinct, the one temporal, the other spiritual and eternal. The one merits the Lord's intervention when Israel is physically threatened; the other merits the Father's everlasting mercy on the souls of men.

A fourth governing pattern divides the book of Isaiah into two broad categories. These reflect respective curses and blessings pertaining to the Lord's covenant with Israel. As the Lord's corporate vassal or servant, Israel would inevitably experience his blessing or his curse, depending on her loyalty to her suzerain King. Unlike the covenant Moses formulated, in which Moses enumerates first the covenant's blessings and then the curses (see Deuteronomy 28), Isaiah emphasizes first the curses (*covenantal malediction*; chaps. 1–39), and then the blessings (*covenantal benediction*; chaps. 40–66). He divides his book to reflect these two broad categories: in the first half, curses predominate; but in the second, blessings.

Many localized exceptions of curses and blessings nonetheless appear in both divisions of Isaiah. Curses appear in the second half of the book, reminding Israel that not all will inherit blessings, only those who remain loyal to the Lord. Blessings appear in the first half of the book, indicating that not all Israel need incur the Lord's wrath. Even in a time of national apostasy and judgment, the Lord makes provision for delivering righteous individuals. Thus, in a chapter wholly devoted to censuring the Lord's people—spelling out the curses they are bringing on themselves—Isaiah inserts a single verse: "Tell the righteous it shall be well with them; they shall eat the fruits of their own labors" (3:10)—covenantal benediction. In a later chapter that depicts the blessedness of strangers and aliens who love the Lord, Isaiah inserts a poignant reminder that even the spiritual leaders of the Lord's people may transgress, to be devoured by wild beasts (see 56:3–12)—covenantal malediction. By drawing on the two extremes of Israelite society, the highest strata (the prophets) and the lowest (the alien), Isaiah makes his point well: all in between also stand to be blessed or cursed.

The dominant idea of curses followed by blessings in the book of Isaiah reflects the order in which these appear in Hittite suzerain–vassal treaties.[6] If the vassal rebels against the suzerain, he will suffer the curses; but if he exercises loyalty toward the suzerain, he will enjoy the blessings. Since Isaiah commences his book by calling on the heavens and the earth—witnesses of the Sinai covenant (see Deuteronomy 30:19)—to testify of Israel's apostasy (see 1:2), the intent is clearly maledictory. All the Lord's judgments upon Israel thereafter take the form of common ancient Near Eastern covenant curses. At the commencement of the second part of the book of Isaiah, the Lord declares Israel's crime expiated—her sins are atoned for (see 40:2). A new, benedictory chapter in Israel's history begins, marked by a wonderful reversal of her curses.

Not only does the Lord reverse Israel's curses, but this same reversal transcends and far exceeds Israel's former glory. The message of Isaiah's structure is that God foreordained Israel's final blessedness, her golden age; however, he destined it to come about only after she had endured a long period of trial. This trial itself, and Israel's loyalty through it, would earn Israel her latter glory. The new Israel of the millennial age would be born a pure people after enduring much affliction. To direct Isaiah's promise of millennial blessedness to any other candidates is unfounded. Yet, Isaiah's pattern of malediction and benediction applies in the short term as well. Forming an overarching idea, it serves as a general principle. All who turn their loyalty to the Lord may experience blessedness. Nevertheless, as exceptions to the pattern tell us, those who have already experienced blessedness may forfeit it. All must pass a test.

Isaiah makes quite clear, for example, that the Lord's people living in the time proximate to the millennial age will experience a sharp rift (see 65:13–15). Since this will affect us all, we may want to examine each group's peculiarities. Some suffer everlasting curse, having been exposed to the Lord's law but having followed their own ways (see 65:1–2). Others enjoy everlasting blessing, having sought

---

[6] See George E. Mendenhall, "Covenant Forms of Israelite Tradition," *Biblical Archaeologist* 17.3 (1954): 50–76; F. C. Fensham, "Malediction and Benediction in Ancient Near Eastern Vassal–Treaties and the Old Testament," *Zeitschrift für die alttestamentliche Wissenschaft* 74 (1962): 1–8.

guidance from the Lord and been diligent in his word (see 66:5). Some, who have known blessedness but consumed it on their pleasures, are cursed forever (see 65:3–7, 11–12). Others, who have known afflictions but remained faithful to the Lord, are blessed forever (see 65:19–25). An eternal gulf divides the two (see 66:23–24).

Isaiah thus transforms ancient Near Eastern literary devices to suit a prophetic purpose. He builds his writings around a diversity of patterns, superimposing their structures one upon another. This layering makes his a sophisticated book, replete with meaning. It also implies that the book is heavily encoded. Its multilayered structure explains why Isaiah reads unevenly, often changing context without any warning. In Isaiah's writings, time appears irrelevant as sequences of events crisscross and overlap. Now he describes one scene, now another, perhaps without any apparent connection between the two. All such scenes are governed by overarching criteria. We must learn what these tell us in order that we may deal more confidently with Isaiah's sayings. Some of Isaiah's words, for example, are so condemnatory that we might get discouraged reading them. Overarching ideas remind us of the light at the end of the tunnel. Isaiah purposefully forces us to wade through much that is harsh before he introduces us to the millennial age. From this we understand that we must keep an overall perspective. We must view passages condemnatory of ourselves in the light of those that hold out the Lord's promise. Conversely, we must deal with promises of glory in the light of the passages that censure us. To every warning there is a bright side; with every promise there is a threat.

A fifth structure pervading the book of Isaiah—by far the most complex—consists of a division of the book into two halves of thirty-three chapters each. Each half divides into seven categories of paralleled subject matter. Isaiah chiastically structures the themes governing the seven categories, as follows:

Ruin and Renascence (chaps. 1–5 and 34–35)
    Recalcitrance and Compliance (chaps. 6–8 and 36–40)
        Punishment and Deliverance (chaps. 9–12 and 41–46)
            Humiliation and Exaltation (chaps. 13–23 and 47)
        Suffering and Salvation (chaps. 24–27 and 48–54)
      Disloyalty and Loyalty (chaps. 28–31 and 55–59)
    Disinheritance and Inheritance (chaps. 32–33 and 60–66)

The progression of thought that characterizes this structure possesses no ancient Near Eastern antecedents; it is entirely original to Isaiah. An idea he establishes in the first unit of chapters in the first half of the book (chaps. 1–5), he develops or complements in the parallel unit in the second half (chaps. 34–35). This developed idea then forms a presupposition in the second unit of the first half of the book (chaps. 6–8), which, in turn, establishes its own concept that Isaiah develops in its parallel unit (chaps. 36–40). All concepts thus far developed then form a presupposition in the third unit (chaps. 9–12), which also develops its own concept together with its parallel unit (chaps. 41–46); and so forth. All theological concepts and ideas Isaiah thus establishes structurally culminate in the seventh unit in the second half of the book (chaps. 60–66), where they appear cumulatively.

The things Isaiah communicates via this *bifid structure* are too many to summarize here.[7] The chiastic nature of the structure, however, tells us that ultimately Israel's destiny (and man's) is to be humiliated or exalted. The governing themes of this pattern express man's behavior and its consequences. In practice, those themes imply that in order to be exalted, Israel must first pass through a period of humiliation—exaltation has a price. The wicked of Israel, and all wicked entities, experience precisely the opposite of this. They exalt themselves now, persecuting the humble, but in the end the Lord humiliates them.

In order to attain exaltation, Israel (and individuals within Israel) must exercise compliance and loyalty toward the Lord. As the Lord's people prove themselves under duress, the Lord delivers them. He saves Israel from perils temporal and spiritual—despite her initial punishment and suffering because of sin. After being ruined and disinherited to pay for her crimes, Israel experiences a renascence; she gloriously reinherits the promised land. Throughout these phenomena, powerful, often dramatic tests present themselves, tests that try Israel's faithfulness to the Lord. Exaltation does not come until Israel passes severe trials. Always there appears the specter of some of Israel being unfaithful to the Lord, playing the traitor while others stand fast amid opposition and oppression.

Isaiah identifies the dominant sins of the Lord's people as injustice and idolatry. While he imputes all Israel with guilt on

---

[7] For a detailed analysis, see my book *The Literary Message of Isaiah* (forthcoming).

account of these and other sins, the righteous repent of them when called on to do so. The wicked of Israel and of the world, on the other hand, distinguish themselves in that they do not repent, even when called on to do so. As a consequence, they suffer ruin, punishment, humiliation, and so forth, without recourse. That constitutes their final state. This, in briefest form, is the message of the bifid structure. How the Lord implements these principles in the last days, the structure sets out in detail.

Like the other structures I have discussed, the bifid structure consists of basic overarching themes. Some familiarity with these is essential if we would grasp any one part of Isaiah's message. It would be bold for us to proceed on the assumption that we could understand Isaiah's words without considering his governing concepts. The tight structuring of the book of Isaiah from beginning to end suggests that Isaiah composed much of the book, particularly its disputed latter sections, to accommodate structural criteria. The correlating of so many governing ideas into a single whole did not materialize spontaneously. It was a life's work, precipitated by an extraordinary spiritual experience.

At a certain point in Isaiah's prophetic ministry, after he had proved his loyalty to the Lord by fulfilling his first commission as prophet, Isaiah experienced an apocalyptic vision, a vision of the end from the beginning.[8] From then on, Isaiah's ministry was characterized by his writing the substance of the vision. He also arranged, added to, and structured his former prophecies and revelations to match the broad picture he had now obtained. His writing style itself took on an elevated quality. Isaiah succeeded in integrating many layers of ideas, compacting into one prophecy a tale of the ages. To unravel it is an adventure.

This transcendent view of Isaiah tells us more about the nature of his prophecies than does the sum of its individual parts. Without it, scholars are left to interpret minute segments of Isaiah's writings, seeking constantly to fit them to some ancient person or event. Rather, Isaiah's message eclipses these historical bounds. His overarching design subordinates the historical origins of his prophecies. These prophecies he recasts into a new, more expansive mold.

---

[8] See Sirach 48:22–25, and J. Flemming and H. Duensing, trans., "Ascension of Isaiah," in *New Testament Apocrypha*, ed. Edgar Hennecke and Wilhelm Schneemelcher (Philadelphia: Westminster, 1965), 2:642–63.

Isaiah's individual prophecies now form pieces of a large puzzle, revealing a panorama of the end from the beginning when all pieces appear in place. Only within this totality do we discover Isaiah's message for our time.

The picture Isaiah builds structurally differs in many respects from the historical one—what happened in Isaiah's day. By subordinating history to prophecy, however, Isaiah does not detract from what transpired anciently. He highlights precisely those historical events that express his newfound purpose. The things Isaiah draws from Israel's history, and from his own background, serve to project his vision of the future. The coherency of his vision tells us that it speaks of a time other than Isaiah's. It leaps across time. Isaiah's vision fills out Israel's history to include the last days, the time when history culminates.

Forms of Speech

Isaiah employs many small literary patterns. He does not compose or utter his words formlessly. Isaiah organizes his sayings so that these compose minor structures of their own. Each of these, too, by its very nature, conveys a message. They include forms of prophetic speech, such as the lawsuit, the messenger speech, the woe oracle, the prophetic lament, the priestly sermon, the parable, and the song of salvation.[9]

The *lawsuit* may range over several verses of scripture, forming a single passage. In the lawsuit, the Lord indicts Israel in a court setting (see 1:10–20). Israel has been rebellious toward the Lord, breaking the covenant. The Lord sits as judge, sentencing Israel for her misdemeanor. Typically, Israel receives a probationary sentence, a brief period in which to repent. But when things come to a head, the Lord metes out judgment and Israel must bear her punishment.

In the *messenger speech*, the prophet assumes the role of the Lord's emissary. He delivers the prophetic message to the people or their king (see 7:3–9; 30:8–17). Often, such a message commences with an account of how the Lord sent the prophet. Following this appears a list of crimes the people have committed, with an

---

[9] See an outline of these forms in Claus Westermann, *Basic Forms of Prophetic Speech*, trans. Hugh C. White (Philadelphia: Westminster, 1967). This list by no means exhausts Isaiah's forms of prophetic speech, which include a variety of psalms, prayers, and declarations.

announcement of the ensuing punishment. The latter announcement usually commences with the prophetic formula, "Thus says the Lord."

The *woe oracle* consists of a series of curses the Lord pronounces upon Israel for breaking the covenant (see 5:8–24). Since Israel's covenant theology largely parallels the framework of ancient Near Eastern suzerain–vassal treaties, these woes mirror ancient Near Eastern curse patterns. All judgments of God upon Israel in the book of Isaiah take this curse form. The prophet pronounces the woes, however, only in specific instances of transgression, thus linking cause and effect.

The *prophetic lament* commences with the word *How?* (see 1:21). This term identifies a lament. The lament bewails a calamity or misfortune. It expresses thoughts that might paraphrase "How could this evil have happened before our eyes? How has Jerusalem, this great city, become so wicked?" Or, from a Book of Mormon context, "How could Zarahemla, our great model city, be taken by our enemies?" To draw an analogy to our day—to show the deep emotional impact of the prophet's words—"How could this great country in which we now live, an exemplar to all the world, become so wicked and be trampled by enemies?" In the Bible, the book of Lamentations forms a classic prolonged lament.

In the *priestly sermon*, the prophet assumes the role of the priest or preacher. These anciently taught the people of Israel, expounding doctrines, urging repentance, and schooling them in the straight way (see 8:11–17). Isaiah frames several prophecies around this pattern. Very often these adopt a personal approach, upholding an example for the people to follow (see 51:1–8).

A *parable* likens one thing to another allegorically to depict a sequence of things. Israel may be like a vineyard (see 5:1–7). The Lord carefully cultivates the vineyard and does everything he can to assure the welfare of his people. But they do not bring forth good fruit. Instead, they bring forth wild fruit. The Hebrew term for this kind of fruit (*běʾûsîm*; 5:2) refers to fruit that does not mature—fruit that rots before it ripens. Hence the Lord allows aliens to break into the vineyard, to trample it down. Briars and thorns rise up in it, signifying that the wicked overrun it. Enemies lay it waste. After the judgment, the Lord reconstitutes the vineyard. Now, however, the vineyard stands for the world at large (see 27:2–6), whither the Lord scattered Israel. A repentant Israel again bears fruit when the Lord restores his ancient covenant people.

In the *song of salvation*, Israel or her spokesman sings the Lord's praises, acknowledging his intervention that brought about Israel's deliverance (see 12:1–6; 26:1–6). When things looked darkest, when the Lord tried the faith of his people past the point of endurance, then he delivered his people from their enemies; then he manifested before the world his glorious power. Such mighty acts of God earn him renown, singling out his people as blessed above all.

The intent of all forms of prophetic speech is to convey a deeper message in the scriptures. The apparent or surface meaning is there when we read the prophecies verbatim. But there exists an additional meaning within the structure itself, one that may not readily appear at first glance. The more of such literary forms we can identify, the richer and more meaningful the prophetic message becomes for us. Although Isaiah modifies, recasts, or synthesizes such structures, particularly in the latter part of his book, we always discern literary forms. The more familiar we become with them, the more alive appear Isaiah's writings.

Parallelism

A literary technique Isaiah commonly uses—determining the smallest structure—is *parallelism*. Most of the text of Isaiah appears in parallel sentences or statements. They are the basic ingredient of Hebrew and ancient Near Eastern poetry. Isaiah employs several types of parallelisms, all important to know and understand. To pass by them, reading the book of Isaiah superficially, would be unfortunate, because not a single part materialized casually. Isaiah organized the book's entire content. As with parallelisms, he even structured individual verses. In one sense, this structuring reflects the patterning and organizing of God's universe. In God's creation all things possess structure, obeying established laws, following set norms, adhering to a well-defined set of principles. The idea of disintegrating into a disorganized whole—literature included—was an abomination to the ancient mind, especially to the Hebrews.

As a rule, parallelisms consist of two synonymous statements—a *synonymous parallelism*. What Isaiah says in one statement, he more or less repeats in a second. The value of this repetition is that the second statement can modify or qualify the first, and vice versa. The reader can thereby draw a better meaning or definition out of what Isaiah says. For example, chapter 60 states:

Arise, shine, your light has dawned,
the glory of the Lord has risen upon you!
(v. 1)

The "light," by parallelistic analogy or definition, *is* "the glory of the Lord"—Isaiah's parallelism equates the one with the other. The light "dawning" and the Lord's glory "rising" (the Hebrew verb *zārah*, "rise/shine," denotes sunrise) complete the parallelism. The Lord commands his people, who form the object of the verse, to rise from slumber at the dawning of the millennial era.

The next verse draws a contrast:

Although darkness covers the earth,
and a thick mist the peoples,
upon you the Lord will shine;
over you his glory shall be visible.
(v. 2)

Here exists a diversion, a contrasting of Israel's light with the darkness that covers the earth. In the first two lines, "darkness" parallels "a thick mist," and "the earth" parallels "the peoples." The darkness, or thick mist, which may be both physical and spiritual, thus envelops all peoples of the earth. The second two lines parallel the Lord's glory with the Lord himself. This signifies the Lord's coming in glory.

The next verse repeats the idea of light:

Nations will come to your light,
their rulers to the brightness of your dawn.
(v. 3)

Here, the "light," by parallelism, *is* "the brightness of [Israel's] dawn." The dawn attracts nations and rulers. But the idea of a light dawning appeared directly in the first verse also. We thus have, in verses 1–3, an instance of *chiasmus*, a kind of parallelistic structure that highlights something. Chiasmus is related to parallelism, and it uses parallelism, but it shows up a central, important idea. In this instance, Israel's light (vv. 1, 3) contrasts the world's darkness, the impenetrable mist of the peoples of the earth (v. 2).

As the Lord's coming grows imminent, some rulers and representatives of nations come out of darkness into the light. From the context of the passage, we learn that these nations and rulers are Israel's descendants among the nations returning home (see vv. 4–9); their return, in verse 3, parallels chiastically Israel's rising in verse 1. Since light is a creation motif and darkness a chaos motif, nations and rulers (Israel's descendants) escape destruction by sharing in Israel's regeneration (compare vv. 10–22). The chiasm of a—light upon Israel (v. 1); b—darkness upon the earth, in contrast to the light (v. 2); and a—light upon Israel, which some seek out (v. 3), thus contains a progression of ideas.

Another parallelism yields some particulars about a major sin the Lord's people commit:

> Their land is full of silver and gold
> > and there is no end to their wealth;
> their land is full of horses
> > and there is no end to their chariots.
> Their land is full of idols:
> > they adore the works of their hands,
> > things their own fingers have made.
> > > (2:7–8)

The expression "their land is full of" occurs three times, introducing three parallel lines. They speak of (1) silver and gold, (2) horses, and (3) idols. Similarly, the synonymous expression "there is no end to" introduces two parallel lines. They speak of (1) wealth and (2) chariots. The parallelistic structuring of these verses (because what is so explicitly parallel appears conceptually synonymous) implies that silver, gold, wealth, horses, and chariots exemplify the summary idea of *idols*—the people's possessions have become their gods. On the other hand, a surface reading only identifies as idols the "works of men's hands" and "things their own fingers have made."

An *antithetical parallelism* contrasts one word or idea with another. Through such a contrast we again obtain a clearer definition or meaning of terms. For example, 45:7 (KJV) reads, "I make peace, and create evil." This parallelism contrasts peace with evil. Both terms come from ancient Near Eastern covenant vocabulary. There, the word *peace* is synonymous with covenant keeping and covenant salvation; the word *evil* is synonymous with covenant breaking and covenant curse—the two terms are antonyms. The Lord, therefore, does not *create* evil, in the abstract sense of the term. No such definition of evil occurs in the writings of the prophets. But the Lord does cause covenant curses to follow those who commit iniquity. That is the "evil" he creates. By this contrast of peace and evil, we also understand better what peace is. Peace must be good—a covenant blessing. By the same token, evil must be the opposite of peace—no peace.

Metaphors

Metaphors in the book of Isaiah pertain to the letter of prophecy. Individual metaphorical terms form key words that uncover important underlying meanings behind Isaiah's writings. Most such key words depict or refer to the two main actors in the drama Isaiah describes—an archtyrant and the Davidic king. In ancient Near Eastern mythology, for example, the terms *Sea* and *River* describe powers of chaos the god Baal must conquer before he assumes the throne of El, the father god.[10] Isaiah, in order to express an important character trait, transforms these powers of chaos, *Sea* and *River*, into pseudonyms of the king of Assyria. Isaiah identifies the king of Assyria by the metaphorical names *Sea* and *River*, thus likening him to a power of chaos. This identification is fitting, because the king of Assyria, a type of archtyrant, causes universal destruction.

Several passages depict the archtyrant as *Sea* or *River*: "In that day my Lord will use a razor hired at the River—the king of Assyria—to shave your head and the hair of your legs, and to cut off even your beard" (7:20). Here, the king of Assyria personifies the *River*, which term at the same time refers to the Euphrates, a river bordering the country of Assyria. Isaiah calls the king of Assyria's power a *razor*, another potentially destructive instrument. The shaving of the hair signifies capitulation and captivity: captive men anciently suffered the indignity of being shorn. The Assyrians shave off Israel's leadership—her "head" (compare 9:15–16)—her virile young men, and even old men (Hebrew *zāqēn*), as implied by the word *beard* (Hebrew *zāqān*).

The same image of a *River* appears in 8:7: "Therefore will my Lord cause to come up over them the great and mighty water of

---

[10] See "Poems about Baal and Anath," trans. H. L. Ginsberg, in *Ancient Near Eastern Texts*, 129–42.

the River—the king of Assyria in all his glory. He will rise up over all his channels and overflow all his banks. He will sweep into Judea like a flood and, passing through, reach the very neck.'' The text thus describes the king of Assyria as a river in flood. His armies constitute a new Flood. They cover the entire earth, including the land of Israel. His reaching the neck signifies that the Lord spares some from this chaotic flood. The neck leaves the head—Zion/Jerusalem. This prophecy relates historically to the Assyrian siege of Jerusalem in the days of King Hezekiah (chaps. 36–38), an event that repeats itself in the last days.

Isaiah 5:30 describes the king of Assyria as the *Sea*, which is stirred up against the Lord's people: ''He shall be stirred up against them in that day, even as the Sea is stirred up.'' This verse summarizes a passage in which the army of the king of Assyria attacks Israel, taking the people captive, with none to rescue them (see 5:25–30). Covenant curses describe the misery the Lord's people suffer as the king of Assyria punishes them: earthquake, unburied corpses (v. 25); rapine, spoil (v. 29); darkness, gloom (v. 30). The effect of Assyria's invasion of the land is chaos.

In contrast to the king of Assyria, Isaiah likens the Davidic king to a power of creation: ''The people walking in darkness have seen a bright light; on the inhabitants of the land of the shadow of death has the light dawned'' (9:2). The ideal king, whom Isaiah describes in this chapter as ascending the throne of David (see 9:6–7), *is* the light. The light constitutes a power of creation that conquers darkness. In ancient Near Eastern mythology, light was seen as a creative power that takes control of chaos, bringing order in the affairs of men. The ruling king was likened to a ''sun'' of his nation. His task was to set in order his kingdom, to establish justice and righteousness among the people. His accession to the throne was seen as the dawning of a new, better day.[11] In Isaiah's theology, the Davidic king conquers the Assyrian power of chaos. Like Baal in the Ugaritic myth, who conquers *Sea* and *River*, the Davidic king accedes to the throne after that victory (compare 9:4–5).

Isaiah applies additional metaphorical pseudonyms to the king of Assyria and the Davidic king. Several of these, such as the terms *hand*, *ensign*, and *staff*, serve to identify both the Davidic king and

---

[11] See Henri Frankfort, *Kingship and the Gods* (Chicago: University of Chicago, 1948), 148–51, 157; W. G. Lambert, *Babylonian Wisdom Literature* (Oxford: Clarendon Press, 1960), 30.

the king of Assyria; each individually shares these pseudonyms. We see, for example, in 11:10 how the Davidic king "stands for an ensign to the peoples"—he personifies the Lord's *ensign* to the nations of the earth. In the ancient Near East, the ensign or banner was a royal symbol. Its function of rallying an army of supporters has remained much the same. Since the Davidic king serves as the Lord's *ensign*, he seeks the people's renewed allegiance to the Lord. He does this by rallying a righteous remnant of the Lord's people from among the nations to Zion. The same verse says, "He shall be sought by the nations." Another passage of Isaiah depicts the Lord's appointing him as a "witness to the nations, a prince and lawgiver of the peoples" (55:4). His task is to summon a nation of the righteous of Israel from captivity and from dispersion (see 55:5, 12).

The word *ensign* parallels the word *hand*: the Lord raises his "hand" to reclaim the remnant of his people out of the nations (11:11); and the Lord raises the "ensign," assembling the exiled of Israel and the scattered of Judah from the four directions of the earth (11:12). From the parallelism of these two verses, we understand that the terms *ensign* and *hand* are synonyms—the Davidic king personifies both the Lord's *hand* and his *ensign*. The Davidic king serves as the Lord's agent of gathering his people in both instances. We again observe the synonymity of these terms and their rallying function in 49:22:

> I will lift up my hand to the nations,
>   raise my ensign to the peoples;
> and they will bring your sons in their bosoms
>   and carry your daughters on their shoulders.

From other contexts of the book of Isaiah we learn that the Davidic king represents the *right hand* of the Lord, his hand of deliverance.[12] As the Lord's right hand, he delivers a remnant of Israel out of calamity in the Lord's day of judgment. He does this by leading them in a new exodus to Zion (compare 41:8–10; 50:2). But the new exodus theme also appears in the passage we are studying: "There shall be a pathway out of Assyria for the remnant of his people who shall be left, as there was for Israel when it came

---

[12] Compare the Davidic theology of the king as the "man of [the Lord's] right hand," Psalms 80:17; 110:1.

up from the land of Egypt" (11:16). This event follows when the Lord dries up the *tongue* of the Egyptian *Sea* by his mighty *wind* (*rûaḥ*, also "spirit") and extends his *hand* over the *River* (11:15). Smiting it into "seven streams," the Lord subdues the Assyrian power and provides a way on foot for the exiles' return (11:15). The exodus takes place when the Lord's *hand*, the Davidic king, subdues the dominant universal power of chaos—Assyria—represented by *Sea* and *River*. The supporting metaphors *tongue* and *wind* denote, respectively, the king of Assyria and the Davidic king. The Davidic king's role thus parallels that of Moses at the exodus out of Egypt, as well as Joshua's at Israel's crossing of the Jordan.

We find also, however, that Isaiah identifies the king of Assyria by the metaphors *hand* and *ensign*. We read in chapter 13: "Raise the ensign on a barren mountain; sound the voice among them! Beckon them with the hand to advance into the precincts of the elite" (v. 2). Historically, the king of Assyria destroyed Babylon, which here comes under attack (v. 1). It was his army that the Lord raised up for this purpose. Isaiah thus depicts the king of Assyria and his army as the Lord's instruments of punishment: "They come from a distant land beyond the horizon—the Lord and the instruments of his wrath—to cause destruction throughout the earth" (v. 5). Thus, the *ensign*, *voice*, and *hand* rallying an army to carry out this destruction (v. 2) identify, metaphorically, a single, warlike individual whom the Lord uses to destroy Babylon. Since these three terms appear in parallel, and their function is the same, they all characterize the king of Assyria.

The text continues: "Hark! A tumult on the mountains as of a vast multitude. Hark! An uproar among kingdoms as of nations assembling: the Lord of Hosts is marshalling an army for war" (v. 4). "Tumult" and "uproar," both chaos motifs, characterize an alliance of nations stirred up against their enemies. The Assyrian army is a universal power of chaos. As the Lord's *ensign*, the king of Assyria rallies an army of nations against Babylon when the peoples of the world have ripened in iniquity. Verse 6 appraises the situation: "Lament, for the day of the Lord is near; it shall come as a violent blow from the Almighty." In the destruction that follows, the sinners, the wicked, the proud, and tyrannical of the earth perish (vv. 9, 11), including those of Israel.

With this, chapter 5 concurs: "Therefore the anger of the Lord is kindled against his people: he draws back his hand against them and strikes them; the mountains quake, and their corpses lie like litter about the streets'' (v. 25). The *hand* of the Lord—the king of Assyria—here parallels the Lord's *anger*. This latter term, therefore, also designates the king of Assyria; he personifies the Lord's anger. *Hand* and *anger* are synonyms, as their parallelism determines. With the hand he draws back against them—his left hand—the Lord smites his people who are ripe in iniquity. When they provoke him, the Lord manifests his anger toward them by means of the king of Assyria. The term *litter*, a chaos motif, again marks the king of Assyria as a power of chaos.

Hand and *anger* again appear in parallel in the following refrain: "Yet for all this his anger is not abated; his hand is upraised still" (v. 25). Isaiah's repeating of this refrain in several contexts (compare 9:12, 17, 21; 10:4) suggests that the Lord's day of judgment, in which Assyria wields power, extends over a prolonged period of time. The king of Assyria rules until he serves fully the Lord's purpose of bringing men to justice (compare 10:6, 12).

In chapter 5's context of retribution, the king of Assyria reappears as an *ensign* rallying the wicked nations of the world against the Lord's people: "He [the Lord] raises an ensign to distant nations and summons them from beyond the horizon. Forthwith they come, swiftly and speedily" (v. 26). The same *ensign* or *hand* that rallies an army of nations against Babylon in chapter 13 rallies such an army against wicked Israel. Wicked Israel suffers the same fate as Babylon. The passage ends with the king of Assyria stirred up like the *Sea* against the Lord's people (v. 30).

In this same passage, Isaiah depicts the archtyrant's army as well disciplined, in contrast to the Lord's people at that time, whom the text describes indirectly: "Not one of them grows weary, nor does any stumble; they do not drowse or fall asleep. Their waist-belts come not loose, nor their sandal thongs undone" (v. 27). Unlike this formidable army, Israel has grown weary in her loyalty to the Lord (compare 43:22); Israel stumbles (compare 59:10); Israel drowses and falls asleep (compare 51:17; 56:10); Israel's waist-belts come loose and Israel's sandal thongs undone (compare 3:7; 8:15)—Israel wallows in apostasy.

The Assyrian army, the Lord's instrument of punishment, does not resemble his people: "Their arrows are sharp; all their bows are strung. The tread of their warhorses resembles flint; their chariot wheels revolve like a whirlwind. They have the roar of a lion; they are aroused like the young lions: growling, they seize the prey and escape, and none comes to the rescue'' (vv. 28–29). To be devoured by wild beasts, in ancient Near Eastern covenant theology, constitutes a curse.[13] The text likens the Assyrians to lions seizing their prey, while their victims remain helpless. This passage is the climax to a series of covenant curses (a *woe oracle*) the Lord pronounces against Israel for crimes she has committed (compare vv. 8–23). A transitional verse explains that the Lord's people ''have despised the law of the Lord of Hosts and reviled the words of the Holy One of Israel'' (v. 24). Their apostasy brings upon them the Assyrians.

Chapter 10, too, portrays the king of Assyria as the Lord's instrument for universally punishing the wicked. The chapter addresses a question to wicked Israel: ''What will you do in the day of reckoning, when the holocaust overtakes you from afar? To whom will you flee for help? Where will you leave your wealth?'' (v. 3). Isaiah answers this question: ''There shall nothing remain but to kneel among the captives or fall among the slain. Yet for all this, his anger is not abated; his hand is upraised still'' (v. 4). The Lord's *anger* and *hand*, as we note, identify the king of Assyria as the Lord's instrument of retribution. In this judgmental context, the Lord now addresses the archtyrant directly: ''Hail the Assyrian, the rod of my anger! He is the staff—my wrath in their hand'' (v. 5). This verse brings together many pseudonyms of the king of Assyria—the *rod, anger, staff, wrath,* and *hand* all describe the archtyrant metaphorically. We see this in other contexts of the chapter as well (compare *rod, staff,* vv. 15, 24; *anger, wrath,* v. 25; *hand,* v. 4).

Chapter 10 continues, ''I will commission him against a godless nation [Israel], appoint him over the people deserving of my vengeance, to pillage for plunder, to spoliate for spoil, to tread underfoot like mud in the streets'' (v. 6). The king of Assyria, whom the Lord thus empowers, makes chaos of wicked Israel. He strips the Lord's people of their wealth and treads them like mud. ''Mud,'' a chaos motif, signifies that he reduces the people to an

---

[13] See F. C. Fensham, ''Common Trends in Curses of the Near Eastern Treaties and *Kudurru*—Inscriptions Compared with Maledictions of Amos and Isaiah,'' *Zeitschrift für die alttestamentliche Wissenschaft* 75 (1963); ''Malediction and Benediction in Ancient Near Eastern Vassal–Treaties and the Old Testament,'' *Zeitschrift für die alttestamentliche Wissenschaft* 74 (1962).

ineffective state (compare 42:22–25). Yet, the king of Assyria remains unaware that he serves the Lord's purpose: "His [the king of Assyria's] purpose shall be to annihilate and to exterminate nations not a few" (v. 7). Although the Lord commissions him to punish the wicked, the archtyrant means to conquer the world. In the process, he decimates the earth's population, destroying the idolatrous peoples of all nations (compare v. 10).

Even as the king of Assyria and his army destroy the wicked of the world, so the Lord destroys him and his horde:

> But when my Lord has fully accomplished his work in Mount Zion and in Jerusalem, he will punish the king of Assyria for his notorious boasting and infamous conceit, because he said,
> > I have done it by my own ability and shrewdness,
> > > for I am ingenious.
> > I have done away with the borders of nations,
> > > I have ravaged their reserves,
> > > I have vastly reduced the inhabitants.
> > > I have impounded the wealth of peoples like a nest,
> > and I have gathered up the whole world
> > > as one gathers abandoned eggs;
> > not one flapped its wings,
> > > or opened its mouth to utter a peep.
> > > > (10:12–14)

This poem of self-adulation shows an extremely egocentric personality; the pronoun *I* appears seven times. But the following verse compares the king of Assyria unceremoniously to an *axe* and a *saw*, again signifying his role as a power of chaos: "Shall an axe exalt itself above the one who hews with it, or a saw vaunt itself over him who handles it?" (v. 15). The Lord wields the *axe* and *saw* to smite the wicked. The king of Assyria possesses no power in himself. The passage as a whole reflects the relative ease with which the king of Assyria conquers the world when thus empowered.

The text continues, "As though the rod wielded him who lifts it up! As though the staff held up the one who is not made of wood!" (v. 15) The king of Assyria's function as a *rod* and *staff* that the Lord wields to smite, parodies the archtyrant's self-aggrandizement. As a world ruler, he seeks to assume the role of God himself (compare 14:13–14; 37:23). Few survive his destruction:

In that day, those who survive of Israel
    and who escape of the house of Jacob
will no longer rely on him who struck them,
    but will truly rely on the Lord, the Holy One of Israel:
of Jacob a remnant will return
    to the one Mighty in Valor.
For though your people, O Israel,
    be as the sands of the sea,
    only a remnant will return;
although annihilation is decreed,
    it shall overflow with righteousness.
For my Lord, the Lord of Hosts, will carry out
    the utter destruction decreed upon the whole earth.

                                        (10:20–23)

A righteous remnant will escape the utter destruction of peoples by the king of Assyria. The Lord intends not merely to punish the wicked but to deliver the righteous of his people from the power of wickedness. At the end of the destruction, only the righteous remain.

The Lord will raise up the Davidic king to break the power of this Assyrian Goliath. A righteous remnant in Zion, besieged by Assyria, is to take comfort: "O my people who inhabit Zion, be not afraid of the Assyrians, though they strike you with the rod or raise their staff over you, as did the Egyptians" (v. 24). Here, the *rod* and *staff* still signify the king of Assyria and his domination over the Lord's people. He seeks control of the entire earth, culminating with Zion. The text continues, "For my anger will very soon come to an end; my wrath will become their undoing" (v. 25). This verse predicts that the king of Assyria—the Lord's *anger* and *wrath*—will soon meet his doom. Exalting himself in the destruction of peoples, he too must be punished.

Isaiah then introduces yet another metaphorical pseudonym: "The Lord of Hosts will raise the whip against them, as when he struck the Midianites at the rock of Oreb" (v. 26). The *whip* identifies an individual who will overthrow the Assyrian power. The reference to the Midianites recalls Gideon's victory over a vast invading force. In that story, Gideon uses a flagellum of briars and thorns with which to whip his enemies (see Judges 7:15–8:16). Isaiah continues, "His staff is over the Sea, and he will lift it over them [the Assyrians], as he did to the Egyptians" (v. 26). The Lord's *staff* over the *Sea* means that the Lord endows his other *staff*—the Davidic king—with power over the forces of chaos. In this context, the parallel terms *whip* and *staff* are both pseudonyms of the Davidic king. The title Lord of Hosts expresses the Lord's omnipotence but here also applies literally.

Isaiah thus depicts the Davidic king as a new Gideon; although vastly outnumbered, he overthrows an invading horde. Isaiah further depicts him as a new Moses; at Moses' outstretched staff the sea closed over the pursuing Egyptians. These roles serve as types of the Davidic king. In him combine the roles of many heroes of biblical history, including Abraham, Moses, Joshua, Gideon, David, Solomon, and Cyrus. In various contexts of his book, Isaiah represents all of them as types of the Davidic king. We thus begin to gain some idea of the important mission the Lord assigns the Davidic king. Although Isaiah here largely depicts that mission as temporal, it is vital to overthrowing the forces of chaos that overwhelm the Lord's people. The Davidic king serves as a counterforce to the power of Assyria. The Lord raises him up to deliver the righteous out of Assyria's hand. The Davidic king puts down Assyria when Assyria's macabre function of punishing the wicked comes to an end.

In the archtyrant, Isaiah combines the roles of the villains of biblical history. These villains are the kings of Assyria and Babylon. Both are known by identical metaphorical pseudonyms (compare *staff*, *rod*, 14:4–6, etc.). The king of Assyria represents primarily the political aspect of the archtyrant, the king of Babylon primarily his spiritual aspect. Historically, kings of Assyria assumed the name "King of Babylon" (14:4) as a religious title.[14] Isaiah's description of the king of Babylon, although it has much in common with the description of the king of Assyria, emphasizes the personality cult of the archtyrant—his self-exaltation as the god of this world.

Isaiah draws on Assyrian mythology to portray the king of Babylon as one who ascends the heavens like a god (see 14:13–14). From his "heavenly" throne, situated above the earth, he rules the world he has conquered. This ominous potentiality in our day, of course, takes on another meaning. The specter Isaiah describes is feasible given today's technology. Isaiah parodies the archtyrant's

---

14 See Seth Erlandsson, *The Burden of Babylon* (Lund, Sweden: Gleerup, 1970), 122, 163–64.

temporal exaltation as a counterfeit of true, spiritual exaltation. After a brief period of rule as demigod, the archtyrant is cast down to earth to suffer the curses of no burial for his corpse, destruction of offspring, and eternal execration (compare 14:12–21).

The Davidic king's victory, which Isaiah depicts in chapter 9, we similarly identify as a victory over the archtyrant. The pseudonyms *staff* and *rod* again typify the king of Assyria: "For thou hast smashed the yoke that burdened them, the staff of submission, the rod of those who subjected them, as in the day of Midian['s defeat]" (v. 4). Isaiah here again shows the Davidic king, who is the subject of this passage (compare vv. 6–7), as having power over the forces of chaos. The expression "as in the day of Midian['s defeat]" links this verse—and thus the Davidic king's accession to the throne that follows—to his victory over Assyria in 10:26. The term *yoke* here parallels those that characterize the king of Assyria. The archtyrant not only typifies the Lord's *staff* and *rod* of punishment but is a *yoke* around the necks of those he conquers.

That the Davidic king and tyrant king share some of the metaphorical pseudonyms Isaiah uses suggests that the two are arch rivals as well as contemporaries. Of course, we see this also in the way Isaiah sets them one against the other in a variety of situations. The very nature of their missions reflects their arch rivalry and contemporaneity; however, the terms that distinguish them, such as *anger*, *wrath*, and *rage*, on the one hand, and *light*, *covenant*, and *right hand*, on the other, show that ultimately one is doomed and one will be victorious. One fulfills the Lord's creative purpose, redeeming the righteous out of physical and spiritual perils; the other chaotically destroys the wicked, fulfilling only an interim role.

A proof of the metaphorical intent of terms such as *ensign*, *rod*, *staff*, and *hand* is that they appear consistently throughout Isaiah. Always they describe the activities either of the Davidic king or of the archtyrant even in contexts where Isaiah mentions neither of the two explicitly. We see the Lord's *voice* and *staff*, for example, subdue Assyria in 30:31–32. The Lord's *ensign* terrifies the Assyrians in 31:9. In 47:6, the Lord gives up the wicked of Israel into a *hand* that shows them no mercy, weighing down even old men with a *yoke*. In 66:14, the Lord manifests his (right) *hand* among his servants but his *rage* among his enemies. The Lord shelters Zion in the shadow of his *hand* in 51:16. In 63:6, the Lord treads the nations underfoot by his *anger* and makes them drunk with his *rage*.

The Lord strengthens with his *right hand* those who return from exile in 41:10, 13. The Lord appoints his servant to be a *light* and a *covenant* to the nations in 42:6; 49:6, 8.

The Lord's servant, his agent for delivering a righteous remnant of Israel in the later chapters of Isaiah, links metaphorically to the Davidic king. Isaiah represents both as the Lord's *right hand*, *ensign*, *light*, and so on. This shows them to be the same individual. Isaiah's servant figure, however, expresses more the spiritual aspect of the ideal Davidic king, whereas Isaiah's earlier expressions emphasize more his political aspect. They thus parallel Isaiah's respective political and spiritual depictions of the archtyrant. Both aspects combine in the book of Isaiah to make up the ideal.

The Davidic king's spiritual mission of preparing Israel for the coming of the Lord underscores his power of survival. Besides gathering a righteous remnant of Israel (compare 11:10–12; 49:6), he also schools them in the law of the Lord (see 42:4; 55:4). In this role he personifies *righteousness* (compare 51:1, 7; 54:14; 61:3), a metaphorical pseudonym unique to him (see 41:2; 46:11–13). *Righteousness* is one of two *arms* of God in the book of Isaiah, the other being *salvation* (see 51:5). The term *salvation* describes the Lord at his coming (see 62:11) and is the complement of *righteousness* (compare 46:13; 56:1; 62:1). The arm of *righteousness* heralds *salvation*, or the coming of the Lord (compare 40:10; 51:5; 52:10). The arm of *salvation* saves his people (compare 12:2; 33:2; 63:5).

The latter group of metaphors shows that although the Davidic king is a separate individual from the Lord himself, their roles are complementary—they function as two spiritual *arms*. The archtyrant enjoys no such intimacy with the Lord but is in reality his enemy. The archtyrant magnifies himself against God, for which God smites him (see 14:14, 19; 37:23, 38). Both *salvation* and *righteousness*— the Lord and his vassal—"endure forever" (see 51:6, 8). They typify Israel's saved condition (see 62:1–2). While the terms *righteousness* and *arm* link by parallelism to the Lord's *right hand* (see 41:10; 62:8)—the Davidic king—none of the metaphorical terms we are discussing, other than *arm* and *salvation*, identify the Lord.

The phenomenon of metaphors—more specifically, metaphorical pseudonyms—hides an entire scenario from the casual reader of Isaiah. Key words both conceal and reveal a drama unlike anything that appears on the surface of the text. Like Isaiah's governing structures, this drama transcends the historical picture of Isaiah's time. By means of it, Isaiah says much more than biblical history actually reflected. Isaiah reproduces a set of events that possesses no single precedent for the kind of outcome he describes. Historically, no Davidic king defeated a king of Assyria or a king of Babylon. On the contrary, successive Assyrian and Babylonian kings defeated Israel and exiled her people.

To express this transcendent drama—how the Lord ultimately overthrows the forces of chaos—Isaiah draws on a variety of biblical types such as Moses, Gideon, David, and Cyrus, each of which exemplifies one or more aspects of the ideal. These Isaiah combines in the Davidic king. The Davidic king's mission of defeating the forces of chaos and delivering temporally the Lord's people evolves out of this synthesis of types, one that fills out the details of Isaiah's picture. Conversely, in the archtyrant Isaiah combines the worst traits of the most notorious of the world's rulers. Isaiah's archtyrant is a veritable monster, the Antichrist himself. As in the ancient Near Eastern myths of Horus and Seth, Marduk and Tiamat, and others, the Lord pits these two figures—the Davidic king and the archtyrant—one against the other to work out their own and the world's destiny. In the book of Isaiah, the struggle between them makes up a real but sublime drama that has a beginning and an end. The archtyrant prevails for a time, so long as he serves the Lord's purpose. The Davidic king gains the final victory on behalf of the Lord.

Hebrew Language

A knowledge of the Hebrew language relates to the letter of prophecy. A translation of Isaiah cannot always fully represent the meanings of Hebrew terms. Particularly is this so with words that possess a double definition. The prophets frequently choose such terms deliberately because these terms enrich their message. The Prophet Joseph Smith reflects this understanding when he says, "My soul delights in reading the word of the Lord in the original."[15] The School of the Prophets in Kirtland hired a Jewish teacher and

---

[15] Joseph Smith, *History of The Church of Jesus Christ of Latter-day Saints* (Salt Lake City: Deseret Book, 1948), 2:396. Joseph Smith adds later, "I . . . take exceptions to the present translation of the Bible [the King James Version] in relation to these matters. Our latitude and longitude can be determined in the original Hebrew with far greater accuracy than in the English version" (Smith, *History of the Church*, 5:342–43).

had access to the Hebrew Masoretic Text as handed down by the Jews. From that text, scholars make translations of the Old Testament. Joseph Smith became proficient in biblical Hebrew, giving a number of explications that show his understanding of the letter of prophecy.[16] I will discuss a passage of Isaiah as an example of how knowing Hebrew helps in understanding Isaiah's words.

Chapter 6 describes Isaiah's receiving his commission as prophet: "In the year of King Uzziah's death, I saw my Lord seated on a throne, highly exalted, the skirt of his robe filling the sanctuary. Seraphs stood by him overhead, each having six wings" (vv. 1–2). In Hebrew, the word *seraph* (*'sārāp*) literally means "a fiery/burning one." Moses uses the same term of the *fiery serpents* at Israel's wandering in the wilderness (see Numbers 21:8). This definition reminds us of Joseph Smith's statement about those who dwell in the presence of the Lord: they dwell amid everlasting burnings.[17] Isaiah's use of *fiery ones* to describe angels that stand about the Lord, instead of the common word for *angels* ("messengers") emphasizes the nature of Isaiah's vision—the angels, here, do not serve as messengers but exemplify a cleansed or purified state.

Each seraph possesses six *wings*. The term in Hebrew (*kĕnāpayîm*) also means "veils." This meaning agrees with the function of their "wings," for the prophet adds, "With two they could veil their presence, with two conceal their location, and with two fly about" (v. 2). Isaiah then describes a hymn the seraphs sing: "They called out to one another, and said, Most holy is the Lord of Hosts; the consummation of all the earth is his glory!" (v. 3).

The Hebrew of the seraphs' anthem, which literally says, "holy, holy, holy," expresses the superlative in that language, the equivalent of the English superlative, "most holy." The superlative again emphasizes a pure and sanctified state, one to which the seraphs themselves look as an ideal. The phrase "the consummation of all the earth is his glory!" the King James Version renders "the whole earth is full of his glory." But the Hebrew word *mĕlō'* ("fulness" or "consummation") is a noun, not an adverb

---

[16] See Joseph Smith, *Teachings of the Prophet Joseph Smith*, sel. Joseph Fielding Smith (Salt Lake City: Deseret Book Company, 1938), 348–52.

[17] Smith, *Teachings of the Prophet Joseph Smith*, 347.

or adjective. Thus, reading the text as "the consummation [or fulness/fulfillment] of all the earth is his glory!" reflects a more correct translation. It also makes good sense in the light of the restored gospel. We know that the consummation of the earth—the earth fulfilling the purpose of its creation—*is* the Lord's glory. The Lord created the earth and man upon it in order that men might have eternal life and glorify God (compare Moses 1:39).

The text continues, "The threshold shook to its foundation at the sound of those who called, and a mist filled the temple" (v. 4). This shows the elements of the earth to be subject to the power of angels—those who are pure and holy. The *mist* (Hebrew *'āšān*, also "cloud/smoke") denotes the presence of the Lord or his entrance into the temple. Seeing the Lord face to face, the prophet is afraid for his life. Isaiah survives the encounter, however, suffering only a partial impairment of his physical functions: "Then I thought, Woe is me: I have been struck dumb, for I am a man of unclean speech, and I live among a people of unclean speech: I have seen the King, the Lord of Hosts, with my own eyes!" (v. 5).

The word translated "struck dumb" (Hebrew *nidmêtî*), which can also mean "ruined/destroyed," the King James Version translates "undone." The term's double meaning possesses added significance. Evidently, the Lord does not ruin or destroy Isaiah, though the term signifies the death of the carnal man. If, on the other hand, we read "struck dumb," then we are reminded of the Opening-of-the-Mouth ceremony such as we find in the Egyptian temple endowment. A person initiated into the rites of passage has his mouth opened so that he may speak. This act typifies his ritual cleansing. In identifying himself closely with his people, Isaiah lets us know that both he and his people partake of the same corrupt human nature. Despite man's nature, however, and although man is prone to sin, the Lord has ordained a way to purify his soul.

Isaiah describes how one of the seraphs flies to him, carrying an ember he has taken with tongs from the altar (see v. 6). There follows a typical Opening-of-the-Mouth ceremony: "Touching it to my mouth, he said, See, this has touched your lips: your sins are taken away, your transgressions atoned for" (v. 7). The tongs the seraph holds compare with an adze of meteoric iron used in

36

the Egyptian endowment.[18] The fiery coal from the altar symbolizes atonement by sacrifice—the seraph opens Isaiah's mouth by virtue of a sacrifice. Having thus been declared cleansed of sin and healed, the prophet is again able to speak. Of course, there is the implication that he can now speak with the tongue of angels.

Isaiah then hears the voice of the Lord saying, "Whom shall I send? Who will go for us?" Isaiah replies, "Here am I; send me!" (v. 8). Isaiah, who before this practically cowered in the Lord's presence, now answers forthrightly and with confidence. He desires to do for his people as has been done for him. Isaiah receives the opposite of the prophetic commission he desires when the Lord says, "Go, and say to these people, 'Go on hearing, but not understanding; go on seeing, but not perceiving!' Make the heart of these people grow fat; dull their ears and shut their eyes, lest they see with their eyes and hear with their ears, understand in their heart, and repent and be healed" (vv. 9–10).

Isaiah, instead of receiving the commission that will lead to "healing" (salvation) for his people, receives a commission to harden their hearts. The conditioned reflex of a people ripened in iniquity,when a prophet preaches repentance and reproves them of wickedness, is to harden their hearts against him. Isaiah finds himself in that predicament. His mission will precipitate Israel's judgment. The expression "these people" describes the Lord's people derogatorily (compare 8:6, 11), repudiating the usual expression that reflects the covenant relationship, "my people." On commissioning Isaiah, the Lord nonetheless makes provision for the healing of those who respond positively to Isaiah's message. The Lord gives an implicit formula for the people's salvation, namely, seeing with the eyes, hearing with the ears, understanding with the heart, repenting, and being healed. In this respect, Isaiah himself serves as a paradigm of the righteous (compare 8:18).

On being commissioned with his prophetic task, Isaiah expresses disappointment. He inquires, "For how long, my Lord?" The Lord answers, "Until the cities lie desolate and without inhabitant, the houses without a man, and the land ravaged to ruin" (v. 11). This answer reflects a bleak prospect for the new prophet, who understands full well that such a judgment comes only as a result of a

---

[18] See Hugh Nibley, *The Message of the Joseph Smith Papyri: An Egyptian Endowment* (Salt Lake City: Deseret Book Company, 1975), 106–13.

people's rejecting the Lord and, thus, his messenger. The Lord's judgment on his people results in their scattering, decimation, and burning: "For the Lord will drive men away, and great shall be the exodus from the centers of the land. And while yet a tenth [of the people] remain in it, or return, they shall be burned. But like the terebinth tree or the oak when it is felled, whose stump remains alive, so shall the holy offspring be what is left standing" (vv. 12–13).

Isaiah here gives us to understand that a two-fold calamity will ensue. First, a desolation of cities and ravaging of the land occurs (see v. 11). This precipitates an exodus of people out of the "centers of the land"—the cities (v. 12). Some of the people remain or return (see v. 13), signifying that initially they escape unharmed. These suffer a second calamity—burning (Hebrew $b\bar{a}'\bar{e}r$, also "consumption"). Isaiah then speaks of a "holy offspring" left standing like the stump of a tree; however, this kind of tree—a terebinth or oak—can renew itself even after it is cut down to its stump. Isaiah here likens Israel to a tree that is able to grow up again after it is destroyed in the Lord's day of judgment.

Two terms are pertinent to this judgment. The first, a *tenth*, is also the word for "tithe" in Hebrew. More specifically, the term stands for "tithe of the Lord" (Hebrew *'a'sîriyâ*, "tithe of Yah"). It is not the usual word for "tenth" or "tithe" (Hebrew *'a'sîrî*). It relates to the *holy offspring* in the same context. The two ideas together recall the tithe of the tithe in the law of Moses. This tithe was called "the holy portion" (Numbers 18:29). The Israelites paid a tithe of their increase to the tribe of Levi, the priestly tribe. In turn, the tribe of Levi paid a tithe of what it received to the family of Aaron, the priests. This tithe of the tithe was consecrated to the Lord—it was called *holy*. In describing those who survive a two-fold destruction in the Lord's day of judgment, Isaiah uses the imagery of the tithe the priests consecrated to the Lord. The chapter thus begins and ends with the idea of holiness.

Searching

In 3 Nephi 23:1–3 Jesus gives two keys for understanding Isaiah. Jesus, who might have spoken his own words, quotes at length from Isaiah (see 3 Nephi 22). That alone signifies the importance of Isaiah's words. Then he says, "I say unto you, that ye ought to search these things. Yea, a commandment I give unto you that ye search these things diligently'' (v. 1). That is the third key. We cannot understand Isaiah without diligent searching; and the Lord made such searching a commandment. In effect, Isaiah is not to be understood simply by our reading his words—we must search them out. When we do that, we make connections, we study things out in our minds, we read between the lines—it involves several techniques, all requiring diligence.

Searching is also a process: we cannot come to a full understanding of Isaiah all at once. We should recognize the implications of this and its effect on us. Those of us who give up and do not search Isaiah will fail to understand his message when it is most needed—to our condemnation and calamity in the last days. On the other hand, those who undertake to search Isaiah diligently will obtain the Lord's help, including his Spirit. By persisting, we will overcome an immense hurdle—Isaiah represents a deliberate challenge. If we persist, his message will eventually crystallize in our minds, bringing increasing recognition of his words. Gaining a mastery of Isaiah's message will prepare us for the events he prophesies—we will know clearly what the Lord expects of us.

Of course, the key of searching relates to all other keys. When I search the scriptures, I often experience the Holy Ghost. This leads me to further searches, adding upon what I have learned. The manner of the Jews also requires searching. In many ways these two keys overlap. Without searching, we cannot analyze Isaiah's words as the Jews do. To become proficient at the letter of prophecy requires practice. It involves us in an ongoing quest. The Jews themselves, not unusually, spend some fifteen years of their lives solely studying the Law and the Prophets. Many Jews do this for an entire lifetime, supported in their endeavor by their wealthy brethren.

The awesome mass of rabbinic commentaries the Jews have accumulated was generated precisely by such searching of texts. The Jews take this for granted. They have had more practice at searching the scriptures than any other people. For more than two thousand years, in the diaspora alone, Jewish academies devoted solely to the study of the Law and the Prophets have flourished. The discoveries the Jews make when searching the word of God keep them motivated. In the Hebrew scriptures, paradoxes are the rule, not the exception. Resolving them is a task the Jews undertake with lively zeal. As far as the word of God is concerned, there exists ever something new and inspiring to learn.

The key of searching, however, may go beyond applying the letter of prophecy. For that reason I regard it as a separate key. Searching the words of Isaiah draws on the manner of the Jews and invites the spirit of prophecy, but it may transcend set literary forms. Thus searching yields a wider, less focused result. Diligent searching leads to a spiritually mature perspective, a deep and abiding commitment. To investigate the scriptures has, for me, always been a rewarding pastime. Where I have had a question, and have sincerely sought, I have obtained an answer. For this reason, searching often becomes a spiritual experience. In order to progress in our salvation, we all must taste its fruits. What we ourselves search out, we assimilate best—it becomes a part of us, our spiritual forage.

In short, there is no substitute for searching—others cannot do it for us. Each must undertake it personally as a prerequisite for growing in the gospel. Because it is a commandment, searching has a purpose. The kind of searching of which Jesus speaks does not regard principles and truths we discover as only of passing interest. It recognizes that there exists a direct equation between our spiritual understanding and the purity and sanctity of our souls. When we apply in our lives all that we learn, knowing that we will thereby become the more enlightened, our knowledge increases but in proportion to our righteousness.

Our searching mind, thus equipped, focuses on the prophets' words without narrowing our view to a single dimension: we observe all things in their place. Proper searching expresses this holistic viewpoint. It recognizes truths as part of a totality, shielding us from intrusive falsehoods. We possess a sure standard by which to judge; we are not easily swayed. We accept truths and assimilate them into this whole. We yield to neither ignorance nor intellectualism. We keep a spiritual perspective.

As with the spirit of prophecy, the intangible elements that are a part of searching—the Holy Ghost, commitment, motivation, perspective—are personal and vary greatly from individual to individual. I therefore limit my discussion to outlining several more practical methodologies, leaving the overall approach to the reader.

Reading between the Lines

Reading between the lines is an integral part of searching the words of Isaiah. This kind of searching we can do in a variety of ways. The ones I suggest by no means exhaust the possibilities. As an example, Isaiah 1:11–12 states, "For what purpose are your abundant sacrifices to me? says the Lord. I have had my fill of offerings of rams and fat of fatted beasts; the blood of bulls and sheep and he-goats I do not want. When you come to see me, who requires you to trample my courts so?" The question the Lord asks at the beginning of verse 11, "For what purpose are your abundant sacrifices to me?" he answers at the beginning of verse 12: "When you come to see me." By reading between the lines, we learn that the purpose of attending the temple is to see the Lord, not to multiply statistics. The true purpose contrasts with the attitude of the people, who presume that their many sacrifices testify of their righteousness and acceptance before the Lord.

The Hebrew for "When you come to see me" (*lērā'ôt pānāi*) the King James Version translates "When ye come to appear before me." The Hebrew verb, however, is active, not passive. The Masoretes, Jewish transcribers of the Hebrew scriptures, nonetheless gave this active verb a passive vocalization. Perhaps they did not believe men could see the Lord in the temple. The various ritually clean animals presented as offerings represent, metaphorically, the Lord's people (compare 5:17; 60:7–9); the people who come to the temple to sacrifice are themselves implied subjects of the sacrifice. They behave much like the brute beasts brought for offerings, "trampling" through the temple's precincts, not knowing why they are there.

A passage of Isaiah may evidence linking words, containing a hidden message, as in chapter 8:

11. The Lord spoke to me, clasping my hand,
     and admonished me not to follow the ways of these people.
     For he said,
12. Do not call a conspiracy all that these people call a conspiracy;
     be not afraid or awed by the thing they fear.
13. But sanctify the Lord of Hosts,
     making him your fear, him your awe.
14. And to you he will be a sanctuary,
     but to the two houses of Israel a stumbling block
     or obstructing rock, and a snare,
     catching unawares the inhabitants of Jerusalem.
15. Many will stumble into them,
     and when they fall shall be broken,
     and when they become ensnared shall be taken captive.

A chain of linking words ties together the first and last ideas to appear. The chain consists of the Lord *speaking/saying* (Hebrew root *'mr*; v. 11); *these people* (vv. 11–12); *a conspiracy* (v. 12); *fear* and *awe* (vv. 12–13); *sanctify/sanctuary* (Hebrew root *qdš*; vv. 13–14); *stumble* and *snare* (vv. 14–15). The first admonition in this word chain concerns the "ways of these people." The last deals with being "taken captive." Reading between the lines, we learn that the present ways of the Lord's people are leading to their captivity. That conclusion could be taken both as a principle—based on the idea of cause and effect—and as an outright prediction: they *will* suffer captivity. The ideas that repeat themselves emphasize underlying conditions.

Important doctrines and theological concepts lie hidden between the lines. A passage in chapter 40, for example, speaks of weariness and nonweariness:

> 28. Is it not known to you; have you not heard?
> The Lord is the God of eternity,
> Creator of the ends of the earth.
> He does not grow faint or weary;
> his intelligence cannot be fathomed.
> 29. He supplies the weary with energy
> and increases in vigor those who lack strength.
> 30. Youth grow faint and weary,
> and young men slump down of exhaustion.
> 31. But they who hope in the Lord
> shall be renewed in strength:
> they shall ascend as on eagles' wings;
> they shall run without wearying,
> they shall walk and not faint.

Verse 28 depicts the Lord as Creator of the ends of the earth. The God of eternity, he does not grow faint or weary. Verses 29–30 contrast those who *do* grow weary—namely, mortal men, even the strongest—the young men on whom Israel depends for physical strength. In effect, even at his best, mortal man grows weary and needs a constant supply of energy. The Lord supplies this. Verse 31 returns to the idea of nonweariness. Those who "hope in" the Lord (Hebrew *qiwê*, also "wait for"), he renews in strength. They "ascend" as on eagle's wings. They run without wearying and walk without growing faint.

42

The concept of nonweariness—God's capacity not to become weary—contrasts with the weariness of mortal man; and the idea of nonweariness recurs: nonweariness designates those who "hope in" the Lord, who are renewed in strength and ascend upward. The word *ascend* (Hebrew *ya'ălû*) also means "progress." In sum, those who progress spiritually become like God in the fact that they become nonwearying. By analogy (because the four verses are structured chiastically: a–b–b–a),[19] the nonweariness of those who ascend is of the same character as the nonweariness of God. The importance theologically of these implicit ideas is self-evident. They come as close to describing man's potential for a glorious immortality as any Hebrew terms.

Rhetorical Connections

Rhetorical links throughout the book of Isaiah pertain to the key of searching. For example, why should Isaiah talk about nations or Gentiles (Hebrew *gôyîm*) "flowing" (Hebrew *nāhărû*) to Zion in the latter days (see 2:2)? Why should he not describe them as "coming" or "going"? He uses the verb flow to link to two other contexts in the book of Isaiah in which he speaks of nations or Gentiles streaming to Zion (see 60:5; 66:12). Those two passages depict the return of Israel's exiles from among the nations. They say nothing, however, about when Israel's return takes place. On the other hand, Isaiah says nothing about the idea of Israel's return home in 2:2. There, he merely describes nations or Gentiles flowing to Zion. By means of rhetorical links between these passages— the ideas they have in common—we thus understand that the nations or Gentiles flowing to Zion in 2:2 represent Israel's exiles returning home and that this return takes place "in the latter days" (2:2).

The term *mountains* links rhetorically to various contexts throughout Isaiah. First, however, we must identify a peculiarity of this term. Isaiah 13:4 reads,

Hark! A tumult on the mountains, as of a vast multitude.
Hark! An uproar among kingdoms, as of nations assembling.

Here, *mountains* parallels *kingdoms*, signifying (because the two lines form a synonymous parallelism) that the term *mountains* serves

---

[19] a—nonweariness (v. 28); b—weariness (v. 29); b—weariness (v. 30); a—nonweariness (v. 31).

as a metaphor of *kingdoms*—we may read *mountains* as *kingdoms*.
The Hebrew preposition *on* (*bĕ*) also reads "in/at/among."

Mountains similarly appears as a metaphor in chapter 64. There,
mountains parallels *nations*:

1. O that thou wouldst rend the heavens and descend,
      the mountains melting at thy presence—
2. as when fire is lit for boiling water,
      which bubbles over from the heat—
   to make thyself known to thine adversaries,
      the nations trembling at thy presence—
3. as when thou didst perform awesome things,
      unexpected by us; thy descent [of old],
   when the mountains quaked before thee!

This passage forms a chiasm of terms. *Nations* (v. 2) appears between
two instances of *mountains* (vv. 1, 3), forming a chiasm (a–b–a).
The expressions "melting at thy presence," "trembling at thy
presence," and "quaked before thee" all parallel one another. The
terms "at thy presence" and "before thee" appear identical in
Hebrew (*mippānêkâ*). The three Hebrew verbs are common
synonyms. Here, then, by means of three synonymous lines, Isaiah
represents *mountains* to be a metaphor of *nations*.

In sum, we may read the term *mountains* in the book of
Isaiah in a secondary sense, as *kingdoms* or *nations*, to yield a
transcendent meaning of the scripture. And, just as we do when
we read literally, so we may read every instance of *mountain/s*
metaphorically—both meanings are valid. Once Isaiah establishes
an idea in one part of his book, it applies in all instances throughout. Let us now relate our discovery to several other contexts.

Chapter 2 refers to mountains and hills in the day of the world's
judgment. A passage begins "The Lord of Hosts has a day in store
for all the proud and arrogant and for all who are exalted, that they
may be brought low" (v. 12). The key idea of this passage is the
humbling of what exalts itself—Isaiah foresees a reversal. He continues, "[It shall come] against all the lofty cedars of Lebanon that
lift themselves up high, and against all the oaks of Bashan" (v. 13).
These names serve as symbols: in the book of Isaiah *Lebanon* and
Bashan represent elite Israel; the *cedars* and *oaks* represent the
people hewn down by the archtyrant, the Lord's *axe* and *saw*

(compare 1:29–30; 10:33–34; 14:8; 37:24). Isaiah says further: "Against all high mountains and elevated hills, against every tall tower and reinforced wall" (vv. 14–15). If we read *nations* or *kingdoms* in place of *mountains*, we see that a divine judgment comes upon all elite peoples. The intent of this judgment, as a concluding verse summarizes, is to bring man's pride low: "The Lord alone shall be exalted in that day" (v. 17).

This intent, therefore, is the hidden meaning of the prophecy. On the surface, verses 13–16 speak of a series of geophysical objects that the Lord levels in his day of judgment. Isaiah does not mention peoples. But if we read these same verses metaphorically, we can understand them to refer to such. The *cedars of Lebanon*, as in other contexts of Isaiah, we define as an exalted people. *Mountains* represent nations or kingdoms. *Tall towers* and *reinforced walls* represent man's prideful institutions (compare 30:13), and so forth. These verses refer to peoples, but only implicitly.

The Book of Mormon version of verse 14 nevertheless identifies peoples directly. After mentioning high mountains and hills, 2 Nephi 12:14 adds, "upon all the nations which are lifted up, and upon every people." The Hebrew preposition *upon* ('*al*) also means "against." This verse in the Book of Mormon adds to Isaiah's context of a series of geophysical objects. It was put there to let us know that the day of judgment comes as much against peoples as against their lands. The Book of Mormon addition reflects the metaphorical meaning of the verse.

We see a similar thing in 5:25, which depicts metaphorically the destruction the archtyrant causes in the Lord's day of judgment:

> Therefore the anger of the Lord is kindled
>   against his people:
> he draws back his hand against them
>   and strikes them;
> the mountains quake, and their corpses
>   lie like litter about the streets.
> Yet for all this his anger is not abated;
>   his hand is upraised still.

As the Lord's *anger* and *hand*, the archtyrant strikes wicked Israel. Reading *mountains* metaphorically, however, we see that nations or kingdoms quake before the archtyrant, that *their* corpses litter the streets. In this metaphorical sense, the Lord's people at that time thus consist of many nations or kingdoms. We confirm this idea rhetorically in the archtyrant's taunt song: "Is this the man who made the earth shake and kingdoms quake?" (14:16). The archtyrant causes the collapse and shaking of the nations of Israel in the Lord's day of judgment.

Many other contexts in which the term *mountain/s* appears would provide a fruitful search. I will discuss a final example. Isaiah 2:2 says, "In the latter days the mountain of the Lord's house shall become established as the head of the mountains." If we read the verse metaphorically, then it says, "In the latter days the nation of the Lord's house shall become established as the head of the nations." The Hebrew preposition *in* (*bĕ*) is sometimes translated "as"—we can read it either way. The Qumran scroll of Isaiah reads literally "as" (Hebrew *kĕ*). The two Hebrew letters are similar; but the former, as in this passage, possesses multiple meanings.

The Lord promises Israel as a covenant blessing that if she abides by the terms of the Sinai covenant, she will become the head of the nations. If she does not, she will be the tail (see Deuteronomy 28:10, 13). This is the substance of what Isaiah is talking about. In the latter days, he says, the nation of the Lord's "house" (a synonym of *temple*; compare 66:1) will again become the head of the nations—as Israel was anciently in the time of David and Solomon. But if we read the verse literally, we can also define the word *head* (Hebrew *rō'š*) as "chief" or "top"— its secondary meanings. In that case the verse says, "In the latter days the mountain of the Lord's house shall become established in the chief/top of the mountains."

Isaiah 2:2, then, exhibits a classic double meaning: (1) Israel will become the head of the nations in the latter days, or, rather, the nation of the Lord's house will become the head of the nations, and (2) the mountain of the Lord's house will be in the chief, or top, of the mountains. When we reflect on the history of America, we see that the head of the nations in the modern age is certainly this country. We also see that the central place and temple built as a result of the Lord's restoring his gospel is located in the chief, or top, of the mountains—in Utah. Isaiah adds, "It shall be pre-eminent among the hills and all nations will flow to it" (2:2). Just as we see a two-fold phenomenon with regard to the head of the nations and the top of the mountains, so we see a two-fold phenomenon here. The United States of America forms a composite of all nations—remnants of all nations have flowed into it to create it. On the other hand, as a result of the gospel's being restored (see 2:3), many people are becoming Latter-day Saints—remnants of all nations come to the high point of the Rocky Mountains.

Rhetorical links identify the Lord's "servant," who appears in passages scattered throughout Isaiah, as the Davidic king. In each of these passages, one or more concepts or motifs link, domino fashion, to similar concepts and motifs in other passages. No one passage describing the Lord's servant is unique—it always contains something others share. This linking establishes a network of common ideas. Taken together, they provide us with a holistic picture of the mission and attributes of the Davidic king. In effect, we cannot gain a full idea of the Davidic king's mission and attributes without examining all interrelated passages. A partial view would handicap our ability to interpret any one such passage. In this respect, rhetorical links serve as a reliable internal check: whatever interpretation we come to we can verify by comparing the descriptive terms Isaiah employs in one passage with the identical terms in others. Isaiah uses such connecting ideas deliberately.

By this means we confirm rhetorically that the Lord's servant and the Davidic king are the selfsame individual—a vassal of the Lord. The term *servant* (see 42:1; 52:13), like the term *son* that Isaiah applies to the Davidic king (see 7:14; 9:6), expresses this vassal relationship.[20] Isaiah's use of the two terms coincides, in the main, with respective political (*son*) and spiritual (*servant*) aspects the Davidic king's mission has. (Familial terms—*son* for a vassal, *father* for a suzerain—express ancient Near Eastern covenant relationships. Such terms, although they may reflect an original familial usage, do not express blood ties between a vassal and suzerain. Vassal kings were generally indigenous to the peoples over whom they ruled. Besides ruling directly over his own people, a suzerain often ruled over many vassal kings in his empire.) Lastly, the term *servant* properly describes a vassal's inferior status toward the suzerain.

While it is not possible here to cite all rhetorical links tying together the many passages about the Davidic king and servant, I

---

[20] Compare King Ahaz's establishing of a vassal–suzerain relationship with the king of Assyria in 2 Kings 16:7: "I am thy servant and thy son." See also Weinfeld, "Berîth," in *Theological Dictionary of the Old Testament*, 2:253–79.

47

nonetheless present the main connecting ideas. First, the Lord commissions the Davidic king, endowing him with his Spirit to gather Israel and Judah and restore them to the Lord's covenant (see 11:2, 10–13; 42:1, 6–7; 48:16; 49:5–6, 8–12; 55:3, 5; 61:1–3). Second, the Lord appoints the Davidic king as Israel's teacher, lawgiver, and judge (see 2:3–4; 11:3–4; 16:5; 42:1–4; 50:4; 55:4). Third, although the Davidic king suffers severe affliction and humiliation, the Lord ultimately vindicates and exalts him (see 49:4–5, 7; 50:5–9; 52:13–15; 53:11–12). Fourth, the Davidic king wins many physical victories for the Lord, overthrowing the forces of chaos or evil both political and spiritual (see 9:4–5; 11:14; 41:2–3, 25; 45:1–2; 48:14). Fifth, the Davidic king undertakes the physical restoring of the promised land (see 44:26–28; 45:13; 49:8; 61:4). And sixth, the Davidic king's rule and ministry are characterized by righteousness (see 2:4; 9:7; 11:4–5; 16:5; 32:1; 41:2; 42:1–4; 61:3).

In marked contrast to the Davidic king, who links rhetorically to many contexts of the book of Isaiah, the suffering figure of 53:1–10 appears unique. That passage stands alone not only in Isaiah but in all of biblical literature. The idea of one man suffering and dying to atone for the sins of a people (see vv. 3–6, 10) possesses no human type or precedent in the Old Testament. It singularly typifies Christ, a divine personage. While suffering the prosecution a rebellious vassal would incur, he himself is innocent. Being buried and having offspring (see vv. 9–10) signifies that although men judge him as guilty and execute him (see v. 8), he remains untouched by covenant curse. To heighten its uniqueness, Isaiah confines rhetorical links to this passage to but a very few terms, such as *arm* of the Lord (v. 1)—a metaphorical pseudonym of the Lord and of the Davidic king (see 33:2; 62:8); *peace* (v. 5)—a synonym of salvation and covenant (see 52:7; 54:10); and *sheep* (v. 6)—a metaphor that describes the Lord's people (see 5:17). By his death, Christ pays the price of salvation for his believing sheep. On their account the Lord reveals his *arm* (v. 1).

An abundance of rhetorical connections between the Davidic king and those whom the Lord spares in his day of judgment illustrates the Davidic king's mission of preparing a people for the coming of the Lord. As the Lord's agent of ransoming Zion, the Davidic king serves as his people's exemplar: what he does, they do. Consequently, the Lord blesses the righteous of his people as he blesses him—they inherit a like glory on the earth.

As the Lord calls *Righteousness*—the Davidic king (see 41:2)—so he calls the followers of righteousness (see 51:1–2); as the Lord endows his servant with his Spirit (see 42:1, 6), so he endows his corporate servant (Israel) with his Spirit (see 44:3, 21); as *Righteousness* calls on the name of the Lord (see 41:1, 25), so the righteous of his people call on the name of the Lord (see 58:9); as the Lord's servant scales the *mountains* to herald the coming of the Lord (see 52:7), so the people of Zion scale the *mountains* to herald the coming of the Lord (see 40:9); as men revile and then worship the Lord's servant (see 49:7), so they revile and then worship the people of Zion (see 60:14; compare 49:23); as moths eat the incriminators of the Lord's servant (see 50:9), so moths eat the incriminators of the righteous (see 51:7–8); as the *arm* of the Lord rises, clothed in power (see 51:9), so Zion rises, clothed in power (see 52:1); as the Lord is glorified in his servant (see 49:3), so he is glorified in the redeemed of Israel (see 44:23); and so forth.

In contrast to this, the Lord's people as a whole do the contrary of what the Davidic king does: the Lord opens the ear of his servant to hear (see 50:4–5), but Israel's ears are closed (see 6:10; 48:8); the Lord's servant possesses a learned tongue (see 50:4), but Israel possesses a perverse tongue (see 3:8; 59:3); the Lord's servant teaches the Lord's law and word (see 42:4; 50:4), but Israel despises the Lord's law and word (see 5:24); the Lord's servant performs the work of justice (see 42:1), but Israel works injustice (see 5:7); *Righteousness* treads upon enemies as on mud (see 41:2, 25), but Israel is trodden as mud by enemies (see 10:6); and so forth. Such rhetorical connections reveal the apostasy of Israel as the Lord's day of judgment approaches. Out of this apostasy and its consequence the Davidic king delivers a righteous remnant of the Lord's people.

Rhetorical links show the new covenant Isaiah prophesies to be a composite of all former covenants the Lord made. At every mention of the covenant idea, Isaiah expresses some aspect of the relationship that prevails between the Lord and his people in the millennial age. By piecing these together rhetorically, we gain a clear idea of what this covenant consists of. Isaiah includes in the new covenant the basic ingredients of the Lord's covenant with Abraham, namely, a promised land and a numerous posterity (see 51:2–3; 60:21–22). The Lord protects the promised land against enemies (see 12:2–6; 26:1–4)—an ingredient of the Davidic covenant. The Lord puts his words in the mouths of his people's posterity (see 51:16; 59:21)—an ingredient of the Levitical covenant. In addition, the Lord regenerates the promised land to a paradisaical state (see 35:1–2; 51:3) and ordains his people's posterity as his priests (see 61:6, 9–10; 66:21).

The Lord makes the new covenant with a corporate group—the righteous of his people—called Zion (see 51:16; 61:8). The new covenant thus resembles the Sinai covenant, which also is a corporate agreement. The new covenant, however, unlike the Sinai covenant, is unconditional. In this respect it resembles the Lord's unconditional covenants with Abraham, with the Levites, and with David. The new covenant, then, draws on the exemplary features of the Lord's former covenants. It embodies in one ideal covenant every blessing pertaining to past sacred agreements with Israel or with individuals. This idea implies that those with whom the Lord makes the new covenant evidence a righteousness comparable to the righteousness of those individuals. It also illustrates how the keys of former dispensations come together in the last days to bless the righteous people of Zion.

Many aspects of the new covenant merge in chapter 54: land and posterity (vv. 1–3); an unconditional covenant replacing a former conditional covenant (vv. 4–8); a covenant with those who survive a cataclysm of the magnitude of the Flood, as in the days of Noah (vv. 9–10); a glorious habitat for the Lord's people (vv. 11–12); a posterity the Lord endows (v. 13); and an assurance of the Lord's protection (vv. 14–17). Personifying the Lord's *covenant* in the book of Isaiah (see 42:6; 49:8) is the Davidic king, who serves as its mediator (see 42:6; 49:8; 55:3–4). Unlike Moses, however, who mediated the Sinai covenant, the Davidic king mediates the new covenant with a people who come out of bondage from among the nations (see 42:4–7; 49:6–13; 55:3–5).

Zion and Babylon

Let us now apply the key of searching in order to define *Zion* according to Isaiah's definition of the term. Isaiah 1:27 consists of a parallelism:

> Zion shall be ransomed by justice,
> those of her who repent by righteousness.

In the first line, *Zion* is the subject of the verb *ransomed*. In the second line, the subject of the verb *ransomed* (implied from the first line) is "those of her who repent." *Justice* and *righteousness*, the grammatical actors, complete the parallelism. The pronoun *her* typifies the woman figure in the book of Isaiah; it represents Israel, or the Lord's people (compare 1:21; 3:26). Here, then, Isaiah gives us a parallelistic definition of who constitutes Zion. We as Latter-day Saints know that Zion consists of the pure in heart (see D&C 97:21). But compare this with Isaiah's definition: Zion (by analogy of the two parallel lines) *is* "those of her [Israel] who repent." The word in Hebrew for *repent* (*šûb*) also means "return" (*šûb*). So the line could read "those of her who return."

Zion as those of Israel who repent/return is a definition we obtain by parallelism. We confirm this definition in 59:20, which says, "He [the Lord] will come as Redeemer to Zion, to those of Jacob who repent of transgression." Again we find the concept that Zion does not comprehend all of Israel—in this instance, "Jacob," which stands for Israel. Zion represents only those of Israel who repent of transgression. In short, the people Zion compose a select group, namely, that portion of the Lord's people that qualifies for ransoming and redeeming because it repents.

Isaiah 35:10 yields another definition of *Zion*, this time not by way of parallelism but by context: "The ransomed of the Lord shall return; they shall come singing to Zion, their heads crowned with everlasting joy" (compare 51:11). Here again, the word *ransomed* designates those who "return." (The latter term is the same one in Hebrew as *repent* in 1:27; 59:20.) The ransomed of the Lord return to Zion. Zion here is a place—the place of return. By putting the several passages together, we find that those of Israel who repent, who constitute Zion (see 1:27; 59:20), are also those who return to the place Zion (see 35:10; 51:11). By Isaiah's double definition, Zion consists of both a people and a place: those who repent and the place of their return.

Isaiah gives justice and righteousness as the criteria for Zion's being ransomed (see 1:27). Although justice and righteousness are general principles that qualify the Lord's people for being ransomed, the term *righteousness* also serves as a metaphorical pseudonym of the Davidic king (see 41:2). It thus alludes to the Davidic king's role in ransoming Zion. By rhetorical definition in the book of Isaiah, to be "ransomed" (Hebrew *pdh*, also "redeemed") means to be delivered temporally in the Lord's day of judgment (compare 29:22; 50:1–2; 51:9–11). In ransoming Zion, the Davidic king serves as a proxy for or agent of the Lord's divine intervention. A synonymous Isaianic term for *ransomed* (Hebrew $g^{)}l$, also "redeemed") spells out this temporal salvation rhetorically as being released from bondage (see 49:25–26; 52:2–3); participating in an exodus out of Babylon (see 48:20–21; 52:9–11); returning from exile (see 35:8–9; 43:1–6); being delivered from death (see 43:1–4; 54:8–9); renewing the covenant (see 54:5–6; 59:20–21); conquering the promised land (see 41:14–16); and inheriting the promised land (see 60:15–16). The effect of being ransomed, Isaiah tells us, is everlasting joy (see 35:10).

In other Isaianic passages we observe how Zion consists of a safe place in the Lord's day of judgment, the day in which he restores universal justice:

> Over the whole site of Mount Zion, and over its solemn assembly, the Lord will form a cloud by day and a mist glowing with fire by night: above all that is glorious shall be a canopy. It shall be a shelter and shade from the heat of the day, a secret refuge from the downpour and from rain.
>
> (4:5–6)

Rhetorically, the word *day* signifies the day of judgment when the Lord metes out justice. The expression "heat of the day" denotes that it is a day of fire and burning. This appears from many other contexts (compare 9:18–19; 33:12–14; 34:8–10; 66:15–16). In the day of the world's judgment, which ushers in the Lord's coming in glory, Zion serves as a safe place for a solemn assembly of his Saints—his "holy ones" (4:3). On that occasion, the Lord restores the pillar of cloud by day and of fire by night (a sign of his presence; see Exodus 13:21) as a protection or canopy. The word *canopy* in Hebrew refers to a marriage canopy (*ḥŭppâ*), implying that the Lord renews the covenant with his people at that time. The "downpour" and "rain" are judgment imagery—Isaiah has in mind a Sodom and Gomorrah type of downpour, a rain from the sky like fire and brimstone, destroying the wicked (compare 13:19; 25:4–5; 34:4, 9).

Another definition by context tells about Babylon. Chapter 13 reads, "An oracle concerning Babylon, which Isaiah the son of Amoz saw in vision" (v. 1). This is the heading of the chapter. But the chapter itself describes a universal destruction. The Lord, in/by his *anger*, signals for a vast and formidable army of nations to gather together to wreak destruction throughout the earth (vv. 2–5). Because the wicked of the Lord's people also come under attack, the Lord calls out his "holy ones" to a place of safety (v. 3). The destruction such a vast army causes, Isaiah calls the "day of the Lord" (v. 6)—the Lord's day of judgment. It makes the whole earth writhe in agony, become terribly desolate, and even jolt out of orbit (vv. 7–13).

So great is the desolation that few men survive it. Those who perish consist of the sinners, the wicked, the proud and tyrannical of the earth (vv. 9, 11–12). The army attacks mercilessly all in its path, committing genocide of entire nations (vv. 14–18; compare 10:7). This worldwide destruction, as the heading of the chapter indicates, Isaiah represents as Babylon's destruction; it is Babylon overthrown like Sodom and Gomorrah (v. 19). The destroyed places men never reinhabit; they become a lair for noxious animals and birds (vv. 20–22). We thus see how Isaiah defines the term *Babylon* by context as both a people and a place, even as *Zion* is both a people and a place. The place consists of the world at large, which the army desolates. The people consist of the sinners, the wicked, the proud, and tyrannical—those who perish.

We now observe how Isaiah contrasts Zion and Babylon. Babylon, as we note, represents the world and the wicked who are ripening for destruction. Zion represents the place to which the Lord's repentant ones return—a place of safety, a people the Lord protects. Isaiah has transformed the names *Zion* and *Babylon* from what they stood for anciently. Historically, Babylon was an idolatrous, materialistic world dominion. Zion was a fortresslike rock, a place adjacent to the temple in Jerusalem. Both names, as Isaiah uses them, symbolize something new—they serve as code names. Isaiah nonetheless retains the ancient connotations these names possessed. *Babylon* now represents universal wickedness, an idolatrous world (compare 21:9), all that the Lord destroys in a fiery holocaust. *Zion* represents a particular definition of the righteous and their place of refuge in the Lord's day of judgment.

Zion and Babylon thus readily appear as two contrasting entities, two mutually exclusive entities. Zion represents what Babylon is not, and vice versa. If Zion consists of those of the Lord's people who repent, who return, and whom the Lord ransoms, then Babylon consists of all who do not repent, who do not return, and whom he does not ransom. If Babylon stands for the world and the wicked whom the Lord destroys in his day of judgment, then Zion stands for what he does not destroy at that time. In the book of Isaiah, there develops an irrevocable dissociation between those who ally themselves with the one and those who ally themselves with the other. As the Lord's day of judgment approaches, all middle ground vanishes.

We see this contrast between Zion and Babylon in 47:1–3. Babylon, who has ruled the world oppressively and despotically, is made to get down off her throne and "sit in the dust" (v.1). Dust, a chaos motif, signifies that her power is at an end—she is going to be reduced to chaos, to a nonentity, so to speak. This happens to Babylon at the time the Lord redeems Zion (see 47:4). Zion, who has suffered oppression as a captive in Babylon (see 47:6), the Lord now causes to "rise from the dust"—from being a nonentity, as it were—to sit on her throne (see 52:1–2). Isaiah identifies this event as the redeeming of Zion (see 52:3). In effect, Babylon's fall heralds Zion's ascendancy. A reversal takes place in the Lord's day of judgment—the Lord wreaks vengeance on the wicked but redeems the righteous (compare 34:8; 63:4).

Our search reveals that not only are the two Isaianic entities, Zion and Babylon, opposites of one another but their antithesis expresses a spiritual condition more than a physical or political one. As code names, *Zion* and *Babylon* possess strong spiritual overtones. They symbolize righteousness, which Isaiah defines as a disposition to repent, and wickedness, a disposition to oppress others, particularly the righteous. The one cannot flourish when the other rules.

Scriptural Links

Extending our search beyond the book of Isaiah helps in understanding Isaiah's words. Both the Book of Mormon and the Doctrine and Covenants, for example, draw substantially on the language and concepts of Isaiah. They often do that indirectly. One unfamiliar with Isaiah's writings might be unaware that these scriptures are quoting Isaiah or that Isaiah's imagery is being presented in the course of a revelation or discourse. The appearance in these scriptures of so much Isaianic material shows how much Isaiah permeates their thought. It also reflects the degree to which Isaiah relates to modern times.

In some instances, the Book of Mormon and the Doctrine and Covenants amplify or explain passages of Isaiah explicitly. That makes searching the words of Isaiah easier. I suggest we commence our

search with such explicit scriptural links. One example of an explana-
tion of Isaiah appears in Doctrine and Covenants 113. It concerns
Isaiah 11:1:

Hebrew	*weyāṣā ḥoṭer miggezaʿ yisāi* *wenēṣer missorāsāw yipreh*
King James Version	And there shall come forth a rod out of the stem of Jesse, and a Branch shall grow out of his roots:
New Translation	A shoot will spring up from the stock of Jesse and a branch from its graft bear fruit.

Doctrine and Covenants 113 identifies the "stock/stem" of Jesse
as Christ (vv. 1–2). Of the "shoot/rod," it says, "it is a servant
in the hands of Christ, who is partly a descendant of Jesse as well
as of Ephraim, or of the house of Joseph, on whom there is laid
much power" (v. 4).

Knowing these identities, we are able to examine Isaiah's allegory
more clearly. But first, we should note that the preceding context
of 11:1 consists of the Lord's day of judgment. The archtyrant levels
the towering trees with terrifying power and batters down the forests
of Lebanon (see 10:33–34). This imagery, as we saw earlier, symbolizes the destruction of the proud of the Lord's people (compare
2:13; 14:8). Second, we recall that a holy offspring of Israel survives the calamity of the day of judgment. It renews itself, growing
up from a stump to become a new tree (see 6:13). While this
imagery does not match precisely that of 11:1, it is nonetheless
important to keep in mind. Common denominators exist: there
comes a day of judgment in which the tree/s are cut down and a
new tree grows up to become a righteous Israel.

Another important idea, one we do not readily discern in the
King James Version of 11:1, is that the three-fold process of *stock*
⟶ *shoot* ⟶ *branch* ends with "fruit." This progression
means that in the implied context of the parable—the Lord's day
of judgment—the tree does not bear fruit. Something new must
happen to cause the tree again to bear fruit. An initial lack of fruit
before the day of judgment (see 5:1–6) and evidence of fruit after

that time (see 4:2) are supporting ideas. The Hebrew verb *bear fruit* (*pārâ*) also translates "sprout/grow forth" (compare KJV). That translation, however, represents a secondary meaning of the verb. Thus, many modern translations of the Bible now translate the verb as "bear fruit." (The Hebrew noun *fruit* [*pĕrî*] derives from the same verbal stem.) In short, what Isaiah represents as happening to the tree eventually leads to fruit. The tree itself, although it at some point may be cut down, renews itself and again becomes acceptable to the Lord.

The Hebrew for *stock/stem* (*geza'*) denotes the lower trunk of a tree. Since Doctrine and Covenants 113 identifies this *stock/stem* as Christ, it reminds us of what Jesus said:

> I am the true vine, and my Father is the husbandman. Every branch in me that beareth not fruit he taketh away: and every [branch] that beareth fruit, he purgeth it, that it may bring forth more fruit. . . . I am the vine, ye [are] the branches: He that abideth in me, and I in him, the same bringeth forth much fruit: for without me ye can do nothing.
>
> (John 15:1–2, 5)

We perceive that the lower trunk of the tree—Christ—is good. The intent of 11:1 is to show how the branch bears fruit and becomes the new tree. If it does, the resulting context of the parable is paradise (compare 11:6–9); if it does not, the context remains destruction in the day of judgment (see 10:33–34)—the world will experience only two immediate destinies.

In order that the tree bear fruit, a shoot springs up from the trunk of the tree. The Hebrew term for this *shoot/rod* (*ḥōṭer*) signifies it to be a watersprout, the sort of growth on fruit trees that farmers lop off in the spring. This cannot, of itself, bear fruit. Characteristic of a watersprout is its rapid growth straight upward from the lower trunk of the tree. It does not bear fruit but instead absorbs much of the moisture of the tree. If, however, the rest of the tree does not bear fruit, yet the lower trunk is good, then one could save such a watersprout and graft into it when it grows sufficiently strong. This procedure is the phenomenon Isaiah depicts in 11:1.

It is the third member of the trio, the *branch* (Hebrew *nēṣer*), that bears fruit. But it can do so only when grafted into the *shoot/rod*—it grows out of the *graft/caudex* (Hebrew *šorāšâw*) of the watersprout. It completes the process that results in a new tree. Only this *branch* can grow into a full-grown, fruit-bearing tree. Unlike the watersprout, which is wild by nature, the *branch* represents a tame, domesticated variety. In depicting the growth of the tree this way, Isaiah expresses something very similar to the parable of the olive tree of the prophet Zenos in the Book of Mormon (compare Jacob 5). There, the wild branches represent the Gentiles who come into the house of Israel. The tame branches represent the house of Israel—the Jews, the Nephites/Lamanites, and the ten tribes. Their being grafted into the tree represents their coming back into the Lord's covenant (compare Jacob 6:1–4).

There remains something else to consider. In Hebrew prophetic thought, the king of a nation (or leader of a community/father of a family) represents, in his person, the entire people. In a figurative sense, he personifies them.[21] If the *stock/stem* of Jesse represents Jesus Christ, then he also represents the tree as a whole—the growth that develops from him (compare John 15:1–2, 5). That is Christianity. But that Christianity no longer bears fruit. A new thing, or restoration, is necessary so that the tree may again bear fruit. The Prophet Joseph Smith and the church he organized typify this new thing. As the *shoot/rod*, he represents or personifies figuratively the Latter-day Saints. Partly a descendant of Jesse as well as of Ephraim, his immediate origins (and the Latter-day Saints') lie among the Gentiles, as the watersprout signifies (compare D&C 109:60).

Similarly, the third member of the trio, the *branch*, represents or personifies figuratively the natural branches of the house of Israel— the Jews, the Nephites/Lamanites, and the ten tribes. When these come into the tree, it again bears fruit—Israel appears in strength. The third party, the *branch*, not only represents the house of Israel but also serves as the Lord's agent of their grafting into the tree.[22] To depict the Davidic king as the agent of this grafting, Isaiah designates him as the Lord's *ensign* and *hand* in the same chapter

---

[21] See the Davidic king personifying "my servant, Israel," in 49:3.

[22] Compare the Prophet Joseph Smith's statement: "Christ, in the days of His flesh, proposed to make a covenant with them [the house of Israel and the house of Judah], but they rejected Him and His proposals, and in consequence thereof, they were broken off, and no covenant was made with them at that time. But their unbelief has not rendered the promise of God of none effect: no, for there was another day limited in David, which was the day of his power; and then His people, Israel, should be a willing people" (*Teachings of the Prophet Joseph Smith*, 14–15).

(see 11:10–11). By means of these two pseudonyms Isaiah then defines the Davidic king's mission metaphorically in his book as a whole. Under the metaphors *ensign* and *hand*, he represents the mission of the Davidic king as gathering Israel (see 49:22), leading the exodus of the Lord's people (see 50:2), delivering temporally the righteous of the Lord's people (see 18:3; 30:17; 51:16), subjugating Assyria (see 31:9), preparing the way of the Lord (see 62:10), reconquering the promised land (see 41:10–16, 20), and dividing the inheritances of the Lord's people (see 34:17).

Doctrine and Covenants 113 concurs with this description of the mission and attributes of the Davidic king. According to this revelation, the *sprig/root* of Jesse (see Isaiah 11:10) is "a descendant of Jesse, as well as of Joseph, unto whom rightly belongs the priesthood, and the keys of the kingdom, for an ensign, and for the gathering of my people in the last days" (v. 6). The *sprig/root* (Hebrew *šōreš*) identifies the early, or grafting phase of the Davidic king's mission. Isaiah defines this phase contextually in the same chapter as gathering Israel and Judah from the four directions of the earth, reuniting Judah and Ephraim, reconquering the promised land, subjugating Assyria, and leading the exodus of the ten tribes (see 11:10–16). This contextual outline of the Davidic king's mission agrees with the metaphorical one we have just noted, as well as with the one we determined rhetorically under a previous heading.

Two further ideas complete this picture. The Davidic king's office in the priesthood (see D&C 113:6) Isaiah details in 61:1–3 as the endowing of Israel's spiritually blind captives. This endowment leads to the captives' conversion (61:1–3), their rebuilding of the promised land, and their becoming universally renowned in the millennial age (61:4–11). The Davidic king's office of holding the keys of the kingdom (see D&C 113:6) Isaiah depicts typologically in 22:20–24. There, "my servant" Eliakim typifies the Davidic king's role of "father" to the house of Judah and the inhabitants of Jerusalem (22:20–21). The Lord invests him with the "keys of the house of David" and he inherits David's posterity (22:22–24).[23] He displaces an apostate holder of this office (22:25).

---

[23] Compare the Prophet Joseph Smith's statement: "The Priesthood that he [David] received, and the throne and kingdom of David is to be taken from him and given to another by the name of David in the last days, raised up out of his lineage" (Smith, *Teachings of the Prophet Joseph Smith*, 339; compare D&C 132:39).

The expression "of Jesse" (11:10) identifies the Davidic king as a descendant of David the son of Jesse. It also signifies that he hails from obscure origins in relation to the establishment of his day. This characterization applies alike to ancient David, Christ, and Joseph Smith. Each arose to assume an important messianic role in his day, but each—like Israel or the Church—came out of obscurity to fulfill it. Partly for that reason, the institution within which each arose opposed them: Saul and his men persecuted David; the Pharisees persecuted Christ; and the Christian sects persecuted Joseph Smith. In 3 Nephi 21:10, Jesus explains that the Davidic king will be "marred" by those who oppose him (compare Isaiah 52:14). Unlike Jesus himself, however, and also the Prophet Joseph Smith—both of whom died—the Davidic king, like King Hezekiah (see 38:5), does not die. The Lord heals him (see 3 Nephi 21:10) and he grows to become universally eminent (see Isaiah 52:15; compare 3 Nephi 21:8; Isaiah 49:5-7).

When we examine Doctrine and Covenants 113 more closely, we note that the lineage of the Davidic king differs somewhat from that of the Prophet Joseph Smith. The latter's lineage, although of Jesse, stems predominantly from Ephraim, the son of Joseph. The tribe of Ephraim early assimilated among the nations (see Hosea 7:8). Thus, Doctrine and Covenants 90:10 largely identifies the house of Joseph with the nations of the world. The Davidic king's lineage, on the other hand, although of Joseph, stems primarily from Jesse, the father of David. The lineage of David (Jesse) predominates among the Jews (see Zechariah 12:10). The name *Jesse*, while identifying ancient David's father, is also a code name (compare Isaiah 11:1). It may, in addition, allude to the fact that the Davidic king will be anointed to his office by the prophet of God—as Samuel anointed David the son of Jesse (see 1 Samuel 16:1-13).

The spirit of discernment and the other spiritual gifts that Isaiah ascribes to the subject of his parable (see 11:2-5) Doctrine and Covenants 113 applies to Christ (see v. 1). It is clear, however, that all three individuals—Christ, Joseph Smith, and the Davidic king—possess these gifts. Because they fulfill messianic roles, all exercise extraordinary spiritual powers. The Davidic king's gift of the Spirit, his office of lawgiver and astuteness as judge, his righteousness and endowment of divine power—all these attributes Isaiah associates with him in various contexts of his book (see 16:5; 41:2, 25; 42:1, 4; 55:4). Similarly, the Prophet Joseph Smith manifested all spiritual gifts at various points in his prophetic ministry. For that reason, the way Isaiah describes the Lord's servant in 61:1–3 also matches the Prophet Joseph Smith. How he describes the Davidic king in 9:6–7 is appropriate to Christ,[24] and so forth—certain messianic attributes appear common to all three. Through the book's internal links we establish the identity of whomever Isaiah describes. Thus, we cannot identify all three individuals rhetorically. In the book of Isaiah, rhetorical connections identify chiefly the Davidic king and the archtyrant.

In 14:29, Isaiah provides a type of the royal succession of *stock* ⟶ *shoot* ⟶ *branch*:

> Rejoice not, all you Philistines,
> > now that the rod which struck you is broken.
> From among the descendants of that snake
> > shall spring up a viper,
> and his offspring shall be a fiery flying serpent.

Isaiah's serpent imagery is messianic. Although one king is dead, another from the loins of David (the "snake/serpent," Hebrew *nāḥāš*) will arise to smite the enemies of the Lord's people. In Isaiah's day, King Hezekiah fulfilled this role. In the latter days, the Davidic king fulfills it. Isaiah's depicting of him as a "seraph" ("fiery serpent," Hebrew *'sārāp*) suggests, by rhetorical association, that the Davidic king's power and authority resemble that of the seraphs who appeared with the Lord to Isaiah (compare 6:2–7).

We have an example of mostly implicit scriptural links in the titles that identify the "son" or vassal of the Lord in 9:6: "Wonderful Counsellor, one Mighty in Valor, a Father for Ever, a Prince of Peace." The Hebrew consists of four couplets: *pele' yô'ēṣ, 'ēl gibbôr, 'abî 'ad, 'sar šālôm*. They express four stages of spiritual perfection the life of Abraham exemplifies; the patriarch Abraham constitutes their type or precedent (compare the Lord's command to Abraham: "Be thou perfect," in Genesis 17:1). Successive narratives in the Genesis account show how Abraham typifies the attributes of *counsel*—in settling the dispute with Lot (see Genesis 13); *valor*—by rescuing Lot from the coalition of

---

[24] See how Matthew frequently applies secondary prophetic meanings (a practice he carries over into Isaiah's prophecies) to Christ (Matthew 2:15, 17; compare Hosea 11:1; Jeremiah 31:15; 40:1).

northern kings (see Genesis 14); *covenantal fatherhood*—after considering two other possible heirs (see Genesis 15–16), by appointing Isaac (see Genesis 17); and *peacemaker/savior*—by interceding with the Lord on behalf of the righteous in Sodom (see Genesis 18). As the Pearl of Great Price records, these attributes parallel four things to which Abraham aspires when he leaves Babylonia: to possess great knowledge, to be a valiant follower of righteousness, to be a father of many nations, and to be a prince of peace (see Abraham 1:2).

In Isaiah's theology, the title "prince of peace" (Hebrew *'sar šālôm*) translates as and equates with the role of "minister of salvation." Abraham exemplifies this role when he pleads with the Lord for the righteous in Sodom. Abraham's role here compares with that of savior on Mount Zion in other scriptures (see Obadiah 21). The title "prince of peace" expresses the spiritual perfection that reflects this mediatory role. Melchizedek, the priest–king of Salem, is also called a "prince of peace" (Alma 13:18). He, too, therefore, having attained to such perfection, typifies the Davidic king.

By drawing on Abraham's example as a type of the Davidic king, Isaiah signifies that the latter's role of proxy for the delivering of his people models in part on Abraham's role in saving the righteous out of Sodom. There, the Lord intervenes to save Lot for Abraham's sake (see Genesis 19:29). In the book of Isaiah, Babylon replaces Sodom as the place the Lord destroys (see 13:19). As he did to Lot, the Lord gathers out the righteous when calamity approaches (see 57:1). He calls the "followers of righteousness" individually, as he did Abraham out of Babylonia (27:12; 51:1–2). Besides applying to the Davidic king the role of meriting and ministering temporal salvation, Isaiah applies to him the attributes of counsel, valor, and covenantal fatherhood (patriarchy) generally (see 11:2; 22:21; 50:4–9). All four attributes appear also in the context of the verse itself: the Davidic king personifies *light*, overthrows the archtyrant, increases his people, and establishes peace (see 9:2–5, 7). The Jews thus view the Davidic king as on a par with Abraham, Isaac, and Jacob—Israel's patriarchs.

A further example of implicit scriptural links concerns the figure of Cyrus. Scholars claim that the mentioning of Cyrus by name (see 44:28; 45:1) indicates that an author other than Isaiah wrote that part of his book. While it is true that Isaiah lived at the time the house of Israel went into exile and Cyrus initiated the Jews' return to Palestine a full century and a half later, Isaiah nonetheless does not represent Cyrus in purely historical terms.

In 44:26–28, Isaiah identifies Cyrus rhetorically as "his [the Lord's] servant"—his vassal. He commands that Jerusalem be rebuilt (vv. 26, 28). The Lord also calls Cyrus "my shepherd" (v. 28) in a context of "the deep" becoming dry (v. 27). This latter combination of terms appears elsewhere only in connection with Moses. Isaiah names Moses as the Lord's "shepherd" who led Israel through "the deep" (63:11–13). For this exodus event, Moses set a biblical precedent; nothing like it had happened before. Thus, by speaking of Cyrus in this way, Isaiah depicts him as a new Moses. The idea of a shepherd of the Lord in a context of the deep becoming dry represents a Moses typology that Isaiah superimposes on the figure of Cyrus. Isaiah nevertheless mentions Cyrus by name because Cyrus set a biblical precedent for ordering the rebuilding of Jerusalem and its temple (v. 28; compare Ezra 1:1–3).

We see a second composite figure of Cyrus in 45:1. There, Isaiah calls Cyrus the Lord's "anointed" (Hebrew *māšiaḥ*, also "messiah"). We know from the Cyrus Cylinder, however, that Cyrus' god was Marduk, the god of Babylon—not the Lord.[25] The expression "his anointed/messiah" (45:1) appears in the Old Testament only when describing Israel's ruling king—initially Saul, but subsequently David and his descendants (compare 1 Samuel 12:3; 22:51; Psalm 18:50). In this instance Isaiah superimposes a David typology on Cyrus. Isaiah's Cyrus again forms a composite of types; Cyrus does not represent a purely historical figure. Isaiah nevertheless names him a second time because Cyrus physically subdued nations and rulers in order to release Israel's exiles (vv. 1, 13). For this event Cyrus too set a biblical precedent. Isaiah, therefore, mentions Cyrus' name in connection with it. Based on Isaiah's methodology, what sets a precedent qualifies as a type with which to predict the future.

In creating this synthesis of types, Isaiah creates an ideal. The ideal combines Moses, David, and Cyrus—no one biblical figure alone expresses all the roles the Davidic king fulfills. That Cyrus himself had yet to be born does not disqualify him from serving as a type of the Davidic king. Isaiah saw both individuals in vision. To reinforce the idea that the two "Cyrus" passages describe roles

---

[25] See A. Leo Oppenheim, trans., "Cyrus (557–529)," in Pritchard, *Ancient Near Eastern Texts*, 315–16.

the Davidic king fulfills, Isaiah repeats his description of these roles in passages that describe the Davidic king elsewhere. Such rhetorical links let us know that Isaiah speaks not of two or more separate figures, all of whom lead out in the same direction, performing identical functions on behalf of the Lord's people, but of a single figure. In serving as the Lord's agent of delivering Israel, the Davidic king fulfills a multiplicity of redemptive roles.

As does "Cyrus," the Lord's servant releases Israel's exiles from captivity (see 42:1, 7; 49:6, 9). The *arm* of the Lord presides for him, shepherding the Lord's flock (see 40:10–11). *Righteousness* leads the exodus of the Lord's people to the promised land (see 58:8, 14). The *arm* of the Lord dries up the deep, enabling the ransomed of the Lord to return to Zion (see 51:9–11). *Righteousness* subdues nations and rulers, reconquering the earth on behalf of the Lord (see 41:2). In this new conquest, those who return from exile aid him: when the Lord's *right hand* strengthens them, the returning Israelites thresh the *mountains* to dust (see 41:13–15; compare vv. 8–12). The historical Cyrus was not so aided in his conquests by Israelites—Isaiah is describing a transcendent event. Isaiah expresses various details of this event metaphorically because what he is predicting possesses no single biblical type. Again, those whom the Lord's anointed endows, who are called the "oaks of righteousness," rebuild the ancient ruins (see 61:1–4). Other Hebrew prophets assign to the Davidic king the task of rebuilding the Lord's temple (see Zechariah 6:12, 15). The Lord enters this temple when he returns to earth (see Malachi 3:1).

A final example of implicit scriptural links comes from chapter 53. Standing out from the rest of the chapter, in which a spokesman of the Lord's people speaks of a suffering figure—Christ—are two verses in which the Lord himself is speaking (vv. 11–12). Here, the Lord refers to "my servant, the righteous one," vindicating many (v. 11). The Hebrew verb *vindicate* (*hiṣdîq*) also means "make righteous"—the Lord's servant makes many righteous. He achieves this in part by serving as their proxy: "Because of his knowledge, and by bearing their iniquities, shall my servant, the righteous one, vindicate many" (v. 1). The "knowledge" the Davidic king possesses is that he—the Lord's vassal—acts as a proxy for his people's deliverance. The Hebrew word for knowledge (*daʿat*) expresses a covenant relationship (compare Hosea 4:6; 6:6–7). According to the terms of the Davidic covenant, the Lord protects the people of the

Davidic king when the latter demonstrates righteousness. In the book of Isaiah, the Davidic king vindicates those who show loyalty towards him before the Lord so that the Lord spares them in the day of judgment (compare 51:1–16; 54:10, 14–17).

Isaiah links several other concepts to the idea of the Davidic king's bearing his people's iniquities: "I will assign him an inheritance among the great, and he shall divide the spoil with the mighty, because he poured out his soul unto death, and was numbered with criminals—he bore the sins of many, and made intercession for the transgressors" (v. 12). Isaiah here presents a synthesis of types, all fused together in the Lord's righteous servant. As we saw previously, the Davidic king embodies in himself the outstanding attributes of Israel's legendary heroes. In the biblical account, Caleb typifies one whom the Lord assigned an inheritance among the great—when the Israelites conquered the land of Canaan (see Numbers 14:24; Joshua 14:6–15; 15:13–17). David typifies one who divided the spoil with the mighty—when he won the victory over the Amalekites (see 1 Samuel 30:16–31). King Hezekiah typifies one who poured out his soul unto death—during his illness, when the Lord assured him that he would deliver his people from the power of Assyria (see Isaiah 38:6, 9–20). Again, David typifies one who was numbered with criminals—when Saul outlawed him (see 1 Samuel 22:1–2). Job typifies one who bore the sins of many—upon the feasting and extravagant life-style of his children (see Job 1:5). Lastly, Moses typifies one who made intercession for transgressors—when Israel became idolatrous in the wilderness (see Exodus 32:11–13; Deuteronomy 9:16–29).

Unlike the multiplicity of biblical types with which Isaiah describes the Davidic king in chapter 53, Isaiah limits his description of the suffering figure (Christ) to Job—whom his friends thought "smitten of God" (v. 4; compare Job 4:7–9); and to David—who at sundry times was "despised . . . by men" (v. 3; compare Psalm 22). Isaiah's depicting of the suffering figure as "a lamb led to slaughter" (v. 7) hints at the sacrificial nature of his death.

By this paucity of human types with which he describes the mission and attributes of the suffering figure, Isaiah alludes to his unique identity. As "a man" (v. 3), he suffers grievously as did Job; men hate him, as they did David. But he is "pierced for our transgressions, crushed because of our iniquities" (v. 5); he is "cut off out of the land of the living for the crime of my people to whom the blow was due" (v. 8). To describe such atonement for sin in terms of a biblical precedent, Isaiah draws on animal sacrifice, more specifically, a passover sacrifice—a slaughtered *lamb* (v. 7). But if the Davidic king, bearing the sins of many, merits his people's temporal salvation, who, then, pays "the price of our peace"— our spiritual salvation—or heals us "with his wounds" (v. 5) except the Lord himself?

To bring this point home to us, Isaiah, who describes the mission and attributes of the Davidic king in the most celebrated and consummate terms, shows how the Davidic king's role flows out of the role the suffering figure fulfills; the Davidic king's function is subservient to that of the suffering figure. Isaiah tells us that the atonement wrought by the suffering figure makes possible the mission of the Lord's servant: "that, if he [Christ] made his life an offering for guilt . . . the purposes of the Lord might prosper in his hand" (v. 10). This transitional verse, which concludes the description of the suffering figure's mission (vv. 1–10), lets us know that the Davidic king's mission, which fulfills the "purposes of the Lord," proceeds out of Christ's atonement. Whatever the Lord sets his *hand* to do, will, on his own account, "prosper" (compare 48:12–16).

In sum, the Davidic king's role of bearing the iniquities of his people does not mean that he atones for their sins. The Atonement is the role and prerogative solely of Christ. It does mean, however, that the Davidic king must answer for the crimes of his people—as a vassal answers to the suzerain for his people's loyalty. The Davidic king's suffering on their account lends substance to his mediating with the Lord on their behalf. As we see in King Hezekiah's case, suffering is a key ingredient of the Davidic king's functioning as a proxy for his people's deliverance.

The Davidic king bears his people's iniquities because of his knowledge of the terms of the Davidic covenant. The ideas of "knowledge" and "bearing iniquity" thus appear in parallel (v. 11). The Davidic covenant itself came into being when Israel failed to maintain a level of righteousness sufficient to merit the Lord's intervention under the terms of the Sinaitic covenant. In effect, the Davidic covenant grew out of iniquity (compare 1 Samuel 8:4–7), the Lord turning evil unto good. The attribute of righteousness, which the Davidic king personifies (compare *righteous one*, v. 11), expresses his acceptability before the Lord when functioning as his people's proxy. His vindicating of "many" signifies that he legitimately represents a remnant of Israel (compare "many," 2:3–4; 52:13–15). These he ransoms in the Lord's day of judgment. All, however, rests on the merits of Christ's atonement.

Types

Jesus gives a fourth key for understanding Isaiah, one closely related to what we have just discussed. After commanding the people to search Isaiah diligently, he says, "For great are the words of Isaiah" (3 Nephi 23:1). He then explains why the words of Isaiah are great: "For surely he spake as touching all things concerning my people which are of the house of Israel" (3 Nephi 23:2). Other prophets may have spoken more or less about the house of Israel, but Isaiah spoke about *all things*: things past, present, and future. He gave an entire accounting of the Lord's people. This idea leads to the next verse, which contains the fourth key: "And all things that he spake have been and shall be, even according to the words which he spake" (3 Nephi 23:3).

Jesus' words contain a paradox. Does he mean that some things Isaiah spoke have been, in the past, while others shall be, in the future? Or does he mean (applying Jesus' own definition that appears in the previous verse) that *all things* Isaiah spoke have been, and *all things* that he spoke shall be? I believe that this latter interpretation is correct, for several reasons. It expresses the very manner in which Isaiah prophesies—using ancient events as types on which to model prophecies of the future. The idea that what has been shall be reflects a well-known definition of typology. The writer of Ecclesiastes says, "The thing that hath been, it is that which shall be; and that which is done is that which shall be done: and there is no new thing under the sun" (Ecclesiastes 1:9). In other words, what has happened in the past will happen again. He continues, "Is there anything whereof it may be said, See, this is new? it hath been already of old time, which was before us" (Ecclesiastes 1:10). Events repeat themselves; history works in cycles. Jesus expresses this concept.

To understand Isaiah in terms of the latter days, then, we need to be familiar with events that occurred in Israel's past, because what happened then will repeat itself. Since Jesus gave this key to the

Nephites about A.D. 34, he was speaking of a fulfillment of Isaiah's words both in the past—in Isaiah's own time, or not long thereafter—and in the future, presumably the latter days.

The Jews have long recognized this double fulfillment of Hebrew prophecy. They traditionally interpret the prophets from this very perspective.[26] First, the Jews apply a prophecy to the prophet's own time, to the events of his day: the historical and spiritual crises of their times caused the prophets to seek answers from the Lord. The Lord gave those answers, which the prophets wrote down as revelations. We thus have prophecies that name the ancient entities of Zion, Babylon, Assyria, Egypt, and so on—names familiar to us from that period. At the same time, the Jews acknowledge that the word of the Lord possesses a transcendent dimension; it has eternal value. In particular do the Jews apply the prophetic word to a parallel context of fulfillment: the latter days. In that case, they view the ancient entities and events that the prophets mention as types of latter-day entities and events. Even today, the Jews interpret the words of the prophets in this manner.

Ezekiel 12:27, for example, shows that the people of Ezekiel's day were all too well aware of this double dimension of prophecy. They exonerated themselves, not wishing to apply Ezekiel's censuring words to themselves. They insisted that Ezekiel must be speaking of someone other than them. His prophecy, they said, must be intended for "the far-off time"—the latter days. On the other hand, we, who live in the latter days, do the reverse. The ancient Hebrew prophecies apply to the time of the prophets themselves, do they not? We, too, exonerate ourselves of hard sayings and unpleasant implications. We keep such at a comfortable distance; human nature has not changed.

Nephi also illustrates this two-fold dimension of prophecy. After giving the first two keys for understanding Isaiah, Nephi makes a paradoxical statement. It nonetheless resonates with what we are discussing. He says, "I have made mention unto my children concerning the judgments of God, which hath come to pass among the Jews . . . according to all that which Isaiah hath spoken" (2 Nephi 25:6). He means that the judgments of God ("according to all that which Isaiah hath spoken") had by this time—some

---

[26] See Daniel Patte, *Early Jewish Hermeneutic in Palestine* (Missoula, Mont.: Scholars Press, 1975).

150 years after Isaiah predicted them—come to pass. But then, in the next verse, Nephi adds, "In the days that the prophecies of Isaiah shall be fulfilled men shall know of a surety, at the times when they shall come to pass" (2 Nephi 25:7).

Nephi, in his second statement, asserts that Isaiah's prophecies will see another fulfillment, besides the one that has occurred. He indicates that this second fulfillment will take place in the last days: "Wherefore, they are of worth unto the children of men, and he that supposeth that they are not, unto them will I speak particularly . . . for I know that they shall be of great worth unto them in the last days; for in that day they shall understand them; wherefore, for their good have I written them" (2 Nephi 25:8).

Nephi thus affirms that the prophecies of Isaiah will see fulfillment a second time—and be understood for what they are—in the last days. Although Nephi's words may appear to contradict themselves, they do not. He is merely expressing the two-fold dimension of Hebrew prophecy as the Jews teach it. I call one the historical interpretation and the other the eschatological (latter-day) interpretation of prophecy. We must account for both if we would understand Isaiah.

Isaiah himself sums up the idea that what has been shall be— that an initial (historical) fulfillment of his words prefigures a latter-day (eschatological) fulfillment. In a classic statement, he represents the Lord as saying, "Who predicts what happens as do I, and is the equal of me in appointing a people from of old as types, foretelling things to come?" (44:7). The ancient Israelites, in their history, in the very things they experienced, foreshadowed what would befall in the latter days. Isaiah is quick to point out that only the Lord can predict history in this way—it is a proof of his divinity (45:21). That is how, in the book of Isaiah, the Lord "foretells the end from the beginning, from ancient times things not yet done" (46:10). This ability to encapsulate the future in Israel's past, and vice versa, is what makes Isaiah's words inimitable and "great."

Of course, this dual fulfillment does not mean that history repeats itself in exactly the same sequence. I do not suggest that the same chronology of events that existed anciently applies in the last days or that all things repeat themselves in precisely the same manner. We have already seen how Isaiah prophesies using composites of types. He often fuses a multiplicity of things ancient to project something new. The principle that what has been shall be ("all things that he spake have been and shall be") selectively chooses events in Israel's past that serve as a type, model, or precedent of what will happen in the future. Isaiah's inspired writings excel at recycling these types to fit a new mold. They do this by drawing from Israel's background those phenomena that apply on two levels: the historical (Isaiah's own era) and the eschatological (the latter days).

This selectivity explains why Isaiah employs no explicit chronology in his writings. Isaiah has scrambled both his chronology and the unfolding of the events themselves. We can unravel them only by diligent searching, linking individual events, domino fashion, to others in the book of Isaiah to form an implicit sequence. We achieve a complete picture of the last days when we identify each piece of the puzzle and link it to those that relate to it. This challenge should not dismay us; it does not lie outside the reach of the reader. Because the Lord has commanded that we search Isaiah's prophecies, his message must lie within our reach. Despite this, since it is not easy to understand Isaiah, we must view as growing pains all that it involves. Once we do understand Isaiah, we will have passed a spiritual milestone in our lives.

New Events

As an example of a typological event, let us take the exodus. Scholars recognize the prominence in the book of Isaiah of a new exodus theme. Just as there occurred an exodus out of Egypt, at which Israel was born as a nation, so a new nation of Israel will be born at a new exodus out of Babylon, on the eve of Babylon's destruction (48:20; 52:11). Isaiah, however, often associates with this event a new wandering in the wilderness (48:21; 52:12). There exists an interim period (during the Lord's day of judgment), after the exodus takes place, when Israel "wanders" to the promised land. In this way, by linking two or more events in various contexts in his book, Isaiah establishes a chronolgy—a new wandering in the wilderness takes place *after* the new exodus. Using this same means, Isaiah alludes to an entire sequence of new events, all of which link to one another implicitly. Always, Isaiah uses episodes out of Israel's history as types upon which to frame prophecies of the future.

More than thirty major events appearing in the book of Isaiah, that set a precedent anciently, prefigure a series of latter-day events.

These include, but are not limited to, Israel's apostasy (1:2–4; compare Amos 3–9; Hosea 1–14)—which takes the form chiefly of injustice (1:21–23; 3:14–15) and idolatry (2:7–8; 8:19); the Babylonian captivity (47:6; 52:5; compare Jeremiah 20:4–6); the Tower of Babel (2:15; 30:25; compare Genesis 11:4–9); the call of Abraham (41:8–9; 51:2; compare Genesis 12:1–3); Lot's deliverance from Sodom (33:14–16; 57:1–2; compare Genesis 19:15–17); the Exodus out of Egypt (43:2, 16–17; 51:9–11; compare Exodus 14:21–31); Israel's wandering in the wilderness (40:3–4; 49:9–12; compare Numbers 14:33); the pilgrimage to Zion (30:29; 35:8–10; compare Psalm 122:1–4); the Lord's protective cloud (4:5–6; 60:2; compare Exodus 14:19–20); the destruction of Sodom and Gomorrah (3:9–11; 13:19; compare Genesis 19:24–25); cosmic cataclysm (13:10, 13; 24:19–20; compare Joshua 10:11–14); chaos (compare Genesis 1:2)—which takes the form of darkness (5:30; 8:22), dust (2:10; 5:24), chaff (17:13; 29:5), refuse/litter (1:31; 5:25), fire (1:7; 9:19), clouds/smoke (9:18; 14:31), ashes (44:20; 61:3), waters (8:7; 17:12–13), mud (10:6; 41:25), clay (41:25; 45:9), fog/mist (5:30; 44:22), and dross (1:22, 25); the Flood (8:7; 28:2; compare Genesis 7:10–24); Assyria's world conquest (10:5–14; 37:11, 17; compare 2 Kings 19:11, 18); Assyria's invasion of the promised land (5:26–30; 10:28–32; compare 2 Kings 18:9–10, 13); the Egyptian bondage (10:24; 52:4; compare Exodus 1:8–14); Assyria's siege of Zion (36:1–2; 37:33–35; compare 2 Kings 19:32–34); the passover (26:20–21; 31:5; compare Exodus 12); the Lord's descent on the Mount (30:30; 31:4; compare Exodus 19:10–20); the Lord's consuming fire (10:16–17; 66:15–16; compare Numbers 11:1; 26:10); Israel's victory over Midian (9:4; 10:26; compare Judges 7–8); Cyrus' universal conquests (41:2, 25; 45:1–2; compare Ezra 1:2); Israel's conquest of the promised land (11:14; 54:2–3; compare Joshua 1–12); the rebuilding of Jerusalem and the temple (44:28; 61:4; compare Haggai 1–2); the reign of the judges (1:26; 32:1; compare Judges 2:16–18); the Davidic monarchy (9:6–7; 11:1–5; compare 2 Samuel 2:4; 5:3); the Lord's covenant (chap. 54); Zion as the Lord's residence (12:6; 24:23; compare Psalm 132:13); the Creation (65:17–18; 66:22; compare Genesis 1); and paradise (11:6–9; 51:3; compare Genesis 2:8).

Around these ancient events Isaiah builds his prophecies. He includes in this sequence the events of his own day or soon thereafter—all serve alike as types of latter-day events. Isaiah's day represents a crucial period in Israel's history. It sets many historical precedents that have a second, latter-day fulfillment. These Isaiah incorporates into the broader sequence of Israel's history to compose a full spectrum of biblical types. They all project Israel's history on two levels—one ancient, the other based on the ancient types. What happens in the last days is thus a composite of all that has happened before. This very recurring of typological events characterizes the last days, enabling us to identify them as such. When the sequence of events Isaiah predicts in this way is set in motion, it lets us know that the last days are here.

Having seen the end from the beginning in a great cosmic vision, Isaiah is able to view these two contexts—Israel's ancient history, particularly his own day; and also the last days, the time of the end—and frame his words in such a way as to capture both in a single prophecy. No other prophet accomplishes this so successfully. No other prophet fills out this picture so completely. In this manner, Isaiah succeeds in speaking about "all things concerning my people which are of the house of Israel" (3 Nephi 23:2).

We must take the words of Isaiah, therefore, as they stand. Modern scholars, notably in the field of archaeology, make remarkable discoveries that verify the history of the Old Testament, including Isaiah's day. We must nonetheless exercise care in reading such historical data back into the book of Isaiah. Certainly Isaiah did not intend that we should read his book in that way. Isaiah does not fulfill the role of a historian, although his book contains historical material that modern discoveries corroborate. On the contrary, Isaiah takes pains to be selective in what he says about nations, persons, and events. He mentions only those things that apply on two levels at one time. In his writings, he exemplifies first and foremost the role of prophet.

Isaiah does not speak, for example, of Assyria's exile of the house of Israel, though that represents a major event of his day. But he does mention Assyria's invading, destroying, and oppressing of Israel, because that episode applies on both a historical and an eschatological level: there will occur an Assyrian type of invasion of the land, a wholesale destruction of peoples, and a siege of Israel's righteous in the last days (see 10:5–11; 36:1–37:13)—Assyria set a precedent for Israel's takeover by an invading foreign power. But to describe Israel's bondage to a foreign power (Assyria), Isaiah draws on the ancient type of the Egyptian bondage (see 10:24). Egypt set the precedent for Israel's bondage, and it, therefore, is the type Isaiah utilizes.

Further, Isaiah does not describe King Hezekiah in a negative light, although historically some grounds for doing so might have existed. Because Hezekiah serves preeminently as a type of the ideal Davidic king, Isaiah preserves only the positive attributes of Hezekiah, which are many. On the other hand, Isaiah does describe King Ahaz disparagingly (see 7:13). Because Ahaz serves as the type of an apostate Davidic dynasty, Isaiah says only those things about him which fit that mold. The books of Kings and Chronicles give a fuller account of the reign of Ahaz.

Many scholars fail to understand Isaiah because they are ever seeking to link his prophecies to their historical base—as if Isaiah were not prophesying but recording history. Whereas Isaiah says, "Never mind the prophecies of bygone events; do not dwell on things of the past. See, I do a new thing!" (43:18–19). It seems to have occurred to but few that the way Isaiah describes what transpired in his day is deliberately fragmentary, not accidentally so. For that reason the historical view of Isaiah has never made good sense. No one has ever understood Isaiah by means of it. The best it has to offer is an impaired view of a remote age. Only typologically is Isaiah coherent. His prophecies wax eloquent as he depicts the scene of the last days. His "sum of vision" (29:11) unfolds to present a detailed and unified picture.

In short, we must accept entities and events as Isaiah describes them. Reading history back into his writings is not a key to understanding Isaiah. That approach leads to confusion because Isaiah's message is *a*historical—his book is typologically oriented. Its overarching literary patterns subordinate all that is historical. Rather, we should adapt our thinking to the prophetic picture Isaiah presents, laying aside our presuppositions until we learn the nature of his transcendent message. For this, Isaiah's own words serve as our best guide.

Assyria and Egypt

How, for example, does Isaiah describe Assyria? As one of two superpowers in the world—as they existed in Isaiah's day—the other being Egypt. He describes Assyria as coming from the North; oppressive and ruthless; a law unto itself; militaristic and bent on world domination; imposing its yoke of servitude on other nations; encroaching on the world by degrees, swallowing up territories; and setting all the surrounding peoples in fear of it. When the world is ripe in iniquity, Assyria suddenly bursts forth like a flood. With its alliance of nations, it sweeps over the entire earth, conquering, destroying by fire and by the sword, leaving havoc and disaster in its wake—capturing the whole world. Only Zion/Jerusalem, a safe place for the Lord's righteous, does Assyria not conquer. Assyria invades even Egypt, the other great superpower; Assyria penetrates Egypt and ravages her land.

After a few years of war and oppression, Assyria lays siege to Zion/Jerusalem, where a remnant of Israel takes refuge. Then occurs Assyria's demise. Because of his covenant with Israel, and because the righteous of his people remain faithful through much trial and tribulation, the Lord utterly destroys the Assyrian army. The 185,000 men who perished overnight in the days of King Hezekiah (see 37:36) serve as the historical type of a latter-day Armageddon. As Isaiah depicts it, this event signals the end of one major Assyrian army (compare 31:8–9). Another is fought to the death by a righteous army of Israel (see 30:30–32). These two victories effectively end Assyrian hegemony. As we saw previously, the Davidic king—a new Cyrus—together with a righteous army of Israel, reconquers the earth on behalf of the Lord (see 41:2, 14–15; 45:1).

Isaiah thus represents both kinds of divine protection that operated in Israel anciently. The first, based on the Sinai covenant, requires that all the Lord's army consist of righteous men. Joshua's army, at the conquest of Canaan, forms its historical type. The second kind of divine protection rests on the Davidic covenant. As we saw, this requires the exemplary righteousness of the Davidic king. He merits the Lord's protection by proxy on behalf of those loyal to the king. King Hezekiah and the people who fled to Jerusalem from the Assyrians serve as its historical type.

The other superpower of Isaiah's time, Egypt, was traditionally a civilized nation. Isaiah describes Egypt as industrious, but now enduring economic problems; stable, but now suffering political decline; religious, but in the main idolatrous; having fertile, irrigated lands, but experiencing drought (see 19:1–15). It possesses vast forces of chariots and horsemen, to which the smaller nations of the world look for protection against Assyria (see 30:1–2; 31:1). Egypt represents the only military power sufficiently strong to counter

Assyria. Many, therefore, ally themselves with Egypt. Their hopes are dashed, however, when Assyria exposes Egypt's weaknesses in a military confrontation (see 20:1–6; 30:3–5; 31:1–3).

Isaiah thus juxtaposes Assyria and Egypt. He presents them as two contrasting political entities, even as he presents Zion and Babylon as two contrasting spiritual entities. The Lord chastises his people for looking to Egypt for help against Assyria, because that sort of trust constitutes an arm of flesh. The Lord requires Israel to trust in him: divine protection is an integral part of the covenant relationship. Trusting in the Lord when enemies threaten death serves as a sure sign of corporate and personal loyalty. This test repeats itself in the last days.

The Hebrew prophets make no qualitative distinction between meriting temporal salvation—being delivered from a mortal threat—and spiritual salvation, which involves forgiveness of sins. The prophets, including Isaiah, hold out deliverance as something the Lord promises his people (compare 49:24–26; 54:14–17) even as he forgives their sins (compare 43:25; 44:22). Divine deliverance rests on the protection clause in the Lord's covenant with his people or their king. It is a covenant blessing, binding upon God when men obey its terms. Assyria might rise to conquer the world, but the Lord protects those who put their trust in him (compare 8:5–15). According to the prophets, meriting salvation, temporal or spiritual, requires an abiding allegiance to the Lord.

An Analogy with Today

To put this fourth key to the test, we should ask ourselves, Does the situation Isaiah describes exist in the world today? Is Isaiah's political and spiritual scenario repeating itself in the latter days? Is there in our day a power in the North, a militaristic superpower, encroaching upon the surrounding nations by degrees, preparing ultimately to launch an all-out flood of destruction and conquest upon a world ripening in iniquity? On the other hand, do we have a major political power to whom the smaller nations of the world look for protection against a latter-day Assyria? Does an Egypt exist—a latter-day arm of flesh? The answer is an unequivocal yes. We see a clear parallel to this very situation.

So too, all things Isaiah describes have their parallel. There exist a latter-day Zion and Babylon—a new, spiritual Israel and an idolatrous world. Yet, many of the Lord's people today still find themselves scattered and divided. Some, like the Latter-day Saints, we can identify. The Latter-day Saints follow the type of Joseph in Egypt. Ephraim, we recall, was born and reared in Egypt. Isaiah's Egypt does not compare with any political nation of the Near East today; those ancient nations no longer exist. Isaiah's Egypt represents one of two great latter-day superpowers. Rhetorically, we also identify it as the land of Ephraim. We see, according to Isaiah's types, that the ancient names *Assyria* and *Egypt* serve as code names of latter-day entities as do *Zion* and *Babylon*. Similarly—applying the fourth key for understanding Isaiah—we find that all Isaianic names typify latter-day phenomena.

Apocalyptic works such as the books of Daniel and Revelation, which also give a picture of the last days, nonetheless do not compare with Isaiah in the amount of detail he provides. Isaiah gives a more complete picture than do even these, the two best-known works of apocalyptic literature. Despite this, they and other apocalyptic writings confirm Isaiah's message of the last days. Apocalyptic books, because they speak explicitly of the last days, by and large describe the same events or portions of them. Isaiah's writings, however, excel because he uses types. To enhance his picture of the last days, Isaiah draws on a multitude of facets of Israel's history. He leaves little unsaid.

Isaiah also depicts events that lead up to the last days, such as the restoration of the gospel. He shows the rise of the Antichrist, the king of Assyria—how he comes to power, the Lord using him to punish the wicked and try the righteous. While promising the world peace, this archtyrant seeks and obtains world dominion and self-aggrandizement, then falls. Isaiah describes the Lord's people at that time as having ripened in iniquity, sunken into idolatry and apostasy, becoming much like the world at large. Few repent, even when challenged. In Isaiah's theology, Israel's apostasy itself serves as the catalyst for a world takeover by the forces of chaos. Except for Israel's unfaithfulness, the antichrist forces could gain no power over the world—the Lord's people would remain the head, not the tail.[27]

How this will affect all of us surely depends on what we do now. When we look at things from Isaiah's perspective, a latter-day

---

[27] See Paul R. Gilchrist, "Israel's Apostasy: Catalyst of Assyrian World Conquest," in *Israel's Apostasy and Restoration*, 99–113.

Assyrian alliance conquering the world has the effect of chastening and refining the Lord's people. While one major segment of Israel, as I note, escapes the holocaust wholly unscathed, another, larger group suffers the consequences of sin by living through that time, somehow surviving. A third group, by far the largest, perishes. Undoubtedly, how we conduct our lives now conditions how we will act then. Where we place our priorities today will at that time receive a severe test. One thing is certain: the world and all nations will experience the Lord's day of judgment.

The three groups of earthly inhabitants we may liken to the three categories in Latter-day Saint theology that identify celestial, terrestrial, and telestial beings. The remnant of the Lord's people whom he ransoms we may liken to celestial beings—in their degree of righteousness. Only these are exempt from the ravaging cataclysm that envelops the world. They pay the price of being delivered by suffering the refiner's fire before that time at the hands of the wicked. Those who endure outer darkness and the devouring fire, yet survive into the millennial age, we may liken to terrestrial beings. These are the more righteous part of all peoples of the earth. Finally, those whom the Lord destroys in the day of wrath represent telestial beings—the earth's wicked.

In preparation for the Millennium, when the Lord cleanses the earth with fire and with the sword, the earth rises from a telestial glory, which it now enjoys, to a terrestrial glory. This terrestrial state compares with paradise, and itself is the new paradise Isaiah prophesies. (Ultimately, at the end of the Millennium, the Lord transforms the earth to a celestial order; it becomes a "sea of glass," a great Urim and Thummim, as the Prophet Joseph Smith describes it; see D&C 130:7–9.) But before this, the Assyrians—a latter-day power of chaos—destroy the wicked of the earth. Then, when the Lord intervenes and lends men his power, the Assyrians themselves perish. The returning ten tribes, whom the ancient Assyrians exiled, make up Assyria's survivors (compare 19:23; 27:13). Thus, only celestial and terrestrial peoples outlive the Lord's cleansing of the earth. By the time the Lord's righteous armies put down Assyria, the earth's population will be greatly diminished. The earth's pristine state will match the righteousness of those who survive into the Millennium.

Applying the Interpretive Keys

Having come thus far in learning the keys for understanding Isaiah, let us now look at a chapter in detail—chapter 28. Appropriately, this chapter addresses Ephraim. We will determine how this chapter fits into the general picture Isaiah projects. Let us seek to apply all four keys for understanding Isaiah.

Chapter 28 begins with a woe, expressing a covenant curse: *Woe to the garlands of glory of the drunkards of Ephraim! Their crowning splendor has become as fading wreaths on the heads of the opulent overcome with wine* (v. 1). Isaiah depicts the Ephraimite nation as drunk, but the "wine" with which the people are drunk refers to wealth and glory. The glory consists of a fading reputation, erstwhile victories, past attainments the people look back upon. This illusion colors the thinking of the Ephraimites about the present. In the Lord's sight, their preeminence is jaded; the crowns on their heads are false. Their wealth has turned the people into "fat proud/opulent ones" (Hebrew *gēʾê šĕmānîm*)[28]—they flaunt their affluence like wreaths and garlands adorning their bodies. The language symbolizes a real condition, warranting a "woe" or curse.

The people of Ephraim, thus given to opulence, live in a state of carnal security, resembling drunkards overcome with wine. In a secondary, rhetorical sense, the "heads" of the people who wear the fading wreaths are political leaders (compare 9:15–16)—the leaders of the Ephraimite nation are drunk and under a curse. The idea of drunkenness links Ephraim rhetorically to Egypt in another passage of Isaiah. By implementing harmful political policies, the leaders of Egypt cause confusion, making the nation stagger like a drunkard into his vomit (see 19:13–14). Such rhetorical links create a typological relationship between Ephraim and Isaiah's Egypt.

Verse 2: *My Lord has in store one mighty and strong: as a ravaging hailstorm sweeping down, or like an inundating deluge of mighty waters, he will hurl them to the ground by his hand.* The flood imagery typifies the king of Assyria and his host. As he does to the land of Judah (see 8:7–8), so he sweeps through the land of Ephraim like an inundating deluge—a new Flood. The "mighty waters" express ancient Near Eastern chaos imagery, denoting

---

[28] So the Qumran Scroll of Isaiah, 1QIsaᵃ; the Masoretic Text reads *gēʾ šĕmānîm*, "fat gully/ravine," evidencing a minor copying error.

particularly the alliance of nations that attacks the Lord's people (compare 5:30; 17:12). The hurling of Ephraim's crowns to the ground "by his hand" signifies that the Lord employs the king of Assyria, his left *hand*, to put down Ephraim's glory. The king of Assyria is one of two mighty and strong in the book of Isaiah, the other being his rival and contemporary, the Davidic king.

Verse 3: *The proud garlands of the drunkards of Ephraim shall be trodden underfoot.* This passage, too, employs chaos imagery. The Lord commissions the tyrant king to tread down the Ephraimite nation when it is ripened in iniquity (compare 10:5–6).

Verse 4: *And the fading wreaths, the crowns of glory on the heads of the opulent, shall be like the first-ripe fruit before summer harvest: he who sees it devours it the moment he has hold of it.* When Ephraim assumes that the victories of former years will repeat themselves in the present (as do the seasons), Ephraim errs. The Assyrians overpower the Ephraimites and plunder the nation. The imagery of harvest denotes the context of the prophecy—the Lord's day of judgment. Isaiah depicts this harvest elsewhere as a harvest of the nations (compare 27:12). In keeping with what Isaiah does generally, however, he thereby lets us know implicitly when the Assyrian attack occurs: Ephraim is overrun at the time of the early harvest (compare 18:3–6).

Verses 5–6: *In that day shall the Lord of Hosts be as a crown of beauty and wreath of glory to the remnant of his people: a spirit of justice to him who sits in judgment, a source of strength to those who repulse the attack at the gates.* The Lord restores his glory to the remnant of Ephraim that survives the Assyrian attack. The covenant formula "his people" signifies that the Lord renews the covenant at that time. The expression "in that day" reiterates the context of the prophecy—the Lord's day of judgment. The crown of beauty and wreath of glory newly worn by the people is the Lord himself. The Lord, again present with his people, has become their head. The people attribute their success and well-being to him, acknowledging his power that makes their victory possible.

The idea of one who judges justly links rhetorically to the Davidic king (compare 11:4; 51:5). Because these Ephraimites have restored justice by appointing a righteous judge or judges, the Lord empowers them to repulse the Assyrian attack at the gates—an army of righteous Ephraimites overthrows the Assyrians flooding into the land (compare a similar deliverance in Egypt, 19:20). This happy ending climaxes a localized cycle of the themes of apostasy (v. 1), judgment (vv. 2–4), restoration (v. 5), and salvation (v. 6). It also concludes Isaiah's addressing of the political aspect of the nation of Ephraim.

Verse 7: *These too have indulged in wine and are giddy with strong drink: priests and prophets have gone astray through liquor. They are intoxicated with wine and stagger because of strong drink; they err as seers, they blunder in their decisions.* Isaiah singles out for condemnation not only political but also religious leaders (compare 9:15–16). In the Old Testament, a prophet is someone who claims to be a spokesman for the Lord, whether he is a true or a false prophet (compare Deuteronomy 13:1–5; 18:20–22). Like the political leaders, Ephraim's religious leaders suffer from being intoxicated with the wine of self-deception. This intoxication causes them to lapse in their ministry. The idea of prophets and seers drunk with wine links rhetorically to a passage of Isaiah that condemns the watchmen of the Lord's people for not watching. They fail to warn the people of the Lord's impending judgment, being oblivious to it themselves:

> Their watchmen are altogether blind and unaware;
>> all of them are but dumb watchdogs unable to bark,
>> lolling seers fond of slumber.
> Gluttonous dogs, and insatiable,
>> such indeed are insensible shepherds.
> They are all diverted to their own way,
>> every one after his own advantage.
> Come, they say, let us get wine
>> and have our fill of liquor.
> For tomorrow will be like today, only far better!
>> (56:10–12)

Verse 8: *For all tables are filled with vomit; no spot is without excrement.* A transitional verse, this imagery relates to the condemning of religious leaders in verse 7 as well as to verse 9, which deals with revelation. It says that the people are being polluted. Like the food that is set out for eating, the "tables" signify not literal tables, but, symbolically, the vehicle for conveying spiritual food. Rhetorically, the idea of tables denotes books or tablets containing the word of God (compare 30:8). The contents of these tables, however, are impure. They abound with partially digested truths,

79

regurgitated for the people to consume. Or they contain excrement, wholly polluted matter that profits nothing.

Verse 9: *Whom shall he give instruction? Whom shall he enlighten with revelation? Weanlings weaned from milk, those just taken from the breast?* Isaiah here introduces the idea of direct revelation, the purest form of the word of God. This is the theme of the chapter, the Lord's answer to the people's self-deception. Isaiah questions their readiness to receive such pure instruction because they live on a diet of vomit and excrement. Even the best of them, Isaiah likens to babes newly weaned who are as yet incapable of digesting solid food. Paul expresses something similar:

> For when for the time ye ought to be teachers, ye have need that one teach you again which be the first principles of the oracles of God; and are become such as have need of milk, and not of strong meat.
>
> For every one that useth milk is unskilful in the word of righteousness: for he is a babe.
>
> But strong meat belongeth to them that are of full age, even those who by reason of use have their senses exercised to discern both good and evil.
>
> (Hebrews 5:12–14)

Verse 10: *For it is but precept upon precept, precept upon precept, measure by measure, measure by measure; a trifle here, a trifle there.* Isaiah uses repetition, assonance, and alliteration in the Hebrew with which to parody satirically the rote method of learning God's word that the people of Ephraim use. The Hebrew says, *kî ṣaw lāṣaw ṣaw lāṣaw qaw lāqāw qaw lāqāw*. It makes a broad allusion to the schoolmaster method of learning, repeating parrot fashion what the mentor articulates. This method allows men to dictate to others what portion of God's word they learn and at what pace they learn it.

The idea of precept upon precept appears in three other instances in the scriptures. All contrast it with a higher form of revelation and follow the King James Version rendering of this expression. Nephi records:

Wo be unto him that shall say: We have received the word of God, and we need no more of the word of God, for we have enough!

For behold, thus saith the Lord God: I will give unto the children of men line upon line, precept upon precept, here a little and there a little; and blessed are those who hearken unto my precepts, and lend an ear unto my counsel, for they shall learn wisdom; for unto him that receiveth I will give more; and from them that shall say, We have enough, from them shall be taken away even that which they have.

(2 Nephi 28:29–30)

The term *more* in this passage expresses the idea that those who receive the Lord's precepts will receive more than precepts. Those who do not, will receive less. A similar idea appears in Doctrine and Covenants 98:12: "He will give unto the faithful line upon line, precept upon precept; and I will try you and prove you herewith." When the Lord tries and proves men, he does it in order to bless them with something greater. The Prophet Joseph Smith speaks of divine communication as "giving line upon line, precept upon precept; here a little, and there a little" and as "giving us consolation by holding forth that which is to come, confirming our hope!" (D&C 128:21).

This latter idea of revelation in a future sense ("that which is to come") mirrors the intent of the passage in Isaiah. It reflects a stage of spiritual progression lying beyond that of weanlings. The revelation the Lord has in mind for his people prepares them for events that will soon occur in rapid succession (compare vv. 16–21). Unfortunately, the people of Ephraim do not put themselves in a position to receive such instruction.

Verse 11: *Therefore, by incomprehensible speech and a strange tongue must he speak to these people.* As I note, the expression "these people" expresses a negative view of the Lord's people, repudiating the covenant relationship. The "incomprehensible speech" refers to the foreign tongue of the Assyrians, whom Isaiah parodies elsewhere as an "insolent people . . . a nation of incomprehensible speech, whose babbling tongue was unintelligible" (33:19). If the Lord's people (Ephraim) do not receive the revelations the Lord desires to give them, then he must speak to them by another, alien means. As that means, the Lord employs the Assyrians, allowing them to overrun his people's land to put them again in mind of him.

Verse 12: *To whom he said, This is rest; let the weary rest! This is a respite! But they would not listen.* The "rest" (Hebrew *měnûḥâ*) refers to the divine instruction and revelation verse 9 mentions. If the people of Ephraim will receive the word of the Lord, it will provide a *rest* or respite for them, not only from the wearisome method of learning God's word via precept upon precept, but by their becoming the confidants of the Lord. The Prophet Joseph Smith refers to this rest above as "consolation."

Isaiah's idea of rest reflects the biblical one. The Lord's *rest* is where he abides (see Psalm 132:14). The prophets see the promised land, particularly the temple, as the Lord's *rest* or *residence* (Hebrew *měnûḥâ*; Deuteronomy 12:9; Isaiah 66:1). Isaiah depicts the Davidic king abiding at the Lord's *residence* (11:10). Doctrine and Covenants 84:23-24 narrows the idea of *rest* even further:

> Now this Moses plainly taught to the children of Israel in the wilderness, and sought diligently to sanctify his people that they might behold the face of God;
>
> But they hardened their hearts and could not endure his presence; therefore, the Lord in his wrath, for his anger was kindled against them, swore that they should not enter into his rest while in the wilderness, which rest is the fulness of his glory.

According to this scripture, *rest* means to be received into the presence of the Lord. In the wilderness, only Moses saw the Lord's glory. The remainder of the people hardened their hearts.

Isaiah equates the *rest* of the Lord with direct revelation, because being instructed by the Lord leads, eventually, into his presence—we may behold his face (compare 40:9). In Isaiah's context—the Lord's day of judgment—the righteous who receive divine instruction find rest and peace (compare 57:1-2). The idea of *rest* thus comprehends both temporal and spiritual salvation. Those whom the Lord saves spiritually, he delivers temporally as well. On the other hand, the wicked in that day find no rest and peace (compare vv. 19-20). Though they know the laws of God, they do not keep them (compare 26:10).

In sum, when the Assyrians, like a flood, invade Ephraim's land, direct revelation will provide the surest guide. *More* of the word of God divides those whom the Lord blesses from those he curses. Unfortunately, the people of Ephraim as a whole will not hear of anything more than the idea of precept upon precept, measure by set measure, a little at a time. To them this one aspect represents the whole word of God. They mistake a preparatory gospel (compare D&C 84:26) for the gospel's fulness.

Verse 13: *So to them the word of the Lord remained: Precept upon precept, precept upon precept, measure by measure, measure by measure; a trifle here, a trifle there, that, persisting, they might lapse into stumbling and break themselves, become ensnared and be taken captive.* This imagery depicts dramatically the effect of being content with anything less than divine revelation. Isaiah sets the idea of precept upon precept—the rote method of learning— over against receiving direct instruction from the Lord. The one leads to *rest*, the other to bondage. This juxtaposition does not mean, of course, that the idea of precept upon precept is not good. Rather, it means that such represents but the first step of growing into the things of God. It is the milk, not the meat, as Paul would say.

The same principle appears in Alma 12:9–11. There Alma contrasts what he calls the lesser portion of the Lord's word with the greater portion:

> It is given unto many to know the mysteries of God; nevertheless they are laid under a strict command that they shall not impart only according to the portion of his word which he doth grant unto the children of men, according to the heed and diligence which they give unto him.
>
> And therefore, he that will harden his heart, the same receiveth the lesser portion of the word; and he that will not harden his heart, to him is given the greater portion of the word, until it is given unto him to know the mysteries of God until he know them in full.
>
> (vv. 9–10)

Alma not only contrasts the lesser portion of the Lord's word with the greater but also leads us to understand that the greater portion consists of the mysteries of God. These, he says, we can learn to such a degree that we can know them in full. Alma continues:

> And they that will harden their hearts, to them is given the lesser portion of the word until they know nothing concerning his mysteries; and then they are taken captive by the devil, and led by his will down to destruction. Now this is what is meant by the chains of hell.
>
> (v. 11)

Alma thus uses a way of expressing himself similar to Isaiah's when he says that if people content themselves with the lesser portion of the Lord's word (Isaiah's idea of precept upon precept), then eventually they are led away captive. The lesser portion does not suffice to deliver us from evil. Hardening our hearts against the greater portion results in our ignorance of saving truths. To regard the lesser portion as an end in itself, not as a preparation for the greater portion, means we forfeit our salvation. Although Alma speaks of these things as a general principle, Isaiah's context of the Lord's day of judgment adds a note of practical urgency as well as a ring of condemnation—for many it may be too late. Like those with Moses in the wilderness, they harden their hearts at a critical time.

The difference between the greater and lesser portions of the Lord's word parallels the difference between the Melchizedek and Aaronic priesthoods:

> The power and authority of the higher, or Melchizedek Priesthood, is to hold the keys of all the spiritual blessings of the church—
>
> To have the privilege of receiving the mysteries of the kingdom of heaven, to have the heavens opened unto them, to commune with the general assembly and church of the Firstborn, and to enjoy the communion and presence of God the Father, and Jesus the mediator of the new covenant.
>
> The power and authority of the lesser, or Aaronic Priesthood, is to hold the keys of the ministering of angels, and to administer in outward ordinances, the letter of the gospel, the baptism of repentance for the remission of sins, agreeable to the covenants and commandments.
>
> (D&C 107:18–20)

The lesser, or preparatory, gospel pertains to the Aaronic Priesthood. The fulness of the gospel—the key to revelation—pertains to the

Melchizedek Priesthood. Doctrine and Covenants 84:19 agrees with this when it says that the Melchizedek Priesthood "holdeth the key of the mysteries of the kingdom, even the key of the knowledge of God." Paul's remedy for spiritual "babes," too, recognizes this distinction. He says, "Therefore leaving the principles of the doctrine of Christ, let us go on unto perfection; not laying again the foundation of repentance from dead works, and of faith toward God" (Hebrews 6:1). Paul's path to perfection—which lies beyond the "first principles" of the gospel—requires a diet of strong meat (Hebrews 5:12).

Verse 14: *Therefore hear the word of the Lord, you scoffers who preside over these people in Jerusalem.* In the context of the Ephraimites' failing to accept direct revelation, the prophet yet offers the leaders of his errant people God's word as He reveals it through the prophet. His word sounds condemnatory because the leaders harden their hearts, deriding the idea of any imminent calamity (compare v. 22). The verse begins a new passage that is a variation on Isaiah's theme of revelation. The idea of self-deception, common to all passages of the chapter, repeats itself. Like the name *Zion* (v. 16), *Jerusalem* serves as a code name, identifying a latter-day place and people of the Lord.

Verse 15: *You have supposed, by taking refuge in deception and hiding behind falsehoods, to have covenanted with Death, or reached an understanding with Sheol, that, should a flooding scourge sweep through [the earth], it shall not reach you.* The people or their leaders are dubiously aware of a day of judgment's coming upon the earth. They deceive themselves, however, about its real nature, hiding behind pretenses, unwilling to admit that it implicates them. The covenant with Death/Sheol (the "underworld/hell") denotes that the people or their leaders presume they can survive by any means other than personal righteousness. Because *Death* and *Sheol* represent mythological powers of chaos in ancient Near Eastern thought, to covenant with them signifies that one trusts or depends on what the Lord will reduce to chaos in his day of judgment. It means relying on human counsel, joining forces with a wicked world, being party to all that the Lord has ordained should pass away.

By referring to Death and Sheol in this way, Isaiah parodies the leaders' delusion. The flood imagery, also mythological and chaotic, links this passage to the deluge of mighty waters in verse 2. The flood again denotes Assyria's inundating of the earth (compare 8:7–8). Like the term *hand* in verse 2, the *scourge* (Hebrew *šôṭ*) serves as a metaphorical pseudonym of the king of Assyria. The term parallels the Davidic king as the Lord's "whip" (Hebrew *šôṭ*; 10:26): the king of Assyria scourges the wicked of the Lord's people, but in the end the Davidic king whips the Assyrians. The king of Assyria's function as the Lord's agent for punishing his people, which Isaiah thus repeats, he nonetheless offsets each time by implicitly mentioning the Davidic king (see following).

Verse 16: *Therefore, thus says my Lord YHWH: I lay in Zion a stone, a keystone, a precious cornerstone, a sure foundation. They who believe it will not do rashly.* In the context of this verse—the Lord's day of judgment (see vv. 15, 17)—the Lord provides the true antidote to calamity. Since the biblical idea of a stone signifies a seer (compare Genesis 49:24; Zechariah 3:9), the verse implies that Zion harbors safety for the Lord's people because Zion enjoys a seer, a revelator of the Lord to his people. This revelation from the Lord serves as a sure foundation, a rock that cannot be moved when the storms and floods come (compare Isaiah 4:5–6; 32:1–2). Those who believe in this revelation do not panic at the onset of the Lord's day of judgment. On the other hand, Isaiah implies that many of the Lord's people will not believe in this as a means of safety. Their vainglory (the fading wreaths) and prejudices (God's word as precept upon precept) prevent them from relying on such an intangible support. The term *Zion*, a code name, links the place and people of Zion to Ephraim's land.

Verse 17: *I will make justice the measure, righteousness the weight; a hail shall sweep away your false refuge and waters flood the hiding place.* The storm and flood imagery again denotes the Assyrian invasion—penetrating every crevice, sweeping before it all the hypocrites of the Lord's people. The only assurance of being delivered from evil comes of justice and righteousness. The Lord in that day weighs all men in the balance. What they meted out to others they themselves receive in full. The idea of justice as a standard links to the first passage of the chapter: with the restoring of justice commences Ephraim's comeback (v. 6). The idea of *righteousness* alludes to the Davidic king, who serves as a touchstone by which the Lord's people may measure themselves. Together with the mention of Zion in verse 16, a localized instance of Isaianic Zion ideology occurs in these verses, namely, the destruction of the wicked and the establishment of the righteous at the presence of the Davidic king.

Verse 18: *Your covenant with Death shall prove void, your understanding with Sheol have no effect: when the flooding scourge sweeps through, you shall be overrun by it.* In the Lord's day of judgment, personal contingency plans come to nought. The invading army of the Assyrian tyrant ingloriously exposes the weaknesses of men and their schemes. The recurring flood and scourge imagery emphasizes the terrible and universal nature of the calamity. The people's wickedness, like a build-up of waters none can check, leads irrevocably to disaster.

Verse 19: *As often as it sweeps through, you shall be seized by it: morning after morning it shall sweep through, by day and by night [it shall seize you]; it shall cause terror merely to hear word of it.* The Lord's judgment, a prolonged ordeal, Isaiah depicts as filled with horror for the wicked. The news of the day holds out no hope for those who do not heed the word of the Lord.

Verse 20: *The couch is too short to stretch out on, the covering too narrow to wrap oneself in.* This proverb of troubled times shows that great deprivation awaits the wicked (compare 3:6–7, 24). Such destitution, together with the storm, flood, and chaos imagery this chapter outlines, denotes covenant curse or malediction. It spells out the nature of the *woe* upon Ephraim that heads the chapter.

Verse 21: *For the Lord will rise up as he did on Mount Perazim, and be stirred to anger, as in the Valley of Gibeon—to perform his act, his unwonted act, and do his work, his bizarre work.* The Lord's rising up bodes ill for the wicked of his people (compare 33:3, 10; 42:13). The parallel idea of anger confirms the judgmental nature of his rising. This judgmental aspect agrees with the two biblical events Isaiah identifies in connection with them. *Mount Perazim* (Hebrew *har pĕrāṣîm*) means "the mount of breakings-forth." The latter term is a plural noun that derives from the Hebrew verb *pāraṣ*, to "break forth/out." It refers to what took place at Mount Sinai during the Israelites' wandering in the wilderness. Once the Lord's destructive power was unleashed, it would break forth upon the unholy of his people and consume them (see Exodus 19:16–24). So the Lord rises in power again and breaks forth upon his people in the day of judgment. When he was stirred to anger upon the wicked, as in the Valley of Gibeon, the Lord rained stones out of the heavens and the sun stood still upon Joshua's men until they had destroyed an army of Amorites (see Joshua 10:8–14).

Such an act by the Lord is "unwonted"—not usual (Hebrew *zār*); it is "bizarre," or strange (Hebrew *nokrîyâ*). The Lord does not seek to impose judgment on the world. Despite this, since his people have alienated themselves, he himself fights against them (compare 1:24; 63:10). Isaiah describes the Lord's work in such negative terms because, as at the flood in the days of Noah, it consists of an entire annihilation of the wicked from the earth—the destroying of many souls. The term *anger*, a metaphorical pseudonym of the king of Assyria, alludes to the part the archtyrant plays in this destruction. The terms *unwonted* and *bizarre* in Hebrew confirm this rhetorically: Isaiah uses their nominative form elsewhere when referring to destructive "aliens" (*zārîm*) and "foreigners" (*běnê nēkār*; compare 1:7; 62:8), namely the Assyrians.

Verse 22: *Now therefore scoff not, lest your bonds grow severe, for I have heard utter destruction decreed by my Lord, YHWH of Hosts, upon the whole earth.* The prophet asks the people and their leaders to hear as he hears. Those who deride his message must inevitably, at the new Flood, perish with the wicked. The "utter destruction . . . upon the whole earth" links rhetorically to Assyria's destroying of those who do not repent (compare 10:23). Only a remnant of the Lord's people survives this calamity (see 10:20–24). By mocking the idea of their own guilt and condemnation, the people and their leaders merely strengthen their covenant with Death. Isaiah implies that its bonds are already almost too secure to release them.

Verses 23–26:

> *Give heed, and hear my voice!*
> > *Be attentive, and listen to what I say!*
> *Will the plowman be forever plowing to sow seed,*
> > *disking and harrowing the same ground?*
> *When he has smoothed its surface,*
> > *does he not sprinkle fennel and scatter cumin?*
> *Does he not demarcate wheat from barley*
> > *and [plant] buckwheat in its own plot?*
> *His God instructs him,*
> > *directing him in the proper procedure.*

The parable of the plowman is a short passage that repeats the idea of direct revelation. Its first and last verses emphasize the roles of God instructing and of people hearing. The term *voice* (v. 23) serves as a metaphorical pseudonym of the Davidic king, as it does elsewhere of the archtyrant (compare 13:2; 30:30). To hear the Lord's *voice*, therefore, is to hear the word of the Lord as he gives it through the Davidic king. The prophet asks the people and their leaders to consider, in a manner equal to the gravity of their situation, what the Lord is telling them. At the same time, Isaiah makes an allusion: those who follow the rural life-style are often more in tune with the Lord's Spirit.

The parable restates the idea of moving from step A (plowing ground) to step B (sowing seed). Just as the plowman does not plow the same ground over and over but continues through the next phase, so the Lord's people (Ephraim) must progress from precept upon precept to divine revelation. Just as the sower does not sow seed carelessly but with precision, so the Lord's people must exercise discretion toward the things of God, pursuing a prudent and perceptive course. The imagery of preparing ground and sowing seed conveys the idea of God's word progressively influencing the souls of men (compare Alma 32:28-43). Its creative action leads to spiritual nurture, expressing well God's purpose.

Verses 27-29:

> *Fennel is not threshed with a sharp-toothed sledge,*
> *   nor is a cartwheel rolled over cumin:*
> *fennel is beaten out with a stick*
> *   and cumin with a rod.*
> *Domestic grain is ground;*
> *   one does not go on endlessly threshing it.*
> *It cannot be ground*
> *   by driving horse and threshing cart [over it].*
> *These things originate with the Lord of Hosts,*
> *   whose counsel is wonderful,*
> *   whose inspiration is surpassing.*

The metaphor of threshing reflects man's capacity to grow increasingly more astute when he places himself under the Lord's influence. Isaiah's repeated emphasizing of a lack of this attribute (endless or improper threshing and grinding of the grain) causes the metaphor to become chaotic: Ephraim's political and religious policies are self-destructive, violating the law of the harvest. In sum, Isaiah adjures the nation of Ephraim and its leaders to live up to their creative potential. That potential must begin with seeking, experiencing, and acting upon divine direction ("counsel/inspiration"), a necessary goal for which all men (plowmen, sowers, threshers) should strive.

Conclusion

I find the four Book of Mormon keys invariably effective for understanding Isaiah. The method we derive from them forms a holistic approach for interpreting Isaiah's words. Although perhaps difficult, at the outset, to apply all the interpretive tools I outline, an interesting phenomenon develops when we do: the more we apply these tools, the more we recognize that many patterns repeat themselves. What Isaiah says in one context, he usually says, with appropriate variation, in another. The things we discover are seldom unique, appearing once, never to recur. Rather, in the book of Isaiah, repetitive patterns are the rule. They serve as points of reference, helping us to tie any given prophecy and how we interpret it into its proper context. When we observe linked phenomena in this way, Isaiah's message soon grows concrete. We see the consistency of his words; a fabric forms. Only by this means—taking note of interrelationships—can we comprehend Isaiah's sweeping vision, his message of judgment and redemption for Israel and for the world.

This method also demonstrates that without examining a thing in its literary context, we easily fall prey to spurious interpretation. The more tools we have to work with (the more we familiarize ourselves with the mechanics that lie behind Isaiah's prophecies), the more we can test and verify what is true. Isaiah did not compose his book to be immediately intelligible, to be transparent to the casual reader. He devised it to be unraveled with effort by those intent on understanding his message. To this end, literary tools serve as a safeguard as well as a key. They enable us to speak with authority on any given prophecy, to show precisely why we interpret something in a given way or why a particular misinterpretation is wrong.

That even among Latter-day Saints there exist conflicting interpretations of scriptures shows that few of us have mastered the tools for interpreting them. We have seen too often the pattern of accepting at face value a thing once spoken or written relevant to a scripture, that seemed, in a certain translation, to appear connected to the theme of a discussion, until, adopted by others and hallowed by time, that interpretation, for want of another, becomes a standard, used widely as a proof text, quoted in books and talks, by such means finally getting established as "gospel" or as the only true interpretation of that prophecy. This phenomenon repeats something that has long occurred in major religions of the world, causing many of the theological differences that divide them. When we misinterpret scriptures this way, we, not those who originated the interpretation, are answerable. The scriptures themselves furnish us with the keys for interpreting them.

For years, in teaching college religion courses on Isaiah, I attempted to explain literary keys to the students incidentally as we progressed, chapter by chapter, through the text. Our courses were structured this way; their emphasis lay not on literary keys but on simple exegesis—explaining what was meant. At first, therefore, students were required to take my word for things. They did not always know whether or why a particular interpretation was correct. They were not immediately given the tools by which to know. Instead, they were required to repeat back the interpretations I gave in order to pass their exams. There thus existed little reason or time for questioning.

But then, toward the end of the semester, most literary keys having been demonstrated along the way, something remarkable would happen. As the students began to catch Isaiah's vision, to see the coherency of his words, they were able, on their own, to determine what Isaiah was saying. From then on, students became self-motivated, often rereading Isaiah, discovering his message afresh for themselves. They no longer needed to take my word for things. Students could interpret Isaiah, and verify their interpretations, without my help. This independence was a new, unexpected dimension in their studying of the scripture, one for which they expressed immense gratitude.

I enjoyed a more fruitful experience in teaching the book of Isaiah subsequently in a class on literary analysis. Here, I taught Isaiah among other courses being taught on the great works of literature: Plato, Paul, Dante, Shakespeare. All such courses emphasized literary skills. Interpretations served not as an end in themselves but to illustrate how and why a particular method worked. After I would outline various literary tools for analyzing Isaiah, providing guidance and citing examples to demonstrate a method, students used these tools on their own. The burden of understanding Isaiah thus fell on the students themselves. They were required to perform their own exegeses, to arrive at their own interpretations.

Students had to write up the results of their analyses weekly, submitting them in a presentable essay form—they were taught both to analyze and to write. Their grades depended not on how well they memorized what I said, but on how they used literary tools to interpret Isaiah's message, on whether their analyses were defensible and complete. I felt no concern that students would spawn spurious ideas. So long as they used proper tools, their interpretations invariably matched—Isaiah's words contain no contradictions.

When I used this approach, the phenomenon of "catching the vision" of Isaiah occurred far more rapidly than with the former. In a short time, students passed the threshold of the unknown—grappling with things for the most part new to them and "different"—becoming quickly motivated on their own to master analytical techniques, to find out for themselves whether an interpretation was correct. From then on, by far the greater part of the semester, students required guidance only as we implemented new tools. Beyond that, they did not depend on me for an interpretation. They could arrive at it themselves each time and confidently defend it in the classroom. I relate these experiences, convinced that anyone can understand Isaiah. In these classes, the Prophet Joseph Smith's famous maxim, "Teach them correct principles and they will govern themselves!" was proven true.

In summary, the holistic method for understanding Isaiah based on the four Book of Mormon keys that I have discussed, works. For one starting out to learn Isaiah's message, I recommend reading more than once the keys I outline. One could then analyze names (using the Index of Terms in the back of the book), such as *Zion* and *Babylon*, *Egypt* and *Assyria*, and the metaphorical terms I mention, or study typological events, such as the new exodus and wandering in the wilderness—in order to obtain a basic understanding of Isaiah's message, the cast of characters he presents and where they lead.

On this framework one can build more detailed and thorough analyses, determining, for example, the roles of the Lord, of the Davidic king, and of the Antichrist; or the many things Isaiah predicts that are grounded in the happenings of his day. Literary structures, particularly the larger ones, because they are more difficult to discern, should follow after. It is important, in the beginning, to understand that they exist and what they imply. But one should seriously attempt to analyze them, commencing with smaller structures and localized patterns, only on becoming familiar with the book of Isaiah as a whole.

Finally, given the four Book of Mormon keys, one cannot fail to learn from Isaiah even by making feeble attempts. Many scholars have tried valiantly to analyze and interpret Isaiah's words. Books have been written, talks given, explaining this or that aspect of Isaiah's message. In most cases, however, authors and commentators have failed to tie a particular aspect of Isaiah's message into the totality of his vision, leaving the reader or listener at a loss of how next to proceed.

While it is true that the book of Isaiah is one of the most complex works of scripture and of literature in general, its message, at the same time, is simple. As far as it concerns the Latter-day Saints, we make up the Israel that Isaiah indicts and censures. As a people, we are the subject of the Lord's judgment on the one hand, while those of us who repent qualify for salvation—spiritual and also temporal—on the other. We can reduce Isaiah's message to these essentials. Because the Latter-day Saints play a key role in the Lord's redeeming of his ancient covenant people, we, as much as any people, may liken his words to ourselves for our profit and learning.

How to Use the New Translation

Words inserted in the text in order to clarify incomplete or difficult phrasing appear in *italics*.

Words or phrases transposed from other parts of the text are set off by brackets [ ].

An italicized letter after a problematic word or phrase in the text,*a* or two identical italicized letters, *b*one before and one after,*b* indicate a footnote.

Footnotes are numbered alphabetically within a chapter and identify a verse by its number.

Abbreviations in the footnotes include—
MT—The Hebrew Masoretic Text from which the New Translation of Isaiah is made.
1QIsa*a*—The complete Hebrew Dead Sea Scroll of Isaiah.
LXX—The Greek Septuagint Version of the Old Testament.

Names and selected terms in the New Translation are referenced in the Index of Terms. Where such terms occur more than once in a verse, the verse number is repeated.

THE BOOK OF ISAIAH

1 The vision of Isaiah the son of Amoz which he beheld
concerning Judea and Jerusalem during the reigns of Uzziah,
Jotham, Ahaz, and Hezekiah, kings of Judah:

> ² Hear, O heavens! Give heed, O earth!
> The Lord*a* has spoken:
> I have reared sons, brought them up,
> but they have revolted against me.
> ³ The ox knows its owner,
> the ass its master's stall,
> but Israel does not know;
> my people are insensible.
> ⁴ Alas, a nation astray,
> a people weighed down by sin,
> the offspring of wrongdoers,
> perverse children:
> they have forsaken the Lord,
> they have spurned the Holy One of Israel,
> they have lapsed into apostasy.
>
> ⁵ Why be smitten further
> by adding to your waywardness?
> The whole head is sick,
> the whole heart diseased.
> ⁶ From the soles of the feet even to the head
> there is nothing sound,
> only wounds and bruises and festering sores;
> they have not been pressed out or bound up,
> nor soothed with ointment.

---

*a*2   Hebrew *YHWH* throughout.

⁷ Your land is ruined,
　　your cities burned with fire;
　your native soil is devoured by aliens in your presence,
　　laid waste at its takeover by foreigners.
⁸ The Daughter of Zion is left
　　like a shelter in a vineyard,
　a hut in a melon field,
　　a city under siege.
⁹ Had not the Lord of Hosts left us a few survivors,
　　we should have been as Sodom,
　or become like Gomorrah.

¹⁰ Hear the word of the Lord,
　　O leaders of Sodom;
　give heed to the law of our God,
　　you people of Gomorrah!
¹¹ For what purpose are your abundant
　　sacrifices to me? says the Lord.
　I have had my fill of offerings of rams
　　and fat of fatted beasts;
　the blood of bulls and sheep and he-goats
　　I do not want.
¹² When you come to see me,
　　who requires you to trample my courts so?

¹³ Bring no more worthless offerings;
　　they are as a loathsome incense to me.
　As for convening meetings at the New Month
　　and on the Sabbath,
　wickedness with the solemn gathering
　　I cannot approve.
¹⁴ Your monthly and regular meetings
　　my soul detests.
　They have become a burden on me;
　　I am weary of putting up with them.
¹⁵ When you spread forth your hands,
　　I will conceal my eyes from you;
　though you pray at length, I will not hear—
　　your hands are filled with blood.

16 Wash yourselves clean:
  remove your wicked deeds
 from before my eyes;
  cease to do evil.
17 Learn to do good: demand justice,
  stand up for the oppressed;
 plead the cause of the fatherless,
  appeal on behalf of the widow.

18 Come now, let us put it to the test,
  says the Lord:
 though your sins are as scarlet,
  they can be made white as snow;
 though they have reddened as crimson,
  they may become *white* as wool.
19 If you are willing and obey,
  you shall eat the good of the land.
20 But if you are unwilling and disobey,
  you shall be eaten by the sword.
 By his mouth the Lord has spoken it.

21 How the faithful city
  has become a harlot!
 She was filled with justice;
  righteousness made its abode in her,
  but now murderers.
22 Your silver has become dross,
  your wine diluted with water.
23 Your rulers are renegades,
  accomplices of robbers:
 with one accord they love bribes
  and run after rewards;
 they do not dispense justice to the fatherless,
  nor does the widow's case come before them.

24 Therefore the Lord, the Lord of Hosts,
  the Valiant One of Israel, declares,
 Woe to them! I will relieve me
  of my adversaries,
  avenge me of my enemies.

²⁵ I will restore my hand over you
>and smelt away your dross as in a crucible,*
>and remove all your alloy.
²⁶ I will restore your judges as at the first,
>and your counsellors as in the beginning.
>After this you shall be called
>the City of Righteousness, a faithful city.

²⁷ For Zion shall be ransomed by justice,
>those of her who repent by righteousness.
²⁸ But criminals and sinners
>shall be altogether shattered
>when those who forsake the Lord are annihilated.

²⁹ And you* will be ashamed of the oaks you cherished
>and blush for the parks you were fond of;
³⁰ you shall become like an oak whose leaves wither,
>and as a garden that has no water.
³¹ The mighty shall be as refuse,
>their works a spark;
>both shall burn up alike,
>and there shall be none to extinguish.

2 A prophecy concerning Judea and Jerusalem which Isaiah the son of Amoz saw in vision:

² In the latter days
>the mountain of the Lord's house
>shall become established
>as* the head of the mountains;
>it shall be preeminent among the hills,
>and all nations will flow to it.
³ Many peoples shall go, saying,
>Come, let us go up
>to the mountain of the Lord,
>to the house of the God of Jacob,

---

*b*25   Hebrew *kabbōr, as with potash/lye,* emended to *kakūr;* compare 48:10.
*c*29   Hebrew *they.*
*a*2   So 1QIsaᵃ; MT has *bet essentiae: in/as.*

that he may instruct us in his ways,
   that we may follow in his paths.
For out of Zion shall go forth the law,
   and from Jerusalem the word of the Lord.

4 He will judge between the nations
   and arbitrate for many peoples.
They will beat their swords into plowshares,
   their spears into pruning hooks:
nation will not lift the sword against nation,
   nor will they learn warfare any more.

5 O house of Jacob, come,
   let us follow the light of the Lord.

6 For thou, *O Lord*, hast forsaken thy people,
   the house of Jacob, because,
like the Philistines,
   they provide themselves with*b*
   mystics from the East
and are content with the infantile heathen.
7 Their land is full of silver and gold
   and there is no end to their wealth;
their land is full of horses
   and there is no end to their chariots.
8 Their land is full of idols:
   they adore the works of their hands,
   things their own fingers have made.

9 Mankind is brought low
   when men thus debase themselves.
Forbear them not!

10 Go into the rocks; hide in the dust
   from the awesome presence of the Lord
   and from the brightness of his glory.
11 The haughty eyes of men shall be lowered
   and man's pride abased;
   the Lord alone shall be exalted in that day.

---

*b*6   Hebrew conjunctive *wĕ* emended to preposition *bĕ*.

99

¹² The Lord of Hosts has a day in store
    for all the proud and arrogant
and for all who are exalted,
    that they may be brought low.

¹³ *It shall come* against all the lofty
    cedars of Lebanon that lift themselves up high,
    and against all the oaks of Bashan,
¹⁴ against all high mountains and elevated hills,
    ¹⁵ against every tall tower and reinforced wall,
¹⁶ against [all vessels at sea,]*c*
    both merchant ships*d* and pleasure craft.
¹⁷ The haughtiness of men shall be abased,
    and man's pride brought low;
the Lord alone shall be exalted in that day.

¹⁸ He will utterly supplant the false gods.

¹⁹ Men will go into caves in the rocks
    and holes in the ground,
from the awesome presence of the Lord
    and from the brightness of his glory,
    when he arises and strikes terror on earth.
²⁰ In that day men will throw away
    to the moles and to the bats
their idols of silver and gods of gold
    which they have made for themselves
    to adore.

²¹ Men will go into crevices in the rocks
    and fissures in the cliffs,
from the awesome presence of the Lord
    and from the brightness of his glory,
when he arises and strikes terror on earth.

²² Desist from *the things of* man,
    in whose nostrils is but breath!
For of what consideration is he?

---

*c*16 So LXX; not in MT.
*d*16 Hebrew *ships of Tarshish*.

3 Even now, the Lord, the Lord of Hosts,
    deprives Judea and Jerusalem
of both staff and crutch—
    all food supply and water supply,
² the valiant man and soldier,
    the magistrate and prophet, the augur and elder,
³ the officer and dignitary,
    advisers, skilled craftsmen, and orators.
⁴ I, *the Lord*, will make adolescents their rulers;
    delinquents will lord it over them.
⁵ People will oppress one another,
    every man his neighbor.
The young will be insolent to the elderly,
    the vile to the honorable.

⁶ Then will a man apprehend a kinsman
    of his father's house, *and say*,
You have a tunic: be our leader
    and take charge of this ruination!
⁷ But he will raise *his hand* in that day
    and swear, I am no physician.
There is neither food nor clothing in my house;
    you cannot make me a leader of the people.

⁸ Jerusalem will falter and Judea fall
    because their tongue and their actions
are contrary to the Lord,
    an affront to his glory before his very eyes.
⁹ The look on their faces betrays them:
    they flaunt their sin like Sodom;
    they cannot hide it.
Woe to their souls;
    they have brought disaster upon themselves!

¹⁰ Tell the righteous it shall be well with them;
    they shall eat the fruits of their own labors.
¹¹ But woe to the wicked
    when calamity *overtakes them*:
they shall be paid back
    for the deeds they have done!

¹² As for my people, babes subject them;
    women wield authority over them.
  O my people, your leaders mislead you,
    abolishing your traditional ways.
¹³ The Lord will take a stand and contend *with them*;
    he has arisen to judge the nations.
¹⁴ He will bring to trial the elders of his people
    and their rulers, *and say to them*,
  It is you who have devoured the vineyard;
    you fill your houses by depriving the needy.
¹⁵ What do you mean by oppressing my people,
    humbling the faces of the poor?
  says the Lord of Hosts.

¹⁶ The Lord says, moreover,
    Because the women of Zion are haughty
  and put on airs, painting their eyes,
    ever flirting when they walk
    and clacking with their feet,
¹⁷ the Lord will afflict the scalps
    of the women of Zion with baldness;
  the Lord will expose their private parts.

¹⁸ In that day the Lord will strip away their finery—the anklets, head ornaments and crescents, ¹⁹ the pendants, chains and scarves, ²⁰ tiaras, bracelets and ribbons, zodiac signs and charm amulets, ²¹ rings for the fingers and for the ears, ²² the elegant dress, the shawl, the kerchief and the purse, ²³ hosiery, sheer linen, millinery, and cloaks.

²⁴ And instead of perfume there shall be a stench,
    instead of the girdle, a piece of twine,
  instead of the coiffure, baldness,
    instead of the festive dress, a loincloth of burlap;
  for in place of beauty
    there shall be ignominy.*
²⁵ Your men shall be felled by the sword,
    your might *overthrown* in war.
²⁶ Her gateways shall lie bereaved and forlorn;
    she shall sit on the ground destitute.

---

*24 So 1QIsaᵃ; term not in MT.

4 Seven women will take hold of one man
    in that day, and say,
We will eat our own food,
    wear our own clothes,
only let us be called by your name—
    take away our reproach!

² In that day the plant of the Lord shall be beautiful and glorious, and the earth's fruit the pride and glory of the survivors of Israel. ³ Then shall they who are left in Zion and they who remain in Jerusalem be called holy—all who were inscribed to be among the living at Jerusalem. ⁴ *This shall be* when my Lord has washed away the excrement of the women of Zion and cleansed Jerusalem of its bloodshed, in the spirit of justice, by a burning wind. ⁵ Over the whole site of Mount Zion, and over its solemn assembly, the Lord will form a cloud by day and a mist glowing with fire by night: above all that is glorious shall be a canopy. ⁶ It shall be a shelter and shade from the heat of the day, a secret refuge from the downpour and from rain.

5 Let me sing for my beloved
    a love song about his vineyard:
My beloved had a vineyard
    on the fertile brow of a hill.
² He cultivated it, clearing it of stones,
    and planted it with choice vines.
He built a watchtower in its midst
    and hewed for it a winepress as well.
Then he expected it to yield grapes,
    but it produced wild grapes.

³ Now, O inhabitants of Jerusalem and you men of Judea,
    please judge between me and my vineyard!
⁴ What more could have been done
    for my vineyard than I have done for it?
When I expected it to yield grapes,
    why did it produce wild grapes?
⁵ Let me now inform you
    what I will do to my vineyard:
I will have its hedge removed
    and let it be burned;

I will have its wall broken through
and let it be trampled.
6 I will make it a desolation:
it shall neither be pruned nor hoed,
but briars and thorns shall overgrow it.
Moreover, I will forbid the rainclouds to rain on it.

7 The vineyard of the Lord of Hosts is the house of Israel
and the people of Judah his cherished grove.
He expected justice,
but there was injustice;
he expected righteousness,
but there was an outcry.

8 Woe to those who join house to house
and link field to field till no place is left,
and you are restricted to dwell
in the centers of the land!
9 The Lord of Hosts *spoke this* in my hearing:
Surely many buildings shall lie desolate,
large and fine *houses* unoccupied.
10 A ten-acre*a* vineyard shall yield but one bath,*b*
a homer*c* of seed but an ephah.*d*

11 Woe to those who go after liquor
as soon as they arise in the morning,
who linger at night parties, inflamed by wine!
12 There are harps and lyres,
drums, flutes, and wine at their banquets,
but they regard not what the Lord does,
nor perceive his hands at work.

13 Therefore are my people exiled
without knowing *why*;
their best men die of famine,
their masses perish with thirst.

---

*a*10   Hebrew *ten-yoke*, viz., the land plowed by ten yoke of oxen in one day.
*b*10   About 6 gallons, or 22 liters.
*c*10   About 6 bushels, or 220 liters.
*d*10   A tenth of a homer.

¹⁴ Sheol becomes ravenous,
  opening her mouth insatiably;
 into it descend their elite with the masses,
  their boisterous ones and revelers.

¹⁵ Mankind is brought low
  when men debase themselves,
  causing the eyes of the high-minded to be downcast.
¹⁶ But the Lord of Hosts will be exalted
  by a just judgment,
 the holy God show himself holy
  by *his* righteousness.
¹⁷ Then shall *his* sheep feed in their pasture,
  and proselytes eat in the ruins of the affluent.

¹⁸ Woe to those drawn to sin by vain attachments,
  hitched to transgression like a trailer,
¹⁹ who think, Let him quickly speed up his work
  so we may see it!
 Let the plan of the Holy One of Israel
  soon come to pass, and we will know!

²⁰ Woe to those who suppose what is evil to be good
  and what is good, evil!
 They put darkness for light
  and light for darkness;
 they make bitterness sweet and the sweet bitter.

²¹ Woe to those who are wise in their own eyes
  and clever in their own view!

²² Woe to those who are valiant at drinking wine
  and champions at mixing liquor!

²³ *Woe to those* who acquit the guilty for a bribe,
  but deny justice to the innocent!
²⁴ As a blazing fire consumes stubble,
  and as dry weeds wane before the flame,
 so shall their roots decay away
  and their blossoms fly up like dust.

 For they have despised the law of the Lord of Hosts
  and reviled the words of the Holy One of Israel.

²⁵ Therefore the anger of the Lord is kindled
    against his people:
he draws back his hand against them
    and strikes them;
the mountains quake, and their corpses
    lie like litter about the streets.

Yet for all this his anger is not abated;
    his hand is upraised still.

²⁶ He raises an ensign to distant nations
    and summons them from beyond the horizon.
Forthwith they come, swiftly and speedily.
²⁷ Not one of them grows weary,
    nor does any stumble;
    they do not drowse or fall asleep.
Their waist-belts come not loose
    nor their sandal thongs undone.
²⁸ Their arrows are sharp;
    all their bows are strung.
The tread of their warhorses resembles flint;
    their chariot wheels revolve like a whirlwind.
²⁹ They have the roar of a lion;
    they are aroused like young lions:
growling, they seize the prey, and escape,
    and none comes to the rescue.

³⁰ He shall be stirred up against them in that day,
    even as the Sea is stirred up.
And should one look to the land,
    there *too* shall be a distressing gloom,
for the daylight shall be darkened
    by an overhanging mist.

6 In the year of King Uzziah's death, I saw my Lord seated on a throne, highly exalted, the skirt of his robe filling the sanctuary. ² Seraphs stood by him overhead, each having six wings—with two they could veil their presence, with two conceal their location, and with two fly about. ³ They called out to one another, and said,

> Most holy is the Lord of Hosts;
>> the consummation of all the earth is his glory!

⁴ The threshold shook to its foundation at the sound of those who called and a mist filled the temple.

⁵ Then I thought, Woe is me: I have been struck dumb, for I am a man of unclean speech, and I live among a people of unclean speech: I have seen the King, the Lord of Hosts, with my own eyes!

⁶ Then one of the seraphs flew to me carrying an ember which he had taken with tongs from the altar. ⁷ Touching it to my mouth, he said, See, this has touched your lips: your sins are taken away, your transgressions atoned for.

⁸ Then I heard the voice of my Lord saying, Whom shall I send? Who will go for us? And I replied, Here am I; send me!

⁹ And he said, Go, and say to these people,

> Go on hearing, but not understanding;
>> Go on seeing, but not perceiving.
> ¹⁰ Make the heart of these people grow fat;
>> dull their ears and shut their eyes,
> lest they see with their eyes
>> and hear with their ears,
> understand in their heart,
>> and repent, and be healed.

¹¹ And I replied, For how long, my Lord? And he said,

> Until the cities lie desolate
>> and without inhabitant,
> the houses without a man,
>> and the land ravaged to ruin.

¹² For the Lord will drive men away,
>> and great shall be the exodus
>> from the centers of the land.
¹³ And while yet a tenth of *the people*
>> remain in it, or return,
>> they shall be burned.
> But like the terebinth or the oak
>> when it is felled, whose stump remains alive,
> so shall the holy offspring be what is left standing.

7 When Ahaz son of Jotham, the son of Uzziah, was king of Judah, Rezin king of Aram and Pekah son of Remaliah king of Israel came up to Jerusalem to wage war against it, but could not overpower it.

2 And when the house of David was informed that Aram was leading Ephraim on, the king's mind and the minds of his people were shaken, as trees in a forest are shaken by a gale.

3 Then the Lord said to Isaiah, Go out and meet Ahaz, you and your son Shear-Jashub,*ᵃ* at the end of the aqueduct of the Upper Reservoir, on the road to the Laundry Plaza. 4 Say to him, See to it that you remain calm and unafraid. Be not intimidated by these two smoking tail ends of kindling, by the burning anger of Rezin and Aram and the son of Remaliah, 5 even though Aram has conceived an evil plot against you, as has Ephraim and the son of Remaliah, who say, 6 Let us invade Judah and stir up trouble there. We will take it for ourselves by force and set a ruler over it—the son of Tabeal.

7 Thus says my Lord the Lord:
    It shall not occur or transpire.
8 For as surely as Damascus is the capital of Aram
        and Rezin the head of Damascus,
    within sixty-five*ᵇ* years shall Ephraim
        be shattered as a nation.
9 But as surely as Samaria is the capital of Ephraim
        and the son of Remaliah the head of Samaria,
    you will not believe it,
        because you are not loyal.

10 Again the Lord addressed Ahaz, and said, 11 Ask a sign for yourself from the Lord your God, whether in the depths below or in the heights above. 12 But Ahaz said, I will not. I will not put the Lord to the test.

13 Then *Isaiah* said, Take heed, O house of David! Is it not enough for you to try the patience of men? Must you also try the patience of my God?

---

*ᵃ*3 That is, *A remnant will return.*
*ᵇ*8 Many commentators: *six or five.*

¹⁴ Therefore will my Lord of himself give you a sign: the young woman with child shall give birth to a son and name him Immanuel.ᶜ ¹⁵ Cream and honey will he eat by the time he has learned to reject what is evil and choose what is good. ¹⁶ But before the child learns to reject the evil and choose the good, the land whose two rulers you loathe shall lie forsaken. ¹⁷ The Lord will bring upon you and your people and your father's house a day unlike any since Ephraim broke away from Judah—*the day of* the king of Assyria.

¹⁸ In that day the Lord will signal for the flies from the far rivers of Egypt and for the bees in the land of Assyria. ¹⁹ And they will come and settle with one accord in the riverbeds of the prairie and in rocky ravines, and by all ditches and water holes. ²⁰ In that day my Lord will use a razor hired at the River—the king of Assyria—to shave your head and the hair of your legs, and to cut off even your beard.

²¹ In that day a man will keep alive a young cow and a pair of sheep. ²² And because of their plentiful milk, men will eat the cream. All who remain in the land will feed on cream and honey.

²³ In that day every plot of ground with a thousand vines worth a thousand pieces of currency shall be briars and thorns. ²⁴ Men will go there with bows and arrows, for the whole land shall revert to wilderness. ²⁵ And on all hillsides cultivated by the hoe you will no longer go for fear of the briars and thorns, but they shall serve as a cattle range, a terrain for sheep to tread down.

8 The Lord said to me, Take a large scroll and write on it in common script: Hasten the plunder, hurry the spoil. ² And I called in reliable witnesses, Uriah the priest and Zechariah the son of Jeberechiah, to witness for me.

³ And when I had been with the prophetess, she conceived and gave birth to a son. And the Lord said to me, Name him Maher-Shalal-Hash-Baz.ᵈ ⁴ For before the child knows how to say, Father, or Mother, the wealth of Damascus and the plunder of Samaria will be brought before the king of Assyria.

ᶜ14   That is, *God is with us.*

ᵈ3   That is, *Hasten the plunder, hurry the spoil.*

⁵ The Lord addressed me again, and said,

> ⁶ Because these people have rejected
>> the waters of Shiloah, which flow gently,
>> and rejoice in Rezin and the son of Remaliah,
> ⁷ therefore will my Lord
>> cause to come up over them
>> the great and mighty waters of the River—
>> the king of Assyria in all his glory.
>> He will rise up over all his channels
>> and overflow all his banks.
> ⁸ He will sweep into Judea *like* a flood
>> and, passing through, reach the very neck;
>> his outspread wings will span
>> the breadth of your land, O Immanuel.
>
> ⁹ Though nations form pacts,
>> they shall be routed.
>> Give heed, all you distant lands!
>> You may take courage in one another,
>> but shall be in fear;
>> you may arm yourselves,
>> but shall be terrorized.
> ¹⁰ Though you hold consultations,
>> they shall come to nought;
>> though you make proposals,
>> they shall not prove firm: God is with us!

¹¹ The Lord spoke to me, clasping my hand, and admonished me not to follow the ways of these people. For he said,

> ¹² Do not call a conspiracy all that these people
>> call a conspiracy;
>> be not afraid or awed
>> by the thing they fear.
> ¹³ But sanctify the Lord of Hosts,
>> making him your fear, him your awe.
> ¹⁴ And *to you* he will be a sanctuary,
>> but to the two houses of Israel
>> a stumbling block or obstructing rock,
>> and a snare, catching unawares
>> the inhabitants of Jerusalem.

¹⁵ Many will stumble into them,
    and when they fall shall be broken,
and when they become ensnared
    shall be taken captive.

¹⁶ *For the Lord has said*, Bind up the testimony;
    seal the law among my disciples.
¹⁷ I will wait for the Lord,
    who hides his face from the house of Jacob,
and expect him.

¹⁸ As for me and the children the Lord has given me, we shall be signs and portents in Israel from the Lord of Hosts, who dwells in Mount Zion.

¹⁹ When men tell you to inquire of mediums and spiritists who huddle together and mutter, *say to them*, Should not a people inquire of their God? Should one inquire*^b* of the dead on behalf of the living ²⁰ for doctrine and for a testimony? Surely, while they utter such words devoid of light, ²¹ they roam about embittered by hunger; and when they are hungry, they become enraged and, gazing upward, curse their king and their God. ²² They will look to the land, but there shall be a depressing scene of anguish and gloom; and thus are they banished into outer darkness.

9 But it shall not be gloomy to those who have been in anguish for her. In the past he humbled the land of Zebulon and Naphtali, but at the last he will exalt the Sea Route by the Jordan *in* Galilee of the nations.

² The people walking in darkness
    have seen a bright light;
on the inhabitants of the land
    of the shadow of death
    has the light dawned.
³ Thou hast enlarged the nation
    and increased its joy;
they rejoice at thy presence
    as men rejoice at harvest time,
    or as men are joyous when they divide spoil.

---

^b19 So LXX; phrase not in MT.

111

⁴ For thou hast smashed the yoke
  that burdened them,
the staff of submission,
  the rod of those who subjected them,
  as in the day of Midian*'s defeat*.
⁵ And all boots used in battle
  and tunics rolled in blood
  have become fuel for bonfires.

⁶ For to us a child is born, a son appointed,
  who will shoulder the burden of government.
He will be called
  Wonderful Counsellor, one Mighty in Valor,
  a Father for Ever, a Prince of Peace—
⁷ that sovereignty may be extended
  and peace have no end;
that, on the throne of David
  and over his kingdom,
his rule may be established and upheld
  by justice and righteousness
  from this time forth and forever.
The zeal of the Lord of Hosts will accomplish it.

⁸ This message my Lord sent to Jacob,
  and it shall befall Israel.
⁹ And the entire people—
  Ephraim and those who dwell in Samaria—
shall know of it,
  who say in pride and arrogance of heart,
¹⁰ The bricks have fallen down,
  but we will rebuild with hewn stone;
the sycamores have been felled,
  but we will replace them with cedars!
¹¹ But the Lord will strengthen
  Rezin's enemies against them
  when he stirs up their adversaries:
¹² Aramaeans from the east
  and Philistines from the west
will devour Israel with open mouth.

  Yet for all this his anger is not abated;
  his hand is upraised still.

¹³ But the people do not turn back
   to him who smites them,
   nor will they inquire of the Lord of Hosts.
¹⁴ Therefore the Lord will cut off from Israel
   head and tail, palm top and reed, in a single day;
¹⁵ the elders or notables are the head,
   the prophets who teach falsehoods, the tail.
¹⁶ The leaders of these people have misled them,
   and those who are led are confused.
¹⁷ My Lord is not pleased with their young men,
   nor does he pity their fatherless and widows,
   because all alike are godless malefactors,
   and every mouth utters profanities.

   Yet for all this his anger is not abated;
   his hand is upraised still.

¹⁸ Wickedness shall be set ablaze like a fire,
   and briars and thorns shall it consume;
   it shall ignite the jungle forests,
   and they shall billow upward
   in mushrooming clouds of smoke.
¹⁹ At the wrath of the Lord of Hosts
   the earth is scorched,
   and people are but fuel for the fire.
   Men will have no compassion for one another.
²⁰ They will snatch on the right, yet remain hungry;
   they will devour on the left, but not be satisfied:
   men will eat the flesh of their own offspring.
²¹ Manasseh *will turn* against Ephraim
   and Ephraim against Manasseh,
   and both will combine against Judah.

   Yet for all this his anger is not abated;
   his hand is upraised still.

10 Woe to those who enact unjust laws,
   who draft oppressive legislation—
² denying justice to the needy,
   depriving the poor of my people of their right,
   making plunder of widows,
   mere spoil of the fatherless!

³ What will you do in the day of reckoning
  when the holocaust overtakes you from afar?
To whom will you flee for help?
  Where will you leave your wealth?
⁴ There shall nothing remain
  but to kneel among the captives
  or fall among the slain.

Yet for all this his anger is not abated;
  his hand is upraised still.

⁵ Hail the Assyrian, the rod of my anger!
  He is a staff—my wrath in their hand.ᵃ
⁶ I will commission him against a godless nation,
  appoint him over the people
  deserving of my vengeance,
 to pillage for plunder, to spoliate for spoil,
  to tread underfoot like mud in the streets.

⁷ Nevertheless, it shall not seem so to him;
  this shall not be what he has in mind.
His purpose shall be to annihilate
  and to exterminate nations not a few.

⁸ He will say, Are not my commanders kings,
  one and all?
⁹ Has not Calno fared like Carchemish?
  Is not Hamath as Arpad,
  Samaria no better than Damascus?
¹⁰ Since I could do this to the pagan states,
  whose statues exceeded
  those of Jerusalem and Samaria,
¹¹ shall I not do to Jerusalem and its images
  even as I did to Samaria and its idols?

¹² But when my Lord has fully accomplished his work in Mount
Zion and in Jerusalem, he will punish the king of Assyria for
his notorious boasting and infamous conceit, ¹³ because he has
said,

ᵃ5 Or, *My wrath is a staff in his hand.*

I have done it by my own ability
   and shrewdness, for I am ingenious.
I have done away with the borders of nations,
   I have ravaged their reserves,
   I have vastly reduced the inhabitants.
14 I have impounded the wealth of peoples like a nest,
   and I have gathered up the whole world
   as one gathers abandoned eggs;
   not one flapped its wings,
   or opened its mouth to utter a peep.

15 Shall an axe exalt itself
   above the one who hews with it,
   or a saw vaunt itself
   over him who handles it?
As though the rod wielded him who lifts it up!
As though the staff held up the one
   who is not made of wood!

16 Therefore will the Lord, the Lord of Hosts,
   send a consumption into his fertile lands,
and cause a fire to flare up like a burning hearth,
   to undermine his glory:
17 the Light of Israel will be the fire
   and their Holy One the flame,
and it shall burn up and devour
   his briars and thorns in a single day.
18 His choice forests and productive fields
   it will consume, both life and substance,
   turning them into a rotting morass.
19 And the trees left of his forest shall be so few,
   a child could record them.

20 In that day those who survive of Israel
   and who escape of the house of Jacob
will no longer rely on him who struck them,
   but will truly rely on the Lord,
   the Holy One of Israel:
21 of Jacob a remnant will return
   to the one Mighty in Valor.

²² For though your people, O Israel,
    be as the sands of the sea,
    only a remnant will return;
  although annihilation is decreed,
    it shall overflow with righteousness.
²³ For my Lord, the Lord of Hosts,
    will carry out the utter destruction
    decreed upon the whole earth.

²⁴ Therefore, thus says my Lord,
    the Lord of Hosts:
  O my people who inhabit Zion,
    be not afraid of the Assyrians,
  though they strike you with the rod
    or raise their staff over you,
    as did the Egyptians.
²⁵ For my anger will very soon come to an end;
    my wrath will become their undoing.

²⁶ The Lord of Hosts will raise the whip against them,
    as when he struck the Midianites
    at the rock of Oreb.
  His staff is over the Sea,
    and he will lift it over them
    as he did to the Egyptians.
²⁷ In that day their burdens shall be lifted
    from your shoulders,
    their yoke *removed* from your neck:
  the yoke *that wore away your fatness*
    shall by fatness wear away.

²⁸ He advances on Aiath, passes through Migron;
    at Micmash he marshals his weaponry.
²⁹ They cross over the pass,
    stopping overnight at Geba.
  Ramah is in a state of alarm,
    Gibeah of Saul is fleeing.
³⁰ Cry out, O Daughter of Gallim!
    Hear her, Laishah; answer her, Anathoth!
³¹ Madmenah has moved out of the way,
    the inhabitants of Gebim are in full flight.

116

32 This same day he will but pause at Nob
 and signal the advance
against the mountain of the Daughter of Zion,
 the hill of Jerusalem.

33 Then will the Lord, the Lord of Hosts,
 shatter the towering *trees* with terrifying power;
the high in stature shall be hewn down,
 the lofty ones leveled.

34 The dense forests shall be battered down
 with *the force of* iron,
and Lebanon fall spectacularly.

11 A shoot will spring up from the stock of Jesse
 and a branch from its graft bear fruit.

2 The Spirit of the Lord will rest upon him—
 the spirit of wisdom and of understanding,
the spirit of counsel and of valor,
 the spirit of knowledge
 and of the fear of the Lord.

3 His intuition will be *guided*
 by the fear of the Lord;
he will not judge by what his eyes see,
 nor establish proof by what his ears hear.

4 He will judge the poor with righteousness,
 and with equity arbitrate for the lowly in the land;
he will smite the earth with the rod of his mouth
 and with the breath of his lips slay the wicked.

5 Righteousness will be as a band about his waist,
 faithfulness a girdle round his loins.

6 Then shall the wolf dwell among lambs
 and the leopard lie down with young goats;
calves and young lions *ᵃwill feedᵃ* together,
 and a youngster will lead them *to pasture*.

7 When a cow and bear browse,
 their young will rest together;
 the lion will eat straw like the ox.

ᵃ6 So 1QIsaᵃ; LXX. MT *and fatlings.*

⁸ A suckling infant will play near the adder's den,
    and the toddler reach his hand
    over the viper's nest.
⁹ There shall be no harm or injury done
    throughout my holy mountain,
for the earth shall be filled
    with the knowledge of the Lord
as the oceans are overspread with waters.

¹⁰ In that day the sprig of Jesse,
    who stands for an ensign to the peoples,
shall be sought by the nations,
    and his residence shall be glorious.
¹¹ In that day my Lord will again *ᵇraiseᵇ* his hand
    to reclaim the remnant of his people—
those who shall be left out of Assyria,
    Egypt, Pathros, Cush, Elam, Shinar, Hamath,
    and the islands of the sea.
¹² He will raise the ensign to the nations
    and assemble the exiled of Israel;
he will gather the scattered of Judah
    from the four directions of the earth.

¹³ Ephraim's jealousy shall pass away
    and the hostile ones of Judah be cut off;
Ephraim will not envy Judah,
    nor Judah resent Ephraim.
¹⁴ But they will swoop on the Philistine flank
    toward the west,
    and together plunder those to the east;
they will take Edom and Moab at hand's reach,
    and the Ammonites will obey them.

¹⁵ The Lord will dry up the tongue
    of the Egyptian Sea ᶜby his mighty wind;ᶜ
he will extend his hand over the River
    and smite it into seven streams
    to provide a way on foot.

ᵇ11   Hebrew *šēnît, a second time,* emended to *śeʾēt;* compare Interpreter's Bible, 5:251.
ᶜ15   Phrase transposed; in text follows *and smite it.*

16 And there shall be a pathway out of Assyria
   for the remnant of his people who shall be left,
as there was for Israel
   when it came up from the land of Egypt.

12 In that day you will say,
   I praise thee, O Lord.
Although thou hast been angry with me,
   thine anger is turned away
   and thou hast consoled me.
2 In*a* the God of my salvation I will trust without fear;
   for the Lord was my strength and *b*my song*b*
   when he became my salvation.
3 Then shall you rejoice in drawing water
   from the fountains of salvation.

4 In that day you will say,
   Give thanks to the Lord; invoke his name.
Make known his deeds among the nations;
   commemorate his exalted name.
5 Sing in praise of the Lord,
   who has performed wonders;
   let it be acknowledged throughout the earth!
6 Shout and sing for joy, O inhabitants of Zion,
   for renowned among you is the Holy One of Israel.

13 An oracle concerning Babylon, which Isaiah the son of Amoz
saw in vision:

2 Raise the ensign on a barren mountain;
   sound the voice among them!
Beckon them with the hand to advance
   into the precincts of the elite.
3 I have charged my holy ones,
   called out my valiant ones:
   *a*my anger is not upon*a* those who take pride in me.

---

*a*2 Hebrew *)el)ēl;* so 1QIsa*a*. A probable haplography in MT.
*b*2 Hebrew *zimrāt yâ,* a probable dittography, emended to *zimrātî.*
*a*3 Hebrew *lĕ)appî (allîzê,* exhibiting a double haplography, emended to *lō))appî (al (allîzê.*

⁴ Hark! A tumult on the mountains,
    as of a vast multitude.
Hark! An uproar among kingdoms,
    as of nations assembling:
the Lord of Hosts is marshalling an army for war.
⁵ They come from a distant land beyond the horizon—
    the Lord and the instruments of his wrath—
to cause destruction throughout the earth.

⁶ Lament, for the day of the Lord is near;
    it shall come as a violent blow from the Almighty.
⁷ Then shall every hand grow weak
    and the hearts of all men melt.
⁸ They shall be terrified, in throes of agony,
    seized with trembling like a woman in labor.
Men will look at one another aghast,
    their faces set aflame.

⁹ The day of the Lord shall come
    as a cruel outburst of anger and wrath
to make the earth a desolation,
    that sinners may be annihilated from it.
¹⁰ The stars and constellations of the heavens
    will not shine.
When the sun rises, it shall be obscured;
    nor will the moon give its light.

¹¹ I have decreed calamity for the world,
    punishment for the wicked;
I will put an end to the arrogance of insolent men
    and humble the pride of tyrants.
¹² I will make mankind scarcer than fine gold,
    men *more rare* than gold of Ophir.
¹³ I will cause disturbance in the heavens
    when the earth is jolted out of place
by the anger of the Lord of Hosts
    in the day of his blazing wrath.

¹⁴ Then, like a deer that is chased,
    or a flock of sheep that no one rounds up,
each will return to his own people
    and everyone flee to his homeland.

¹⁵ Whoever is found shall be thrust through;
    all who are caught shall fall by the sword.
¹⁶ Their infants shall be dashed in pieces before their eyes,
    their homes plundered, their wives ravished.
¹⁷ See, I stir up against them the Medes,
    who do not value silver, nor covet gold.
¹⁸ Their bows shall tear apart the young.
    They will show no mercy to the newborn;
    their eye will not look with compassion on children.

¹⁹ And Babylon, the most splendid of kingdoms,
    the glory and pride of Chaldeans, shall be *thrown down*
    as God overthrew Sodom and Gomorrah.

²⁰ Never shall it be reinhabited;
    it shall not be resettled through all generations.
    Nomads will not pitch their tents there,
    nor will shepherds rest their flocks in it.
²¹ But wild animals will infest it,
    and its buildings overflow with weasels;
    birds of prey will find lodging there
    and demonic creatures prance about in it.
²² Jackals will cry out from its palaces,
    howling creatures from its amusement halls.
    Her time draws near;
    *Babylon's*ᵇ days shall not be prolonged.

14 The Lord will have compassion on Jacob
    and once again choose Israel;
    he will settle them in their own land,
    and proselytes will adhere to them
    and join the house of Jacob.
² The nations will take them
    and bring them to their own place.
    And the house of Israel will possess them
    as menservants and maidservants
    in the land of the Lord:
    they will take captive their captors
    and rule over their oppressors.

ᵇ22 Hebrew *Her.*

³ In the day the Lord gives you relief from grief and anguish and from the arduous servitude imposed on you, ⁴ you will take up this taunt against the king of Babylon, and say,

> How the tyrant has met his end
>   and tyranny*ᵃ* ceased!
> ⁵ The Lord has broken the staff of the wicked,
>   the rod of those who ruled—
> ⁶ him who with unerring blows
>   struck down the nations in anger,
> who subdued peoples in his wrath
>   by relentless oppression.
> ⁷ Now the whole earth is at rest and at peace;
>   there is jubilant celebration!
> ⁸ The pine trees, too, rejoice over you,
>   as do the cedars of Lebanon:
> Since you have been laid low,
>   no hewer has risen against us!
>
> ⁹ Sheol below was in commotion because of you,
>   anticipating your arrival;
> on your account she roused all the spirits
>   of the world's leaders,
> causing all who had ruled nations
>   to rise up from their thrones.
> ¹⁰ All alike were moved to say to you,
>   Even you have become powerless as we are!
> You have become like us!
>
> ¹¹ Your glory has been cast down to Sheol,
>   along with the music of your lyres.
> Beneath you is a bed of maggots;
>   you are covered with worms.
> ¹² How you have fallen from the heavens,
>   O morning star, son of the dawn!
> You who commanded the nations
>   have been hewn down to earth!
>
> ¹³ You said in your heart, I will rise in the heavens
>   and set up my throne above the stars of God;

---

*ᵃ*4   Or, *rage;* so 1QIsaᵃ; LXX. MT rendering is unknown.

I will seat myself
    in the mount of assembly *of the gods*,
    in the utmost heights of Zaphon.
14 I will ascend above the altitude of the clouds;
    I will make myself like the Most High!

15 But you have been brought down to Sheol,
    to the utmost depths of the Pit.
16 Those who catch sight of you
    stare at you, wondering,
Is this the man who made the earth shake
    and kingdoms quake,
17 who turned the world into a wilderness,
    demolishing its cities,
permitting not his captives to return home?

18 All rulers of nations lie in state,
    each among his own kindred.
19 But you are cast away unburied
    like a repugnant fetus,
exposed like the slain disfigured by the sword,
    whose mangled remains are thrown in a gravel pit.

20 You shall not share burial with them,
    for you have destroyed your land
    and murdered your people.
May the brood of miscreants
    never more be mentioned!
21 Prepare for the massacre of their sons,
    in consequence of their fathers' deeds,
lest they rise up again
    and take possession of the world,
and fill the face of the earth with cities.

22 I will rise up against them, says the Lord of Hosts.
    I will cut off Babylon's name and remnant,
    its offspring and descendants, says the Lord.
23 I will turn it into swamplands, a haunt for ravens;
    I will sweep it with the broom of destruction,
says the Lord of Hosts.

123

²⁴ The Lord of Hosts made an oath, saying,

> As I foresaw it, so shall it happen;
>> as I planned it, so shall it be:

²⁵ I will break Assyria in my own land,
>> trample them underfoot on my mountains;
> their yoke shall be taken from them,
>> their burden removed from their shoulders.

²⁶ These are things determined upon the whole earth;
>> this is the hand upraised over all nations.

²⁷ For what the Lord of Hosts has determined,
>> who shall revoke?
> When his hand is upraised, who can turn it away?

²⁸ In the year King Ahaz died, came this oracle:

²⁹ Rejoice not, all you Philistines,
>> now that the rod which struck you is broken.
> From among the descendants of that snake
>> shall spring up a viper,
> and his offspring shall be a fiery flying serpent.

³⁰ The elect poor shall have pasture,
>> and the needy recline in safety.
> But your descendants I will kill with famine,
>> and your survivors shall be slain.

³¹ Wail at the gates; howl in the city!
>> Utterly melt away, you Philistines!
> From the North shall come *pillars of* smoke,
>> and no place he has designated shall evade it.

³² What shall then be told the envoys of the nation?
>> The Lord has founded Zion;
> let his longsuffering people find refuge there.

15

An oracle concerning Moab:

> When in one night Ar is devastated,
>> Moab shall be silenced;
> when in one night Kir is razed,
>> Moab shall be destroyed.

² They will go up to the sanctuaries,
>> and in Dibon to the hill shrines, to weep;
> they will wail in Moab over Nebo and Medeba.
>> Every head shall be bald, every beard cut off.

3 They will wear sackcloth openly;
  on the housetops and in the streets
they will altogether wail and give way to weeping.

4 Heshbon will cry for help, as will Elealeh;
  their appeal shall be heard as far as Jahaz.
They will sound the alarm
  to summon the armed men of Moab,
but their spirit shall be broken.
5 My heart will cry out for Moab;
  its fugitives will reach Zoar
  and as far as Eglath Shelishiah.
In tears they will ascend the slopes of Luhith;
  on the road to Horonaim
they will raise the cry of catastrophe.

6 For the waters of Nimrim shall be desolate;
  the grass shall dry up, vegetation disappear,
  and no green foliage shall remain.
7 The surplus they have acquired,
  and their personal belongings,
  they will carry away
    over the Valley of the Willows.
8 The cry of calamity
    shall encompass the land of Moab;
  the sound of it shall reach Eglaim
    and echo as far as Beer Elim.

9 Although the waters of Dibon shall flow with blood,
    yet will I impose more than this upon Dibon:
  I *will bring* lions upon the fugitives of Moab
    and on those who remain in the land.

16 Send couriers to those who rule in the earth,
    from Sela in the desert
    to the mountain of the Daughter of Zion.
2 Like fluttering birds forced out of the nest,
    so are Moab's women at the fords of Arnon.
3 Provide a solution, *they say*; judge our case!
    Overshadow us at high noon as though it were night!
  Shelter those dispossessed;
    betray not the refugees!

⁴ Let the exiles of Moab dwell with you;
   be a refuge to them from the aggressors!

When oppressors are no more
   and violence has ceased,
when tyrants are destroyed from the earth,
⁵ then, in loving kindness,
   shall a throne be set up in the abode of David,
and in faithfulness a judge sit on it
   who will maintain justice and expedite righteousness.

⁶ We have heard of the glories of Moab,
   of its excessive pride and its boasting,
   of its outbursts of false propaganda.
⁷ For this shall the Moabites *be made to* lament,
   and all *have cause to* bewail Moab:
they shall groan at the ruin of Kir Hareseth
   in utter dejection.

⁸ For the vineyards of Heshbon shall wither;
   the ruling nations will smite Sibmah's vines.
Its runner vines reached Jazer,
   trailing through the desert;
its branches spread abroad across the sea.
⁹ Therefore I will mourn as Jazer mourns
   for the vines of Sibmah;
I will water you with my tears,
   O Heshbon and Elealeh,
when your shouts of cheer
   over the summer fruit and harvest are stilled.
¹⁰ The joyful festivity will be gone from the orchards;
   no shouts of delight shall sound in the vineyards.
The wine treaders will tread no wine in the presses;
   the vintage shout I will bring to an end.

¹¹ My breast will vibrate like a harp for Moab,
   my inmost being for Kir Hareseth.
¹² For when the Moabites weary themselves
   with petitioning on the hill shrines,
and enter their sanctuaries to pray,
   it shall be to no avail.

13 These things the Lord spoke hitherto about Moab. 14 But now the Lord has said, Within three years, as the term of a lease, Moab's glory shall become ignominy. For all its large populace there shall be very few left, and those of no account.

17 An oracle concerning Damascus:
　　Damascus shall cease to be a city
　　　and become a heap of ruins.
　2 The cities of Aroer shall lie forsaken
　　　and become places for herds to recline,
　　where no one will disturb them.
　3 When Ephraim's defense comes to an end,
　　　so shall the sovereignty of Damascus:
　　as with the glory of the children of Israel,
　　　so shall it be with Aram's remnant,
　　says the Lord of Hosts.

　4 In that day Jacob's glory shall wane,
　　　and his fatness of body become leanness.
　5 After being like a harvest of ripe grain,
　　　whose ears are reaped by the armful,
　　he will become like ears plucked
　　　in the Valley of Rephaim
　　　6 when only the gleanings are left,
　　or when an olive tree is beaten,
　　　having two or three berries in the topmost bough,
　　or four or five in its most fruitful branch,
　　　says the Lord, the God of Israel.

　7 In that day men will have regard to their Maker,
　　　and their eyes look to the Holy One of Israel,
　8 and regard not the altars,
　　　the works of their hands,
　　nor look to things made by their fingers—
　　　the idols of prosperity and the shining images.

9 In that day their mighty cities shall be like the deserted towns of the *Hivites and Amorites,* which they abandoned before the Israelites during the desolation.

---

*a*9　So LXX; MT *groves and treetops.*

¹⁰ For you have forgotten your God, your salvation,
    and not remembered the Rock, your fortress.
Therefore, though you plant choice crops
    and sow hybrid seed,
¹¹ and though you make them thrive
    the day you plant them,
causing them to sprout
    the very morning you sow them,
yet shall the harvest vanish
    in a day of diseases and incurable pain.

¹² Woe to the many peoples in an uproar,
    who rage like the raging of the seas—
tumultuous nations, in commotion
    like the turbulence of mighty waters!
¹³ Nations may roar like the roaring of great waters,
    but when he rebukes them they will flee far away;
they will be driven before the wind
    like chaff on the mountains,
    or as whirling *dust* in a storm.
¹⁴ At evening time shall be the catastrophe,
    and before morning they shall be no more.
This is the lot of those who plunder us,
    the fate of those who despoil us.

18 Woe to the land of buzzing wings
    beyond the rivers of Cush,
² which sends emissaries by sea,
    in swift craft across the water.
They say, Go speedily, you messengers!
    Go to a people perpetually on the move,
a nation dreaded far and wide,
    a people continually infringing,
whose rivers have annexed their lands.

³ All you who live in the world,
    you inhabitants of the earth,
look to the ensign
    when it is lifted up in the mountains;
heed the trumpet when sounded!

4 For thus said the Lord to me:
    I will watch in silence over my dwelling place
when the searing heat overtakes the reapers,^a
    and when the rainclouds *appear*
    amid the fever of reaping.
5 For before the harvest,
    when the *time of* flowering is past
and the set blossoms are developing into young fruit,
    they will cut down the fruit-bearing twigs with knives
    and remove the new branches by slashing.
6 All shall be left to the birds of prey
    of the mountains
    and to the beasts of the land:
the birds of prey will feed on them all summer
    and the beasts of the land all winter.

7 At that time shall tribute be brought
    to the Lord of Hosts
from a nation perpetually on the move,
    from a nation dreaded far and wide,
a people continually infringing,
    whose rivers have annexed their lands,
to the place of the name of the Lord of Hosts:
    Mount Zion.

19 An oracle concerning Egypt:

When the Lord enters Egypt riding on swift clouds,
    the idols of Egypt will rock at his presence
    and the Egyptians' hearts melt within them.

2 I will stir up the Egyptians against the Egyptians;
    they will fight brother against brother
and neighbor against neighbor,
    city against city and state against state.
3 Egypt's spirit shall be drained from within;
    I will frustrate their plans,
and they will resort to the idols and to spiritists,
    to mediums and witchcraft.

---

*a*4   Hebrew *)ôr, light,* emended to *)ôreh.*

⁴ Then will I deliver the Egyptians
    into the hand of a cruel master;
a harsh ruler will subject them,
    says my Lord, the Lord of Hosts.

⁵ The waters of the lakes shall ebb away
    as streambeds become desolate and dry.
⁶ The rivers shall turn foul,
    and Egypt's waterways recede and dry up.
Reeds and rushes shall wither;
    ⁷ vegetation adjoining canals and estuaries,
and all things sown along irrigation channels,
    shall shrivel and blow away and be no more.

⁸ Fishermen will deplore *their lot*
    and anglers in canals bemoan themselves;
those who cast nets on water
    will be in misery.
⁹ Manufacturers of combed linen
    and weavers of fine fabrics will be dismayed.
¹⁰ The textile workers will know despair,
    and all who work for wages ªsuffer distress.ª

¹¹ The ministers of Zoan are utter fools;
    the wisest of Pharaoh's advisers give absurd counsel.
How can you say to Pharaoh,
    We ourselves are as wise as the first rulers?
¹² Where are your wise men indeed?
    Let them please tell you, if they can discern it,
what the Lord of Hosts has in mind for Egypt!

¹³ The ministers of Zoan have been foolish,
    the officials of Noph deluded;
    the heads of state have led Egypt astray.
¹⁴ The Lord has permeated them
    with a spirit of confusion;
they have misled Egypt in all that she does,
    causing her to stagger like a drunkard into his vomit.
¹⁵ And there shall be nothing the Egyptians
    can do about it,
    neither head nor tail, palm top or reed.

ª10   Hebrew ʾagmê nepeš, *ponds for life*, emended to ʿagmê nepeš.

¹⁶ In that day the Egyptians will be as women, fearful and afraid at the brandishing hand the Lord of Hosts wields over them. ¹⁷ The land of Judah shall become a source of terror to the Egyptians; all reminded of it shall dread what the Lord of Hosts has in store for them.

¹⁸ In that day five Hebrew-speaking cities in the land of Egypt will swear loyalty to the Lord of Hosts. One shall be known as the City of Righteousness.ᵇ

¹⁹ In that day there shall be an altar *erected* to the Lord in the midst of the land of Egypt and a monument to the Lord at its border. ²⁰ They shall serve as a sign and testimony of the Lord of Hosts in the land of Egypt: when they cry out to the Lord because of the oppressors, he will send them a savior, who will take up their cause and deliver them.

²¹ The Lord will make himself known to the Egyptians, and the Egyptians shall know the Lord in that day. They will worship by sacrifice and offerings, and make vows to the Lord and fulfill them. ²² The Lord will smite Egypt, and by smiting heal: they will turn back to the Lord, and he will respond to their pleas and heal them.

²³ In that day there shall be a highway from Egypt to Assyria. Assyrians shall come to Egypt and Egyptians go to Assyria, and the Egyptians shall labor with the Assyrians.

²⁴ In that day Israel shall be the third party to Egypt and to Assyria, a blessing in the midst of the earth. ²⁵ The Lord of Hosts will bless them, saying, Blessed be Egypt my people, Assyria the work of my hands, and Israel my inheritance.

20 In the year the general who was sent by Sargon king of Assyria came to Ashdod and took it by combat, ² the Lord had spoken through Isaiah the son of Amoz, saying, Go and ungird the sackcloth from your loins and remove the shoes from your feet. And he had done so, going naked and barefoot.

³ Then the Lord said, Just as my servant Isaiah has gone naked and barefoot for three years as a sign and portent against Egypt and Cush, ⁴ so shall the king of Assyria lead away the captives of Egypt and the exiles of Cush, both young and old, naked and barefoot,

---

ᵇ18 So LXX. MT *city of destruction;* 1QIsaᵃ *city of the sun.*

with buttocks uncovered—to Egypt's shame. ⁵ Men shall be appalled and perplexed at Cush, their hope, and at Egypt, their boast.

⁶ In that day shall the inhabitants of this isle say, See what has become of those we looked up to, on whom we relied*a* for help and deliverance from the king of Assyria! How shall we ourselves escape?

21

An oracle concerning the Wilderness of the West:
  Like tornadoes sweeping through the South,
    they come from the steppes, a land of terror.
² A grim vision has been revealed to me:
    the traitor in the act of treachery,
    the destroyer laying waste.
  Attack, O Elamites! Lay siege, you Medes!
    All the sighing that *Babylon*a has caused
    I will bring to an end.

³ Therefore my whole frame is racked with trembling;
    throes of agony have seized me like a woman in labor.
  I am tormented beyond giving heed;
    I am too distraught to see.
⁴ My mind reels, I am paralyzed with fear;
    the nightfall I longed for has become a horror to me:
⁵ They prepare tables;
    they deck them with candlesticks.
  They are eating and drinking . . .
    Mobilize, you commanders! Oil the armor!

⁶ Because of this my Lord said to me,
    Go and appoint a watchman
    who will report what he sees.
⁷ Let him watch for chariots with teams of horses,
    riders on asses and riders on camels.
  He must be most vigilant, fully alert.
⁸ Then the lookout*b* cried,
    I have been standing on the watchtower
  day in and day out, my Lord;
    night after night I have stood guard.

---

*a*6   So 1QIsa*a*; MT *to whom we fled.*
*a*2   Hebrew *she.*
*b*8   So 1QIsa*a*; MT *a lion.*

⁹ Now they come: cavalry and teams of horses!
    And he gave the reply,
She has fallen; Babylon has fallen.
    All her idol gods he has razed to the ground.

¹⁰ ᶜTo you who know me, who are of my fold,ᶜ
    I have reported what I heard
from the Lord of Hosts, the God of Israel.

¹¹ An oracle concerning Dumah:

Men call to me from Seir,
    Watchman, what remains of the night?
    Watchman, how much of the night is left?
¹² The watchman replies,
    Morning comes, though it is still night.
If you would ascertain it,
    do so by repenting and coming back.

¹³ An oracle concerning those in Arabia:

You wandering bands of Dedanites,
    who sojourn in the forests of Arabia,
¹⁴ bring water to greet the thirsty;
    meet the fugitives with food,
O inhabitants of the land of Tema.
¹⁵ For they flee from destruction,
    from the bared sword, the drawn bow
    and the severity of war.

¹⁶ On account of this, my Lord said to me, Within a year, as the term of a lease, Kedar's glory shall fully expire. ¹⁷ And the number of valiant archers remaining of the sons of Kedar shall be few. The Lord, the God of Israel, has spoken it.

22 An oracle concerning the Arena of Spectacles:

Whatever is the matter with you,
    causing you all at once
    to climb onto the housetops?
² You resounded with loud cheers—
    a tumultuous town, a city of revelry!

ᶜ10 So 1QIsaª; MT *My threshed and winnowed ones.*

But your slain were not killed by the sword;
  they did not die in battle!
³ Your chiefs, altogether in flight,
  are captured without using the bow;
all of you left behind are caught easily
  before you can get away.

⁴ Because of this I said,
Turn your attention from me,
  though I weep bitterly;
hasten not to comfort me
  at the ruin of the Daughter of my People.

⁵ For my Lord, the Lord of Hosts, has in store
a day of commotion and trampling and riot
  in the Arena of Spectacles,
a day of battering down walls,
  and of crying in distress, To the mountains!

⁶ When Elam takes up the quiver,
  and horses are harnessed to the chariots of Aram,*
  and Kir uncovers the armor,
⁷ then shall your choice valleys fill with chariots,
  and cavalry take up positions at your gateways.
⁸ And in the day Judea's defensive screen is removed,
  you will look to the forest home as protection.

⁹ When you saw the city of David increasingly breached,
  you conserved water in the Lower Reservoir.
¹⁰ You took a census of the buildings in Jerusalem,
  tearing down buildings to fortify your wall.
¹¹ You built cisterns between the walls
  for the water from the Old Reservoir,
but you did not look to its Maker,
  nor have regard for the One who designed it long ago.

¹² In such a day my Lord, the Lord of Hosts,
  calls for weeping and lamentation,
  for austerity and wearing sackcloth.

---

*a*6 Hebrew *ʾādām*, *man/men*, emended to *ʾărām*.

¹³ Instead, there is mirth and merrymaking,
the killing of cattle and slaughter of sheep,
eating meat and drinking wine:
Let us dine and drink, for tomorrow we die!

¹⁴ The Lord of Hosts revealed this to my ears: Such wickedness cannot be forgiven you till you die, says my Lord, the Lord of Hosts.

¹⁵ Thus said my Lord, the Lord of Hosts:
Go and see that steward, Shebna,
overseer of the palace.
¹⁶ *Say to him*, What are you up to?
Who do you think you are,
that you have hewn yourself a tomb here,
like those who hew their sepulchres up high,
carving out graves for themselves in the rock?

¹⁷ The Lord will hurl you away
as an athlete hurls a missile;
he will make you soar like a dart.
¹⁸ He will bind you tightly about
and send you spinning like a top
into an open country.
There shall you die,
and your *in*glorious conveyance there
shall be a disgrace to your master's house.
¹⁹ I will thrust you out of office;
you will be expelled from your post.

²⁰ In that day I will commission my servant Eliakim the son of Hilkiah: ²¹ I will clothe him with your robe and bind your girdle on him; I will appoint him your jurisdiction. And he will be a father to the inhabitants of Jerusalem and to the house of Judah. ²² I will invest him with the keys of the house of David: when he opens none shall shut, when he shuts none shall open. ²³ I will fasten him as a nail in a sure place, and he will be a throne of glory to the house of his father. ²⁴ Upon him shall be hung all the glory of his father's house: his descendants and posterity, including all the lesser vessels, from ordinary bowls to the most common containers.

²⁵ In that day, says the Lord of Hosts, the nail that was fastened in a sure place shall be removed. It shall be dislodged and fall, and the burden hanging on it cut off. The Lord has spoken it.

23 An oracle concerning Tyre:

Sound your sirens, O merchant ships!
  For *Tyre*[a] is laid waste,
  stripped of warehouse and wharf.
On their way from the land of Kittim
  shall they be informed of it.
² Be dumbfounded, you inhabitants of the isles,
  who were amply replenished
  by the traders of Sidon crossing the seas.
³ The grain of Shihor, the harvest of the Nile,
  was her source of revenue upon the high seas
when she became the merchant of nations.

⁴ Be dismayed, O Sidon, because the Sea,
  the mighty haven of the Sea, has declared,
I no longer labor and bear children!
  I no longer rear young men or raise virgins!
⁵ When the news of Tyre reaches Egypt,
  men will be in anguish at the report.

⁶ Move on to Tarshish lamenting,
  you inhabitants of the isles.
⁷ Is this your festive *city* of ancient origin,
  whose feet led her to settle far-off *lands*?
⁸ Who devised this stratagem against Tyre,
  the imperial *city*,
whose traders were princes,
  whose merchants the world's celebrities?
⁹ The Lord of Hosts devised it,
  to make all glorying in excellence a profanity,
and the world's celebrities an utter execration.

¹⁰ Overflow your land like the Nile,
  O Daughter of Tarshish: the harbor is no more.
¹¹ The Lord will stretch out his hand over the Sea
  and distress kingdoms;
he will give orders concerning the merchant *city*
  that her ports of haven be destroyed.

---

[a]1   Hebrew *she*.

12 He will say, You will frolic no more,
  O ravished virgin, Daughter of Sidon.
Get up and cross over to Kittim,
  though even there you will find no rest.

13 So too with the land of the Chaldeans,
  the people who founded *Tyre*[b] for shipping.
Was it not the Assyrians who set up observatories,
  exposed its fortifications, and caused her downfall?
14 Sound your sirens, O merchant ships;
  your haven is desolate!

15 In that day Tyre shall be forgotten seventy years, the lifetime
of a king. And at the end of seventy years, Tyre shall be as the harlot
in the song:

16 Take a lyre and go about the town,
  O forgotten harlot.
Play skillfully; sing song after song,
  that you may be remembered.

17 For after seventy years, the Lord will revisit Tyre. And she will
return to her trade and hire herself out to all the kingdoms of the
world on the face of the earth. 18 Her merchandise and hire shall
be consecrated to the Lord; it shall not be hoarded or stored up.
Her commerce shall provide for those who dwell in the presence
of the Lord, that they may eat their fill and be elegantly clothed.

24 Lo! The Lord will lay waste the earth and empty it;
  he will disfigure its surface
  and scatter its inhabitants.
2 And it shall be with priest as with people,
  with master as with servant,
with mistress as with maid,
  with seller as with buyer,
with lender as with borrower,
  with creditor as with debtor—
3 when the earth is sacked,
  it shall be utterly ravaged.
The Lord has given word concerning it.

---

[b]13 Hebrew *her*.

⁴ The earth shall pine away,
    the world miserably perish;
    the elite of the earth shall be made wretched.
⁵ The earth lies polluted under its inhabitants:
    they have transgressed the laws,
  changed the ordinances,
    set at nought the ancient covenant.
⁶ The curse devours the earth,
    for those who dwell on it have incurred guilt;
  because of it the population of the earth
    shall be diminished*
and little of mankind remain.

⁷ The new wine withers on languishing vines,
    making all the lighthearted lament.
⁸ The rhythm of drums ceases,
    the revelers' din stops;
    the pulsating of lyres comes to an end.
⁹ Men no longer drink wine amid song;
    liquor has turned bitter to drinkers.
¹⁰ The towns of disorder are broken up;
    all houses are shuttered, that none may enter.
¹¹ Outside is *heard* the clamor for wine,
    though all joy has become gloom:
    the earth's vitality is gone.
¹² Havoc remains in the city;
    the gates lie battered to ruin.

¹³ Then shall it happen in the earth among the nations
    as when an olive tree is beaten,
    or as grapes are gleaned when the vintage is ended.
¹⁴ Then will these lift up their voice and shout for joy,
    and *those* from across the sea
    exult at the Lord's ingenuity.
¹⁵ Because of it they will give glory to the Lord
    in the regions of sunrise,
  and in the isles of the sea
    to the name of the Lord, the God of Israel.

ᵃ6   So 1QIsaᵃ; MT *burned*.

¹⁶ From a sector of the earth we hear singing:
   Glorious are the righteous!
Whereas I thought, I am wasting away;
   I am weakening:
woe is me; the traitors have been treacherous,
   the turncoats have deceitfully betrayed!

¹⁷ Terrors and pitfalls and traps await you,
   O inhabitants of the earth:
¹⁸ those who flee at the sound of terror
   shall fall into a pit,
and those who get up from the pit
   shall be caught in a trap.
For when the windows on high are opened,
   the earth shall shake to its foundations.

¹⁹ The earth shall be crushed and rent;
   the earth shall break up and cave in;
   the earth shall convulse and lurch.
²⁰ The earth shall reel to and fro like a drunkard,
   sway back and forth like a shanty;
its transgressions weigh it down,
   and when it collapses it shall rise no more.

²¹ In that day will the Lord deal on high
   with the hosts on high
   and on earth with the rulers of the earth.
²² They shall be herded together
   like prisoners to a dungeon
   and shut in confinement many days, as punishment.
²³ The moon will blush and the sun be put to shame,
   when the Lord of Hosts manifests his reign
   in Mount Zion and in Jerusalem,
and *his* glory in the presence of his elders.

25 *In that day you will say,*
   O Lord, thou art my God;
I will extol thee by praising thy name.
   For with perfect faithfulness
 thou hast performed wonders,
   things planned of old.

2 Thou hast made the city a heap of rubble,
   fortified towns a ruin—
heathen mansions shall no more form cities,
   nor ever be rebuilt!
3 For this will powerful peoples revere thee,
   a community of tyrannous nations fear thee.

4 Thou wast a refuge for the poor,
   a shelter for the needy in distress,
a covert from the downpour
   and shade from the heat.
When the blasts of tyrants beat down
   like torrents against a wall,
5 or like scorching heat in the desert,
   thou didst quell the onslaughts of the heathen:
as burning heat by the shade of a cloud,
   thou subduest the power of tyrants.

6 In this mountain will the Lord of Hosts prepare
   a sumptuous feast for all peoples,
a feast of leavened cakes, succulent and delectable,
   of matured wines well refined.
7 In this mountain he will destroy
   the veil that veils all peoples,
the shroud that shrouds all nations,
   8 by abolishing Death forever.
My Lord the Lord will wipe away
   the tears from all faces;
he will remove the reproach of his people
   from throughout the earth.
The Lord has spoken it.

9 In that day you*a* will say, This is our God,
   whom we expected would save us.
This is the Lord for whom we have waited;
   let us joyfully celebrate his salvation!

10 For in this mountain rests the hand of the Lord,
   and under him Moab shall be trampled down
   as straw is trampled in a dung pit.

---

*a*9   So 1QIsaᵃ; MT *he*.

¹¹ For when he stretches his hands
 into the midst of it,
 as a swimmer spreads his hands to swim,
  he will pull down his pride in the attempt.
¹² Your highly walled fortifications
 he will lay low by razing them to the ground,
 even with the dust.

26 In that day shall this song be sung in the land of Judah:

Our city is strong; salvation he has set up
 as walls and barricades!
² Open the gates to let in the nation
 righteous because it keeps faith.
³ Those whose minds are steadfast, *O Lord*,
 thou preservest in perfect peace,
 for in thee they are secure.

⁴ Ever trust in the Lord,
 for the Lord Yah is an everlasting Rock.
⁵ He has put down the elite inhabitants
 of the exalted city
 by casting it to the ground,
  laying it even with the dust.
⁶ It is trodden underfoot by the feet of the poor,
 by the footsteps of those impoverished.

⁷ The path of the righteous is straight;
 thou pavest an undeviating course for the upright.
⁸ In the very passage of thine ordinances
 we anticipate thee, O Lord;
 the soul's desire is to contemplate thy name.
⁹ My soul yearns for thee in the night;
 at daybreak my spirit within me seeks after thee.
 For when thine ordinances are on the earth,
  the inhabitants of the world learn righteousness.

¹⁰ Though favor be shown the wicked,
 they will not learn righteousness;
 in a land of uprightness they remain perverse
 and see not the glory of the Lord.

¹¹ O Lord, thy hand is lifted up,
    but they perceive it not.
Let them perceive with dismay
    thy zeal for thy people
when the fire prepared for thine enemies
    consumes them.

¹² O Lord, thou bringest about our peace;
    even all that we have accomplished
    thou hast done for us.
¹³ O Lord, our God, lords other than thou
    have ruled over us,
    but thee alone we recall by name.
¹⁴ They are dead, to live no more,
    spirits who will not rise up;
thou appointest them to destruction,
    wiping out all recollection of them.
¹⁵ Thou hast enlarged the nation, O Lord,
    and by enlarging it gained glory for thyself;
thou hast withdrawn all borders in the earth.

¹⁶ O Lord, in their distress they remembered thee;
    they poured out silent prayers
    when thy chastisements were upon them.
¹⁷ As a woman about to give birth
    cries out from her pangs during labor,
so were we at thy presence, O Lord.
¹⁸ We were with child; we have been in labor,
    but have brought forth only wind.
We have not wrought salvation in the earth,
    that the inhabitants of the world might not fall.ᵃ

¹⁹ Yet shall thy dead live when their bodiesᵇ arise.
    Thou wilt say to them,
Awake, and sing for joy,
    you who abide in the dust:
your dew is the dew of sunrise!
    For the earth shall cast up its dead.

ᵃ18 Or, *abort.*

ᵇ19 Hebrew *my body.* MT evidences incomplete third person pronoun suffix; compare LXX.

²⁰ Come, O my people, enter your chambers
and shut the doors behind you;
hide yourselves a little while
until the wrath is past.
²¹ For now will the Lord come out of his dwelling place
to punish the inhabitants of the earth
for their iniquities;
the earth will uncover the blood shed upon it
and no more conceal its slain.

27 In that day will the Lord,
with his great and powerful sword,
punish severely*ᵃ* Leviathan,
the evasive maritime serpent,
Leviathan, that devious sea monster,
when he slays the dragons of the Sea.

² In that day, sing of *the earth*ᵇ
as of a delightful vineyard
³ of which I, the Lord, am keeper.
I water it constantly, watch over it night and day,
lest anything be amiss.
⁴ I have no more anger *toward her.*
Should briars and thorns come up,
I will ruthlessly attack them
and altogether set them ablaze.
⁵ But should they take hold of me for a refuge
and make peace with me,
they shall be reconciled to me.
⁶ For *in days* to come, when Jacob takes root
and Israel bursts into blossom,
the face of the earth shall fill with fruit.

⁷ Was he smitten as were his smiters?
Or was he slain as were they who slew him?
⁸ Thou hast dealt with them
by utterly banishing them, *O Lord.*
By his fierce blasts they were flung away
in the day of the burning east wind.

ᵃ1   Term modifies *sword,* an incongruity in translation.
ᵇ2   Hebrew *her;* compare 26:21; 27:6.

⁹ But by this shall Jacob's iniquity be expiated,
 as a result of this his sins removed:
when he makes like crushed chalkstone
 all altar stones,
leaving no idols of prosperity
 and shining images standing.
¹⁰ Because *of them* the fortified cities lie forlorn,
 deserted habitations, forsaken like a wilderness;
steers forage and recline there,
 stripping bare the young branches *of trees*.
¹¹ A harvest of twigs dries, broken off by women
 who come to light their fires with them.
They are not a discerning people.
Therefore their Maker shows them no mercy;
 he who formed them favors them not.

¹² In that day the Lord will thresh out *his harvest* from the torrent of the River to the streams of Egypt. But you shall be gleaned one by one, O children of Israel.

¹³ In that day a loud trumpet shall sound, and they who were lost in the land of Assyria and they who were outcasts in the land of Egypt shall come and bow down to the Lord in the holy mountain at Jerusalem.

28

Woe to the garlands of glory
 of the drunkards of Ephraim!
Their crowning splendor has become as fading wreaths
 on the heads of *the opulent* overcome with wine.

² My Lord has in store one mighty and strong:
 as a ravaging hailstorm sweeping down,
or like an inundating deluge of mighty waters,
 he will hurl them to the ground by his hand.
³ The proud garlands of the drunkards of Ephraim
 shall be trodden underfoot.
⁴ And the fading wreaths, the crowns of glory
 on the heads of *the opulent*,
shall be like the first-ripe fruit
 before summer *harvest*:

---

*a*1, *a*4 Hebrew *gê'ê šĕmānîm;* so 1QIsa*a*. MT *gê' šĕmānîm, fat gully/ravine.*

he who sees it devours it
    the moment he has hold of it.

5 In that day shall the Lord of Hosts
    be as a crown of beauty and wreath of glory
  to the remnant of his people:
6 a spirit of justice to him who sits in judgment,
    a source of strength
to those who repulse the attack at the gates.

7 These too have indulged in wine
    and are giddy with strong drink:
priests and prophets have gone astray through liquor.
    They are intoxicated with wine
and stagger because of strong drink;
    they err as seers, they blunder in their decisions.
8 For all tables are filled with vomit;
    no spot is without excrement.

9 Whom shall he give instruction?
    Whom shall he enlighten with revelation?
Weanlings weaned from milk,
    those just taken from the breast?
10 For it is but precept upon precept,
    precept upon precept,
measure by measure, measure by measure;
    a trifle here, a trifle there.

11 Therefore, by incomprehensible speech
    and a strange tongue
  must he speak to these people,
12 to whom he said, This is rest; let the weary rest!
    This is a respite! But they would not listen.
13 So to them the word of the Lord remained:
    Precept upon precept, precept upon precept,
measure by measure, measure by measure;
    a trifle here, a trifle there, that,
persisting, they might lapse into stumbling
    and break themselves,
become ensnared and be taken captive.

14 Therefore hear the word of the Lord, you scoffers
    who preside over these people in Jerusalem.

145

¹⁵ You have supposed, by taking refuge in deception
and hiding behind falsehoods,
to have covenanted with Death,
or reached an understanding with Sheol, that,
should a flooding scourge sweep through *the earth*,
it shall not reach you.

¹⁶ Therefore, thus says my Lord the Lord:
I lay in Zion a stone, a keystone,
a precious cornerstone, a sure foundation.
They who believe it will not do rashly.

¹⁷ I will make justice the measure,
righteousness the weight;
a hail shall sweep away your false refuge
and waters flood the hiding place.
¹⁸ Your covenant with Death shall prove void,*ᵇ*
your understanding with Sheol have no effect:
when the flooding scourge sweeps through,
you shall be overrun by it.
¹⁹ As often as it sweeps through,
you shall be seized by it:
morning after morning it shall sweep through,
by day and by night *it shall seize you*;
it shall cause terror merely to hear word of it.
²⁰ *Then shall come to pass the proverb*:
The couch is too short to stretch out on,
the covering too narrow to wrap oneself in.

²¹ For the Lord will rise up
as he did on Mount Perazim,
and be stirred to anger, as in the Valley of Gibeon—
to perform his act, his unwonted act,
and do his work, his bizarre work.
²² Now therefore scoff not,
lest your bonds grow severe,
for I have heard utter destruction decreed
by my Lord, the Lord of Hosts,
upon the whole earth.

ᵇ18 Hebrew *kŭppar, expiated,* emended to *hŭpar.*

²³ Give heed, and hear my voice!
   Be attentive, and listen to what I say!
²⁴ Will the plowman be forever plowing to sow seed,
   disking and harrowing the same ground?
²⁵ When he has smoothed its surface,
   does he not sprinkle fennel and scatter cumin?
   Does he not demarcate wheat from barley
   and *plant* buckwheat in its own plot?
²⁶ His God instructs him,
   directing him in the proper procedure.

²⁷ Fennel is not threshed with a sharp-toothed sledge,
   nor is a cartwheel rolled over cumin:
   fennel is beaten out with a stick
   and cumin with a rod.
²⁸ Domestic grain is ground;
   one does not go on endlessly threshing it.
   It cannot be ground
   by driving horse and threshing cart *over it*.
²⁹ These things originate with the Lord of Hosts,
   whose counsel is wonderful,
   whose inspiration is surpassing.

29 Woe to Ariel—
      Ariel, the city where David lodged!
   Though you add year to year,
      and the feastdays recur in succession,
   ² yet will I distress Ariel:
      there shall be mourning and sorrow
      when she becomes as my *altar hearth.*
   ³ I will encamp against you round about,
      and beleaguer you with assault posts,
      and erect siege installations against you.
   ⁴ And when you have been laid low,
      you will speak from the ground,
      your words uttering out of the dust:
   your voice from the ground
      shall be like that of a medium;
   your sayings shall whisper out of the dust.

---

*a*2   Or, *Ariel,* a wordplay.

⁵ Suddenly, in an instant,
    your crowds of evildoers*ᵇ* shall become as fine dust,
    your violent mobs like flying chaff.
⁶ She shall be chastened by the Lord of Hosts
    with thunderous quakings,
resounding booms, tempestuous blasts
    and conflagrations of devouring flame.

⁷ And the nations amassed to fight against Ariel,
    all who congregate at her stronghold
    to distress her,
shall be as a dream seen in the night:
⁸ like a hungry man who dreams he eats,
    but awakens famished,
or like a thirsty man who dreams he drinks,
    but wakes up faint and craving.
So shall be all the nations
    that amass to fight against Mount Zion.

⁹ Procrastinate, and become bewildered;
    preoccupy yourselves, until you cry for help.
Be drunk, but not with wine;
    stagger, but not from strong drink.
¹⁰ The Lord has poured out on you
    a spirit of deep sleep:
he has shut your eyes, the prophets;
    he has covered your heads, the seers.

¹¹ For you the sum of vision has become as the words of a sealed book that they give to one who is learned, saying, Please read this, and he answers, I cannot; it is sealed. ¹² Or if they give it to one who is unlearned, saying, Please read this, he answers, I am unlearned.

¹³ But my Lord says, Because these people
    approach me with the mouth
and pay me homage with their lips,
    while their heart remains far from me—
their piety toward me consisting of
    commandments of men learned by rote—

---

*ᵇ*5   So 1QIsaᵃ; LXX. MT *of strangers.*

14 therefore it is that I shall again astound these people
    with wonder upon wonder,
  rendering void the knowledge of their sages,
    the intelligence of their wise men insignificant.

15 Woe to those who contrive
    to hide their schemes from the Lord!
  They work in the dark, thinking,
    Who will see us? Who will know?
16 What a contradiction you are!
    Shall the potter be regarded as the clay?
  Shall what is made say of its maker,
    He did not make me,
  or a work of its designer, He doesn't understand?
17 In a very little while, shall not Lebanon
    again become a fruitful land,
  and lands now fruitful be considered backwoods?

18 In that day shall the deaf hear
    the words of the book
  and the eyes of the blind see
    out of gross darkness.
19 The lowly shall obtain an increase of joy in the Lord,
    and the poorest of men rejoice
    in the Holy One of Israel.

20 For tyrants shall come to nought and scorners cease;
    all who persist in wickedness shall be cut off—
21 those who at a word adjudge a man to be guilty,
    who ensnare the defender at court,
  who for nothing turn away him who is in the right.

22 Therefore thus says the Lord,
    who redeemed Abraham, to the house of Jacob:
  No longer shall Jacob be dismayed;
    his face shall pale no more.
23 For when he sees among him his children,
    the work of my hands, hallowing my name,
  devoted to the Holy One of Jacob,
    reverencing the God of Israel,
24 then will the erring in spirit gain understanding
    and they who murmured accept instruction.

30 Woe to you, rebellious sons, says the Lord,
for drawing up plans, but not by me,
for making alliances without my approval,
only adding sin to sin!
2 They are bent on going down to Egypt—
but have not inquired at my mouth—
on seeking protection in Pharaoh's forces,
on taking shelter in Egypt's shadow.

3 But Pharaoh's protection shall turn to your shame,
shelter in Egypt's shadow to embarrassment.
4 For all their officials at Zoan,
and their envoys' travels to Hanes,
5 they shall be utterly disgusted
with a people who will avail them nothing;
they shall be of no help or benefit,
but a humiliation and disgrace.

6 An oracle concerning the Beasts of Negeb:

Through a land of hardship and vicissitude,
of lions and the *a*roaring*a* king of beasts,
of vipers and the fiery flying serpent,
they carry their wealth
on the backs of young asses,
their riches on the humps of camels,
to a people who cannot profit them.
7 Egypt's help shall be futile and vain;
therefore I refer to her as an idle boast.

8 Go now, write on tablets concerning them;
record it in a book for the last day,
as a testimony forever.
9 They are a rebellious people, sons who break faith,
children unwilling to obey the law of the Lord,
10 who say to the seers, See not!
and to those with visions,
Predict not what is right for us:
flatter us; foresee a farce!

---

*a*6 Hebrew *mēhem, of them,* emended to *nôhēm.*

¹¹ Get out of the way; move aside, off the path!
    Cease confronting us with the Holy One of Israel!

¹² Therefore, thus says the Holy One of Israel:
    Because you have rejected this word,
  and rely on manipulation and double dealing,
    and on them are dependent,
¹³ this iniquity will be to you as a perilous breach
    exposed in a high wall
    which suddenly and unexpectedly collapses.
¹⁴ It shall shatter with a crash
    like an earthenware vessel ruthlessly smashed,
  among whose fragments shall not be found a shard
    with which to scoop lit embers from a fireplace,
    or dip water from a tank.

¹⁵ For thus says my Lord the Lord,
    the Holy One of Israel:
  By a calm response triumph;
    with quiet confidence gain the victory.
  But you would have none of it.
¹⁶ For you thought, Not so; we will flee on horses!
    Therefore shall you flee indeed.
  We will ride on swift mounts!
    Therefore shall your pursuers be swifter.
¹⁷ You will flee by the thousand at the threat of one,
    by thousands at the threat of five,
  till you are left as a flagstaff on a mountaintop,
    an ensign on a hill.

¹⁸ Then will the Lord delay *his coming*,
    that he may favor you;
    out of mercy toward you he will remain aloof.
  For the Lord is the God of justice;
    blessed are all who wait for him.

¹⁹ O people of Zion, O inhabitants of Jerusalem,
    you shall have no cause to weep.
  He will graciously respond at the cry of your voice;
    he will answer you as soon as he hears it.

20 Though my Lord give you the bread of adversity
and the water of affliction,
yet shall your Teacher remain hidden no longer,
but your eyes shall see the Master.
21 Your ears shall hear words from behind you
saying, This is the way; walk in it!
should you turn left or right.
22 You will discard as unclean
your graven idols plated with silver,
your cast idols gilded in gold;
you will eject them
as a menstruous woman *her impurity*
and say, Away with you!

23 Then will he water with rain
the seed you sow in the ground,
that the land's increase of food
may be rich and abundant.
In that day your cattle shall graze
in ample pasture lands,
24 and the oxen and asses that till the soil
eat grain silage winnowed with shovel and fork.

25 On all mountain heights and prominent hills
shall appear streams of running water,
on the day of the great slaughter,
when the towers fall.
26 The light of the moon
shall be as the light of the sun,
and the light of the sun increase sevenfold;
as the light of seven days shall it be,
in the day the Lord binds up
the fracture of his people
and heals their open wound.

27 Behold, the Lord Omnipotent*b* coming from afar!
His wrath is kindled, heavy is his grievance;
his lips flow with indignation,
his tongue is like a devouring fire.

*b*27 Literally, *the name of the Lord.*

²⁸ His breath is like a raging torrent
　　that severs at the neck.
He comes to sift the nations
　　in the sieve of falsehood;
with an erring bridle on their jaws
　　he will try the peoples.

²⁹ But for you there shall be singing,
　　as on the night when a festival commences,
and rejoicing of heart, as when men march
　　with flutes [and drums and lyres]ᶜ
on their way to the mountain of the Lord,
　　to the Rock of Israel.

³⁰ The Lord will cause his voice to resound,
　　and make visible his arm descending in furious rage,
with flashes of devouring fire,
　　explosive discharges and pounding hail.
³¹ At the voice of the Lord
　　the Assyrians will be terror-stricken,
they who used to strike with the rod.
³² At every sweep of the staff of authority,
　　when the Lord lowers it upon them,
they will be fought in mortal combat.

³³ For Tophet has been prepared of old,
　　a hearth indeed, made ready for rulers;
broad and deep is its fire pit and ample its pyre;
the Lord's breath burns within it
　　like a river of lava.

31

Woe to those who go down to Egypt for help,
　　relying on horses,
putting their trust in immense numbers
　　of chariots and vast forces of horsemen,
but who do not look to the Holy One of Israel,
　　nor inquire of the Lord!

ᶜ29 Terms brought up from verse 32, where they follow *they will be fought,* a probable textual dislocation.

2 Yet he too is shrewd
and will bring disaster *upon them*,
and not retract his words.
He will rise up against the brood of miscreants
and allies of evildoers.
3 The Egyptians are human, not divine;
their horses are flesh, not spirit:
when the Lord stretches out his hand,
those who help them will stumble
and those helped will fall;
both shall come to an end together.

4 For thus said the Lord to me:
As a lion or a young lion growls over the prey
when the shepherds muster in full force against him,
and is not dismayed at the sound of their voice
nor daunted by their numbers,
so shall the Lord of Hosts be when he descends
to wage war upon Mount Zion and upon its heights.
5 As birds hover over [the nest],*
so will the Lord of Hosts guard Jerusalem;
by protecting it he will deliver it,
by passing over it, preserve it.

6 Return to him from whom you have contrived to go far astray,
O children of Israel. 7 For in that day every one of you will despise
your idolatrous silver and gold by which your hands have incurred
guilt.

8 And Assyria shall fall by a sword not of man;
a sword not of mortals shall devour them:
before that sword they shall waste away
and their young men melt;
9 their captain* shall expire in terror
and their officers shrink from the ensign,
says the Lord, whose fire is in Zion,
whose furnace is in Jerusalem.

---

*5   Text emended to include Hebrew direct object *qēn* before the similar sounding adverb
kēn, so.
*9   Literally, *rock*, a probable military term.

154

32 A king shall reign in righteousness
    and rulers rule with justice.
2 And a man shall become as a shelter
    from the wind or refuge from the storm,
like brooks of water in a desert place,
    or the shade of a large rock in arid country.

3 The eyes of those who see shall not be shut,
    and the ears of those who hear shall listen.
4 The minds of the rash shall learn understanding,
    and the tongues of the stammerers master eloquence.
5 The godless shall no longer be regarded as noble
    nor rogues considered respectable.

6 For the godless utter blasphemy;
    their heart ponders impiety:
how to practice hypocrisy and preach
    perverse things concerning the Lord,
leaving the hungry soul empty,
    depriving the thirsty *soul* of drink.
7 And rogues scheme by malevolent means
    and insidious devices to ruin the poor,
and with false slogans and accusations
    to denounce the needy.
8 But the noble are of noble intent,
    and stand up for what is virtuous.

9 Up, and listen to my voice, O complacent women;
    you careless daughters, hear my words!
10 In little more than a year
    you shall be in anguish, O carefree ones,
for when the harvest is over,
    the produce shall fail to arrive.

11 Be alarmed, you complacent women;
    be perturbed, O careless daughters!
Strip yourselves bare;
    put sackcloth around your waists.
12 Beat your breasts for the choice fields
    and flourishing vines.

¹³ For my people's land
    shall be overgrown with briars and thorns.
Mourn for all the amusement houses
    in the city of entertainment,
¹⁴ for the palaces shall lie abandoned,
    the clamorous towns deserted.
High rises and panoramic resorts
    shall become haunts for ever after,
the playground of wild animals,
    a browsing place for flocks.

¹⁹ᵃ For by a hail shall forests be felled,
    cities utterly leveled.
¹⁵ Then*ᵇ* shall a Spirit from on high
    be poured out on us;
the desert shall become productive land
    and lands now productive
    be reckoned as brushwood.

¹⁶ So shall justice inhabit the desert,
    and righteousness abide in the farmland.
¹⁷ And the effect of justice shall be peace,
    and the result of righteousness
    an assured calm forever.
¹⁸ My people shall dwell in peaceful settlements,
    in safe neighborhoods, in comfortable dwellings.
²⁰ Blessed are you, who shall then sow by all waters,
    letting oxen and asses range free.

33

Woe to you, despoiler,
    who yourself was not despoiled;
O treacherous one,
    with whom none have been treacherous:
when you have done with devastating,
    you shall be devastated;
when you are through betraying,
    they shall betray you!

ᵃ19 Verse appears out of sequence in text.
ᵇ15 Hebrew ʿad, until, emended to ʾaz.

² O Lord, be favorable toward us;
> we have waited for thee.
> Be our*ᵃ* *strength of* arm from morning to morning,
> our salvation in troubled times.

³ The peoples fled from thy thunderous voice;
> at thine uprising the nations scattered.
⁴ Their spoil was harvested
> in the manner of caterpillars;
> like insatiable locusts they rushed upon it.
⁵ But the Lord is supreme, for he dwells on high;
> with justice and righteousness he will replenish Zion.
⁶ Your faithfulness in time *of trial*
> shall prove to be a strength,
> your wisdom and knowledge your salvation;
> your fear of the Lord shall be your riches.

⁷ See, their stalwarts sob in public;
> the champions of peace weep bitterly.
⁸ The highways are desolate, travel is at an end.
> The treaties have been violated,
> their signatories*ᵇ* held in contempt;
> man is disregarded.
⁹ The Land lies withered and forlorn,
> Lebanon wilts shamefully;
> Sharon has been turned into a dry waste,
> Bashan and Carmel are denuded.

¹⁰ Now will I arise, says the Lord;
> I will now become prominent,
> now gain preeminence.
¹¹ You who conceived chaff and brought forth stubble,
> the fire of your own breath devours you!
¹² Whole nations have been burned like lime,
> mown down like thorns and set ablaze.

¹³ Take heed what I have done, you who are far off;
> you who are near, be apprised of my might!

---

*ᵃ*2 Hebrew *their.*
*ᵇ*8 So 1QIsaᵃ; MT *cities.*

¹⁴ The sinners in Zion are struck with fear;
    the godless are in the grip of trembling:
Who among us can live through the devouring fire?
Who among us can abide eternal burning?
¹⁵ They who conduct themselves righteously
    and are honest in word,
who disdain extortion
    and stay their hand from taking bribes,
who stop their ears at the mention of murder,
    who shut their eyes at the sight of wickedness.
¹⁶ They shall dwell on high;
    the impregnable cliffs are their fortress.
Bread is provided them, their water is sure.

¹⁷ Your eyes shall behold the King in his glory
    and view the expanse of the earth.
¹⁸ You shall recount in your mind the terror:
    Where are those who conducted the census?
Where are those who levied the tax?
    Where are the ones who appraised the towers?
¹⁹ The insolent people are not to be seen,
    a nation of incomprehensible speech,
whose babbling tongue was unintelligible.

²⁰ Behold Zion, the city of our solemn assemblies;
    let your eyes rest upon Jerusalem,
the abode of peace—an immovable tent,
    whose stakes shall never be uprooted,
    nor any of its cords severed.
²⁴ᶜ None who reside there shall say, I am ill;
    the people who inhabit it
    shall be forgiven their iniquity.

²¹ May the Lord ᵈcause us to dwellᵈ there,
    a country of rivers and broad streams,
where no warships sail
    or majestic fleets pass by.

ᶜ24 Verse appears out of sequence in text.
ᵈ21 Hebrew ʾaddîr, *mighty one,* emended to yādîr.

23[e] Their riggings hang loose;
    they hold not the mast in place
    nor spread out the sail.
Now shall spoil in abundance be divided,
    and even the lame take part in the plunder.
22 For the Lord is our Judge,
    and the Lord our Lawgiver.
The Lord is our King; he himself will save us.

34

Come near, you nations, and hear!
    Pay attention, you peoples!
Let the earth give heed, and all who are upon it,
    the world, and all who spring from it.
2 The Lord's rage is upon all nations,
    his fury upon all their hosts;
he has doomed them,
    consigned them to the slaughter.

3 Their slain shall be flung out
    and their corpses emit a stench;
[a]their blood shall dissolve on the mountains,
  4 their fat decompose [on the hills][a]—
when the heavens are rolled up as a scroll,
    and their starry hosts shed themselves with one accord,
like withered leaves from a vine,
    or shrivelled fruit from a fig tree.
5 When my sword drinks its fill in the heavens,
    it shall come down on Edom in judgment,
on the people I have sentenced to damnation.

6 The Lord has a sword that shall engorge with blood
    and glut itself with fat—
the blood of lambs and he-goats,
    the kidney fat of rams.

---

[e]23   Verse appears out of sequence in text.
[a]3, [a]4   A problematic couplet, whose literal translation of MT reads *the mountains shall dissolve with their blood, and all the host of heaven decompose.* Hebrew *kol ṣĕbā' haššamayîm*, emended to *gib'ôt mēḥelbām* and the sense of the passage rendered congruous with its context; compare the parallelism *blood/fat*, verses 6–7, and the reading *hills* for *host of heaven*, LXX.

For the Lord will hold a slaughter in Bozrah,
    an immense massacre in the land of Edom;
⁷ among them shall fall bison, bulls, and steers.
    Their land shall be saturated with blood,
        their soil enriched with fat.

⁸ For it is the Lord's day of vengeance,
    the year of retribution on behalf of Zion.

⁹ *Edom's*[b] streams shall turn into lava
    and her earth into brimstone;
        her land shall become as burning pitch.
¹⁰ Night and day it shall not be quenched;
    its smoke shall ascend forever.
It shall remain a wasteland
    from generation to generation;
        through endless ages none shall traverse it.
¹¹ But hawks and falcons shall possess it,
    and owls and ravens inhabit it.
It shall be surveyed with muddled measure
    and chaotic weight.

¹² Shall they summon its nobles when it is no kingdom,
    when all its lords no longer exist?
¹³ For thorns shall overgrow its palaces,
    thistles and briars its strongholds;
    it shall become the haunt of howling creatures,
        a reserve[c] for birds of prey.
¹⁴ Prairie wolves shall greet jackals,
    and wild goats call to one another.
There too shall the night owl find repose
    and discover for herself a resting place.
¹⁵ There shall the hawk owl nest and lay eggs,
    hatch them and brood over her young.
There too shall kites come together,
    each one accompanying her mate.

¹⁶ Search, and read it in the book of the Lord:
    None is unaccounted for, not one lacks her mate.

---

[b]9 Hebrew *Her.*
[c]13 Hebrew *ḥāṣîr, grass,* emended to *ḥāṣēr.*

By his mouth he decreed it,
 by his Spirit he brings them together.
17 It is he who allots them an inheritance,
 his hand that divides it by measure.
They shall possess it forever,
 inhabit it from generation to generation.

35

Wilderness and arid land shall be jubilant;
 the desert shall rejoice
when it blossoms like the crocus.
2 Joyously it shall break out in flower,
 singing with delight;
it shall be endowed with the glory of Lebanon,
 the splendor of Carmel and Sharon.
The glory of the Lord and the splendor of our God
 they shall see *there*.

3 Strengthen the hands grown feeble,
 steady the failing knees.
4 Say to those with fearful hearts,
 Take courage, be unafraid!
See, your God is coming to avenge and to reward;
 God himself will come and deliver you.

5 Then shall the eyes of the blind be opened
 and the ears of the deaf unstopped.
6 Then shall the lame leap like deer,
 and the tongue of the dumb shout for joy.
Water shall break forth in the wilderness
 and streams *flow* in the desert.
7 The land of mirages shall become one of lakes,
 the thirsty place springs of water;
in the haunt of howling creatures
 [shall marshes break out],[a]
in the reserves[b] shall come rushes and reeds.
8 There shall be highways and roads
 which shall be called the Way of Holiness,
[c]for they shall be for such[c] *as are holy*.

---

[a]7 Hebrew *ribṣâh, her resting place*, emended to *tiprōṣ biṣṣâ*.
[b]7 Hebrew *ḥaṣîr, grass*, emended to *ḥāṣēr;* compare 34:13.
[c]8 Phrase transposed; in text follows *traverse them*.

The unclean shall not traverse them;
  on them shall no reprobates wander.
⁹ No lions *shall be encountered there,*ᵈ
  nor shall wild beasts intrude.
But the redeemed shall walk them,
  ¹⁰ the ransomed of the Lord shall return;
they shall come singing to Zion,
  their heads crowned with everlasting joy.
They shall have won joy and gladness
  when sorrow and sighing flee away.

36 In the fourteenth year of King Hezekiah*'s reign*, Sennacherib king of Assyria marched against all the fortified cities of Judea and seized them. ² And the king of Assyria sent Rabshakeh with a large army from Lachish to King Hezekiah at Jerusalem. And he took up a position by the aqueduct of the Upper Reservoir, on the road to the Laundry Plaza. ³ And Eliakim the son of Hilkiah, overseer of the palace, Shebna the secretary, and Joah the son of Asaph, the record keeper, went out to him.

⁴ And Rabshakeh said to them, Please tell Hezekiah, Thus says the great king, the king of Assyria: On what grounds do you behave with such confidence? ⁵ Do you suppose that in war mere words are *sufficient* tactics or *show of* strength? In whom have you put your trust, that you have rebelled against me? ⁶ It is clear you depend on the support of Egypt, that splintered reed which enters and pierces the palm of any man who leans on it. Such is Pharaoh king of Egypt to all who rely on him! ⁷ But if you tell me, We rely on the Lord our God, is he not the one whose shrines and altars Hezekiah abolished, telling Judea and Jerusalem to worship *only* at this altar? ⁸ Come now, wager with my lord the king of Assyria: I will give you two thousand horses, if you are able to put riders on them. ⁹ How then shall you repulse even one of the least of my lord's servants, depending as you do on Egypt for chariots and horsemen? ¹⁰ Moreover, could I have marched against this land and destroyed it without the Lord? For the Lord told me to come against this land and destroy it.

ᵈ9   Text emended to replace Hebrew *lō' yihyeh šām, shall not be there,* with *lō' yimmāṣē' šām,* which occurs as a duplication (fem.) following *intrude.*

¹¹ Then Eliakim, Shebna and Joah said to Rabshakeh, please speak to your servants in Aramaic, which we understand. Do not speak to us in Judean in the ears of the people who are on the wall.

¹² But Rabshakeh replied, Did my lord send me to say these things to you and to your lord and not to the men sitting on the wall, who with you are to eat their own dung and drink their own urine?

¹³ Then Rabshakeh stood and called out in a loud voice in Judean, Hear the words of the great king, the king of Assyria! ¹⁴ Thus says the king: Do not let Hezekiah delude you! He cannot deliver you. ¹⁵ Do not let Hezekiah make you trust in the Lord by saying, The Lord will surely save us; this city shall not be given into the hand of the king of Assyria.

¹⁶ Do not listen to Hezekiah! Thus says the king of Assyria: Make peace with me by coming out to me. Then every one of you will eat from his own vine and his own fig tree and drink water from his own cistern, ¹⁷ until I come back and take you to a land like your own, a land of grain and wine, a land of grain *fields* and vineyards.

¹⁸ *Beware*, lest Hezekiah mislead you by saying, The Lord will save us. Were any gods of the nations able to save their lands out of the hand of the king of Assyria? ¹⁹ Where are the gods of Hamath and Arpad? Where are the gods of Sepharvaim? Did they deliver Samaria out of my hand? ²⁰ Who of all the gods of those countries saved his land from my hand, that the Lord should save Jerusalem from my hand?

²¹ But they remained silent, replying nothing, for the king had commanded them not to answer him.

²² Then Eliakim the son of Hilkiah, overseer of the palace, Shebna the secretary, and Joah the son of Asaph, the record keeper, went to Hezekiah with their clothes rent and reported to him the things Rabshakeh had said.

37 When King Hezekiah heard it, he rent his clothes and put on sackcloth and entered the house of the Lord. ² And he sent Eliakim the overseer of the palace, Shebna the secretary, and the elders of the priests in sackcloth to the prophet Isaiah the son of Amoz.

⁵ᵃ And when King Hezekiah's servants came to Isaiah, ³ they said to him, Thus says Hezekiah: This is a woeful day, a day of reproof

---

ᵃ5   Verse appears out of sequence in text.

and disgrace. Children have reached the point of birth, but there is no strength to deliver them. ⁴ It may be that the Lord your God has heard the words of Rabshakeh, whom his lord the king of Assyria has sent to scorn the living God, and will rebuke him for the things the Lord your God has heard, were you to offer up prayer on behalf of the remnant that is left.

⁶ And Isaiah said to them, Tell your lord, Thus says the Lord: Be not afraid because of the words with which you have heard the king of Assyria's subordinates ridicule me. ⁷ See, I will give him a notion to return home upon hearing a rumor, and will cause him to fall by a sword in his own land.

⁸ And when Rabshakeh heard that the king of Assyria had left Lachish, he withdrew and found him fighting against Libnah.

⁹ Now *Sennacherib*ᵇ received a report that Tirhakah king of Cush had set out to fight against him. And when he heard it, he sent messengers to Hezekiah, telling them, ¹⁰ Speak thus to Hezekiah king of Judah: Let not your god in whom you trust delude you into thinking that Jerusalem shall not be given into the hand of the king of Assyria. ¹¹ You yourself have heard what the kings of Assyria have done, annexing all lands. Shall you then escape? ¹² Did the gods of the nations my fathers destroyed deliver them? *Did they deliver* Gozan and Haran, Rezeph and the Edenites in Tel Assar? ¹³ Where are the kings of Hamath and Arpad and the kings of the cities of Sepharvaim, Hena, and Ivvah?

¹⁴ And Hezekiah received the letter from the messengers and read it. Then Hezekiah went up to the house of the Lord and unrolled it before the Lord. ¹⁵ And Hezekiah prayed to the Lord and said,

¹⁶ O Lord of Hosts, God of Israel, who sittest enthroned between the cherubim, thou alone art God over all the kingdoms of the earth. It is thou who madest the heavens and the earth . . .

¹⁷ O Lord, give ear and hear; O Lord, open thine eyes and see. Listen to all the words Sennacherib has sent to mock the living God.

¹⁸ O Lord, the kings of Assyria have indeed destroyed all peoplesᶜ and their lands, ¹⁹ committing their gods to the fire. For they were no gods, but mere works of men's hands, of wood and of stone, and so they could destroy them. ²⁰ But now, O Lord our God, deliver us out of his hand, that all kingdoms on earth may know that thou alone art Lord.

ᵇ9 Hebrew *he*.

ᶜ18 Hebrew *hāʾărāṣôt, lands,* emended to *haggôyîm;* compare 2 Kings 19:17.

21 Then Isaiah the son of Amoz sent word to Hezekiah, saying, Thus says the Lord, the God of Israel: Because you have prayed to me concerning Sennacherib king of Assyria, 22 this is what the Lord has spoken against him:

> The Virgin Daughter of Zion holds you in contempt;
>   she laughs you to scorn.
> The Daughter of Jerusalem shakes her head at you.

23 Whom have you mocked and ridiculed?
    Against whom have you raised your voice,
        lifting your eyes to high heaven?
    Against the Holy One of Israel!
24 By your servants you have blasphemed the Lord.
        You thought, On account of my vast chariotry
    I have conquered the highest mountains,
        the farthest reaches of Lebanon.
    I have felled its tallest cedars, its choicest cypresses.
        I have reached its loftiest summit, its finest forest.
25 I have dug wells and drunk of foreign^d waters.
        With the soles of my feet
    I have dried up all Egypt's rivers!

26 Have you not heard
        how I ordained this thing long ago,
    how in days of old I planned it?
        Now I have brought it to pass.
    You were destined to demolish fortified cities,
        turning them into heaps of rubble,
27 while their timorous inhabitants
        shrank away in confusion,
    becoming as wild grass, transiently green,
        or like weeds on a roof
        that scorch^e before they grow up.

28 But I know where you dwell,
        and your comings and goings,
    and how stirred up you are against me.

---

^{d}25 So 1QIsa^a; 2 Kings 19:24. Term not in MT.

^{e}27 So 1QIsa^a; MT reading obscure.

²⁹ And because of your snortings
 and bellowings against me,
 which have mounted up to my ears,
 I will put my ring in your nose
 and my bit in your mouth
 and turn you back by the way you came.

³⁰ But to you this shall be a sign:
 This year eat what grows wild,
 and the following year what springs up of itself.
 But in the third year sow and harvest,
 plant vineyards and eat their fruit:
³¹ the remnant of the house of Judah that survives
 shall once more take root below and bear fruit above.
³² For out of Jerusalem shall go a remnant,
 and from Mount Zion a band of survivors.
 The zeal of the Lord of Hosts will accomplish it.

³³ Therefore, thus says the Lord
 concerning the king of Assyria:
 He shall not enter this city or shoot an arrow here.
 He shall not advance against it with armor,
 nor erect siegeworks against it.
³⁴ By the way he came he shall return;
 he shall not enter this city, says the Lord.
³⁵ I will protect this city and save it,
 for my own sake and for the sake of my servant David.

³⁶ Then the angel of the Lord went out and slew a hundred and eighty-five thousand in the Assyrian camp. And when men arose in the morning, there lay all their dead bodies!

³⁷ So Sennacherib king of Assyria broke camp and withdrew. And he returned to Nineveh, where he dwelt.

³⁸ And as he was worshiping in the temple of Nisroch his god, his sons Adrammelech and Sharezer slew him with a sword and fled to the land of Ararat. And his son Esarhaddon succeeded him as king.

38 In those days Hezekiah became gravely ill. And the prophet Isaiah the son of Amoz came to him and said, Thus says the Lord: Put your house in order. You will die; you will not recover.

2 At this Hezekiah turned his face toward the wall and prayed to the Lord: 3 I beseech thee to remember, O Lord, how I have walked before thee faithfully and with full purpose of heart and have done what is good in thine eyes. . . . And Hezekiah wept disconsolately.

4 Then the word of the Lord came to Isaiah: 5 Go and tell Hezekiah, Thus says the Lord, the God of your father David: I have heard your prayer and seen your tears. I will add fifteen years to your life. 6 And I will deliver you and this city out of the hand of the king of Assyria; I will protect this city.

21ᵃ And Isaiah gave instructions to take fig packs and apply them to the swelling so that he could recover.

22ᵃ But Hezekiah said, What of a sign that I shall *again* go up to the house of the Lord?

7 *And Isaiah replied,* This shall be a sign to you from the Lord, that the Lord will do the thing he has promised: 8 See, I make the shadow cast by the afternoon sun on the dial of Ahaz recede the ten degrees it has gone down. So the sun reversed its descent by ten degrees on the dial.

9 Hezekiah king of Judah's account of his illness, *written* upon his recovery:

> 10 I said, in the prime of life
>> must I depart through Sheol's gates,
>> deprived of the balance of my years?
> 11 I thought, I shall not see ᵇthe Lordᵇ
>> in the land of the living;
> I shall not now behold Man
>> among those dwelling in mortality.
> 12 My tabernacle is being uprooted,
>> carried away from me like a shepherd's tent.
> My life is cut off like woven fabric;
>> he is severing me from the loom.ᶜ
>
> 13 Can I contain myself until morning,
>> while like a lion he racks my whole frame?
> *Surely*, as night has followed day,
>> thou art bringing on my end!

ᵃ21, ᵃ22   Verse appears out of sequence in text.

ᵇ11   Hebrew *yāh yāh* emended to *YHWH*.

ᶜ12   MT adds *as night has followed day, thou art bringing on my end!* (so v. 13), a probable duplication. Compare LXX.

¹⁴ Like a mounting lark I twitter,
    like a dove I murmur.
My eyes are drawn looking heavenward;
    [I am utterly sleepless*d*
    from bitterness of soul. . . .]*e*
O Lord, I am in straits; be my surety!

¹⁵ But what shall I say
    when he has *already* spoken for me,
    when he himself has brought it about?
¹⁶ O my Lord, by means of such *trials*
    comes *a newness of* life,
    and throughout them all the renewal of my spirit.
¹⁷ Surely, for my own good I am in such dire distress;
    by its means thou drawest my soul
    out of the Pit of dissolution.
For thou hast cast all my sins behind thee,
    [restoring and reviving me].*f*

¹⁸ For Sheol cannot praise thee, nor Death glorify thee;
    those who go down into the Pit
    have no *further* hope of thy faithfulness.
¹⁹ But the living, only they bring thee praise,
    as I do this day; from father to sons
    they pass on the knowledge of thy faithfulness.
²⁰ O Lord, *may it please thee* to save me,
    and we will perform music
    all the days of our lives in the house of the Lord.

39 At that time Merodach-Baladan the son of Baladan, king of Babylon, sent letters and gifts to Hezekiah, for he had heard of his illness and recovery. ² And Hezekiah was glad of them and showed *the envoys*ᵃ his treasury—the silver and gold, the spices and fragrant oils, and his entire armory and all that was in his treasuries. There was nothing in his palace or in all his realm that Hezekiah did not show them.

---

*d*14 Hebrew *ʾeddaddeh kol šĕnôtai, I will wander all my years,* emended to *nôddĕdâ kol šĕnâtî.*

*e*14 Line brought up from verse 15, where it follows *brought it about.*

*f*17 Phrase brought down from verse 16, where it follows *my spirit.*

*a*2 Hebrew *them.*

3 Then the prophet Isaiah came to King Hezekiah and said, What did those men say to you, and where did they come from? And Hezekiah replied, They came from a distant land; *they came* to me from Babylon. 4 And *Isaiah*[b] asked, What did they see in your palace? And Hezekiah said, They saw everything there is in my palace. There is nothing in my treasuries that I did not show them.

5 Then Isaiah said to Hezekiah, Hear the word of the Lord of Hosts: 6 The time shall come when everything in your palace, and all that your forefathers have treasured up until now, shall be carried away to Babylon. Nothing shall be left, says the Lord. 7 And from among your own sons, your future offspring and descendants, they shall take *some* to serve as eunuchs in the palace of the king of Babylon.

8 But Hezekiah said to Isaiah, The word of the Lord you have spoken is good. For he thought, Then there shall be peace and loyalty during my reign.

40

Comfort and give solace to my people,
    says your God; 2 speak kindly to Jerusalem.
Announce to her that she has served her term,
    that her guilt has been expiated.
She has received from the Lord's hand
    double for all her sins.

3 A voice calls out,
    In the desert prepare the way for the Lord;
in the wilderness
    pave a straight highway for our God:
4 every ravine must be raised up,
    every mountain and hill made low;
the uneven ground must become level
    and rough terrain a plain.

5 For the glory[a] of the Lord shall be revealed
    and all flesh see it at once.
By his mouth the Lord has spoken it.

---

[b]4 Hebrew *he.*

[a]5 Or, *presence.*

⁶ A voice said, Announce it.
　　And I asked, How shall I announce it?
　All flesh is grass,
　　and at its best like a blossom of the field.
⁷ ᵇThough the Spirit of the Lord breathe within it,
　　the people themselves are but herbage—
⁸ grass that withers, flowers that fade—
　　only the word of our God endures forever.

⁹ Scale the mountain heights,
　　O Zion, herald of good tidings.
　Raise your voice mightily,
　　O Jerusalem, messenger of good news.
　Make yourself heard, be not afraid;
　　proclaim to the cities of Judah: Behold your God!

¹⁰ See, my Lord the Lord comes with power;
　　his arm presides for him.
　His reward is with him; his work precedes him.
¹¹ Like a shepherd he pastures his flock:
　　the lambs he gathers up with his arm
　　and carries in his bosom;
　the ewes that give milk he leads gently along.

¹² Who measured out the waters
　　with the hollow of his hand
　and gauged the heavens
　　by the span of his fingers?
　Who compiled the earth's dust by measure,
　　weighing mountains in scales,
　　hills in a balance?
¹³ Who has comprehended the Spirit of the Lord,
　　that a man should let him know his plan?
¹⁴ Of whom was he counselled
　　that he might be enlightened,
　by whom instructed in the path of discretion,
　　imparting to him knowledge,
　　acquainting him with the way of understanding?

ᵇ7　MT adds *Grass that withers, flowers that fade* (so v. 8), a probable duplication.
Compare 1QIsaᵃ; LXX.

¹⁵ The nations are but drops from a bucket,
    counting no more than dust on a balance;
  the isles he displaces as mere specks.
¹⁶ Lebanon would not suffice to kindle a fire,
    nor *all* its beasts be adequate for sacrifice.
¹⁷ Before him all nations are as nothing;
    as less than the ether they are reckoned by him.

¹⁸ To whom then will you liken God?
    What does he resemble in your estimation?
¹⁹ A figure cast by the artisan,
    overlaid by the smith with gold,
  fitted with a silver chain from the craftsman?
41:7ᶜ The artisan encourages the smith,
    and he who beats with a hammer
    urges him who pounds the anvil.
They say of the welding, It is good,
    though they fasten it with riveting
    that it may not come loose.
²⁰ Those too poor for this *type of* sacrifice
  select a wood that resists decay.
They seek an expert sculptor
    to carve them an image that will not deteriorate.

²¹ Are you so unaware, that you have not heard?
    Have you not been told before,
that you do not understand
    by whom the earth was founded?
²² By him who sits enthroned above the earth's sphere,
    to whom *its* inhabitants are as grasshoppers,
who suspends the heavens like a canopy,
    stretching them out as a tent to dwell in.
²³ By him who brings potentates to nought
    and makes the authorities of the world null and void.
²⁴ When scarcely they are planted,
    or scarcely they are sown,
when hardly their stalk has taken root in the earth,
    he puffs at them and they wither,
  and a storm sweeps them off as chaff.

ᶜ41:7 Verse appears out of sequence in text.

²⁵ To whom then will you liken me,
  to whom can I be compared? says the Holy One.
²⁶ Lift your eyes heavenward and see:
  Who formed these?
He who brings forth their hosts by number,
  calling each one by name.
Because he is almighty and all powerful,
  not one is unaccounted for.

²⁷ Why then do you say, O Jacob,
  and speak thus, O Israel:
Our path has become obscured from the Lord;
  our cause is overlooked by our God?

²⁸ Is it not known to you; have you not heard?
  The Lord is the God of eternity,
  Creator of the ends of the earth.
He does not grow faint or weary;
  his intelligence cannot be fathomed.
²⁹ He supplies the weary with energy
  and increases in vigor those who lack strength.
³⁰ Youths grow faint and weary,
  and young men slump down *of exhaustion.*
³¹ But they who hope in the Lord
  shall be renewed in strength:
they shall ascend as on eagles' wings;
  they shall run without wearying,
they shall walk and not faint.

41

Be silent before me, O isles;
  become still, you peoples!
Let them come forward and state their case;
  let us stand trial together.

² Who has raised up Righteousness from the east,
  calling him to *the place of* his foot?
Who has delivered nations to him,
  toppled their rulers,
rendering them as dust to his sword,
  as driven stubble to his bow?
³ He puts them to flight, passing on unhindered
  by paths his feet have never trod.

4 Who is at work accomplishing *this*,
    foreordaining dynasties?
I, the Lord, first and last, am he.

5 The isles look on in fear;
    the ends of the earth are in trembling.
They flock together*
    and come 6 to one another's aid,
saying, each to his fellow, Courage!

8 But you, O Israel, my servant,
    Jacob, whom I have chosen,
    offspring of Abraham my beloved friend,
9 you whom I have taken from the ends of the earth,
    called from its farthest limits—
to you I say, You are my servant;
    I have accepted you and not rejected you.
10 Be not fearful, for I am with you;
    be not dismayed, for I am your God.
I will strengthen you; I will also succor you
    and uphold you with my righteous right hand.

11 See, all who are enraged at you
    shall earn shame and disgrace;
    your adversaries shall come to nought, and perish.
12 Should you look for those who contend with you,
    you shall not find them;
whoever wars against you
    shall be reduced to nothing.
13 For I, the Lord your God,
    hold you by the right hand and say to you,
Have no fear; I will help you.

14 Be not afraid, you worms of Jacob;
    O men of Israel, [be not dismayed]:*
I am your help, says the Lord;
    your Redeemer is the Holy One of Israel.
15 I will make of you a sharp-toothed threshing sledge
    of new design, full of spikes:

---

5   So 1QIsa; term not in MT.
*14   A reconstruction based on meter and parallelism; compare verse 10.

you shall thresh mountains to dust
and make chaff of hills.
16 As you winnow them, a wind shall take them away,
a tempest dispel them.
Then will you rejoice in the Lord
and glory in the Holy One of Israel.

17 When the poor and needy require water,
and there is none,
and their tongue becomes parched with thirst,
I the Lord will answer their want;
I, the God of Israel, will not forsake them.
18 I will open up streams in barren hill country,
springs in the midst of the plains;
I will turn the desert into lakes,
parched lands into fountains of water.
19 I will bring cedars and acacias,
myrtles and oleasters in the wilderness;
I will place cypresses,
elms and box trees in the steppes—
20 that all may see it and know, consider it,
and perceive that the Lord's hand did this,
that the Holy One of Israel created it.

21 Present your case, says the Lord;
submit your evidence, says the King of Jacob.
22 Let them come forward and recount to us
their prophecies of events heretofore.
What were they? Tell us,
that we may examine them
and know whether they were fulfilled.
Or predict the future for us:
23 Tell us of events to come hereafter,
so that we may know you are gods.
Perform something good or evil
at which we will be dazzled and all stand in awe.
24 It is clear you are of no account,
that your works ᶜamount to nothing;ᶜ
whoever accepts you is himself an abomination.

ᶜ24 Hebrew ʾāpaʿ (unknown) emended to ʾāpes.

²⁵ I have raised up one from the north
    who calls on my name,
    who shall come from the direction of sunrise.
He shall come upon dignitaries as on mud,
    tread them as clay like a potter.

²⁶ Who announced this beforehand, so we would know,
    declared it ahead of time,
    that we might say, *ᵈ*He was right?*ᵈ*
Indeed, not one could foretell it,
    not one make it known;
no one has heard from you
    any [prophetic]*ᵉ* utterance.
²⁷ But to Zion, he shall be her harbinger;*ᶠ*
    I will appoint him as a herald of tidings to Jerusalem.

²⁸ For when I looked there was no one,
    not one who could offer counsel,
or when I questioned them,
    who could answer a word.
²⁹ Surely they are all iniquitous,
    their works worthless;
    their outpourings are but wind and emptiness.

42 My servant whom I sustain,
    my chosen one in whom I delight,
him I have endowed with my Spirit;
    he will dispense justice to the nations.*ᵃ*
² He will not shout or raise his voice
    to make himself heard in public.
³ Even a bruised reed he will not break;
    a dim wick he will not snuff out.
He will perform the work of justice
    in the cause of truth.

---

*ᵈ*26 Literally, *The righteous one,* a pun on the subject of verses 2, 25.

*ᵉ*26 Hebrew *riš⁾ôn,* a probable corruption (compare plural *ri⁾šōnôt,* v. 22; *mēr⁾ōš,* v. 26), included in present verse; term commences verse 27 in MT.

*ᶠ*27 Hebrew *hannōmeh* (compare Arabic); so 1QIsaᵃ. MT *hinnām, behold them/here they are.*

*ᵃ*1 Hebrew *gôyîm,* also *Gentiles.*

⁴ Neither shall he himself grow dim or be bruised
   until he has brought about justice in the earth.
The isles await his law.

⁵ Thus says the Lord God,
   who frames and suspends the heavens,
who gives form to the earth and its creatures,
   the breath of life to the people upon it,
   spirit to those who walk on it:
⁶ I the Lord have rightfully called you
   and will grasp you by the hand;
I have created you and appointed you
   to be a covenant for the people,
   a light to the nations,*b*
⁷ to open eyes that are blind,
   to free captives from confinement
and from prison those who sit in darkness.

⁸ I am the Lord; that is my name.
   I will not relinquish my glory to another,
   nor my praise to wrought idols.
⁹ The prophecies of the former events
   indeed came to pass,
but new things I yet foretell.
   Before they spring up I declare them to you.

¹⁰ Sing to the Lord a new song;
   sing his praise from the end of the earth.
ᶜLet the sea roar,ᶜ and all that lives in it,
   the isles and they who inhabit them.
¹¹ Let the desert and its cities raise *their voice,*
   and the villages where Kedar dwells;
let the inhabitants of Sela sing for joy
   and cry out from the tops of the mountains.
¹² O let them give glory to the Lord,
   and in the isles speak out in praise of him.

¹³ The Lord will come forth like a warrior,
   his passions aroused like a fighter;

---

*b*6 Hebrew *gôyîm,* also *Gentiles.*
*c*10 Hebrew *yôrdê hayyām, they who go down to the sea,* emended to *yirᶜam hayyām.*

he will give the war cry,
    raise the shout of victory over his enemies.
14 For a long time I have been silent,
    keeping still and restraining myself.
But now I will scream like a woman in labor
    and breathe hard and fast all at once.
15 I will lay waste mountains and hills
    and make all their vegetation wither;
I will turn rivers into dry land and evaporate lakes.

16 Then will I lead the blind by a way they did not know,
    and guide them in paths unfamiliar;
the darkness confronting them I will turn into light,
    and the uneven ground make level.
These things I will not fail to perform.
17 But those who trust in idols
    and esteem their images as gods
shall retreat in utter confusion.

18 O you deaf, listen; O you blind, look and see!
19 Who is blind but my own servant,
    or so deaf as the messenger I have sent?
Who is blind like those I have commissioned,
    as uncomprehending as the servant of the Lord—
20 seeing much but not giving heed,
    with open ears hearing nothing?

21 It is the will of the Lord, that,
    because of his righteousness,
    they magnify the law and become illustrious.
22 Instead, they are a people plundered and sacked,
    all of them trapped in holes,
    hidden away in dungeons.
They have become a prey, yet no one rescues them,
    a spoil, yet none demands restitution.

23 Who among you hearing this
    will take heed of it hereafter,
    and be mindful and obey?
24 Who is it that hands Jacob over to plunder
    and Israel to despoilers, if not the Lord,
    against whom we have sinned?

For they have no desire to walk in his ways
    or obey his law.
25 So in the heat of his anger
    he pours out on them the violence of war,
till it envelopes them in flames—
    yet they remain unaware—
till it sets them on fire;
    yet they take it not to heart.

43 But now, thus says the Lord—
    he who formed you, O Jacob,
    he who created you, O Israel:
Do not fear, for I have redeemed you.
    I have called you by name; you are mine.
2 When you cross the waters, I will be with you;
    when you traverse the rivers,
    you shall not be overwhelmed.
Though you walk through the fire,
    you shall not be burned;
its flame shall not consume you.

3 For I the Lord am your God,
    I, the Holy One of Israel, am your Savior;
Egypt I have appointed as ransom for you,
    Cush and Seba *I give* in place of you.
4 Because you are precious and revered in my eyes,
    and because I love you,
I give men in return for you,
    peoples in exchange for your life.

5 Do not fear, for I am with you.
    I will bring your offspring from the east
    and gather you from the west;
6 I will say to the north, Give up!
    to the south, Withhold not!
Bring my sons from afar
    and my daughters from the end of the earth—
7 all who are called by my name,
    whom I have formed, molded and wrought
    for my own glory.

⁸ Let go the people who are blind, yet have eyes,
　who are deaf, yet have ears.

⁹ When all nations unitedly assembled,
　when the peoples were gathered together,
who among them foretold these things,
　or predicted events that have come to pass?
Let them bring their witnesses
　and justify themselves,
　that those within hearing may say, It is true.
¹⁰ But you are my witnesses, says the Lord,
　my servant whom I have chosen,
to the end that you may recognize it and believe me,
　and perceive that I was the one *who foretold them*—
before me no god was formed,
　nor shall one exist after me.

¹¹ I myself am the Lord;
　apart from me there is no savior.
¹² It is I who foretold and wrought salvation,
　making it known
　when there was no strange god among you.
You are my witnesses, says the Lord,
　that I am divine,
¹³ that from the first I have been present—
　from my hand none can deliver;
when I work, who can thwart it?
¹⁴ Thus says the Lord, the Holy One of Israel,
　your Redeemer:
For your sake I launch *an attack* on Babylon
　and bring down as fugitives all the Chaldeans,
　they who sing the praises of shipping.
¹⁵ I the Lord, your Holy One,
　Creator of Israel, am your King.

¹⁶ Thus says the Lord—
　who provides a way in the Sea,
　a path through the mighty waters,
¹⁷ who dispatches chariots and horses,
　armies of men in full strength;
they lie down as one, to rise no more,
　they flicker and die, snuffed out like a wick—

¹⁸ Never mind the prophecies of bygone events;
    do not dwell on things of the past.
¹⁹ See, I do a new thing; it is now springing up.
    Surely, you are aware of it:
I am making roads through the desert,
    streams in the wasteland.
²⁰ The wild beasts do me honor,
    the jackals and birds of prey,
for bringing water to the wilderness,
    streams to the dry land,
that I may give drink to my chosen people,
    ²¹ the people I formed for myself
    to speak out in praise of me.

²² But you do not call upon me, O Jacob;
    you have grown weary of me, O Israel.
²³ Yet *I required* not that you bring me
    offerings from your flocks
    or pay me homage by sacrificial slaughter;
I have not burdened you with oblations
    or wearied you with burning incense.
²⁴ *Nor have I burdened you* to buy
    me the fragrant calamus
    or sate me with the fat of immolations.
Yet you have burdened me with your sins,
    wearied me with your iniquities.
²⁵ But it is I myself, and for my own sake,
    who blot out your offenses,
    remembering your sins no more.

²⁶ Recount for me *the past*;
    let us plead each our case.
    Speak up and vindicate yourself.
²⁷ Your first father transgressed;
    your spokesmen sinned against me.
²⁸ Therefore I let *the holy cities* be profaned;
    I gave Jacob to be ostracized, Israel to execration.

---

*28 Hebrew *śārê qōdeš*, *the princes of the sanctuary*, emended to *'ārê qōdeš*; compare 47:6; 64:10.

44 Hear now, Jacob my servant,
and Israel whom I have chosen.
2 Thus says the Lord, your Maker,
who formed you from the womb and succored you:
Be not afraid, O Jacob, my servant,
and Jeshurun whom I have chosen.

3 I will pour water on the thirsty *soil*,
showers upon the dry ground;
I will pour out my Spirit on your offspring,
my blessing upon your posterity.
4 They shall shoot up like grass
among streams*^a* of water,
like willows by running brooks.
5 One will say, I am the Lord's,
and another name himself Jacob.
Yet others will inscribe on their arm, To the Lord,
and adopt the name Israel.

6 Thus says the Lord, the King of Israel,
the Lord of Hosts, their Redeemer:
I was at the first and I am at the last;
apart from me there is no God.
7 Who predicts *^bwhat happens^b* as do I,
and is the equal of me
in appointing a people from of old *^cas types,^c*
foretelling things to come?
8 Be not perturbed or shaken.
Have I not made it known to you from of old?
Did I not foretell it, you being my witnesses?
Is there a God, then, apart from me?
There is no Rock unknown to me.

9 All who manufacture idols are deranged;
the things they cherish profit nothing.
Those who promote them are themselves
sightless and mindless, to their own dismay.

---

[a]4   So LXX; term not in MT.

[b]7   Hebrew *yiqrā'*, *will call*, emended to *yiqrâ*.

[c]7   Hebrew *wĕ'ōtiyôt*, *the coming things*, emended to *kĕ'ōtōt*; compare 8:18; 1QIsa^a, 45:11.

¹⁰ Who would fashion a god or cast an idol
  that cannot benefit them?
¹¹ Their whole society is confused;
  their fabricators are mere mortals.
 Were they all to assemble
  and take their stand *before me,*
 they would at once cringe in fear.

¹² The smith with his tools works the iron over the coals
  and gives it shape by hammering;
 he forges his *god* by the strength of his arm:
  when he becomes hungry, he no longer has strength;
 if he fails to drink water, he begins to grow faint.

¹³ The woodworker draws a diagram,
  sketching his *idol* with a marker.
 He creates it by chiselling to the outline of the dividers;
  he gives it a human likeness, resembling man's beauty,
 fit to lodge in a house.

¹⁴ He is required to cut down cedars;
  he must select holms and oaks
 and care for them among the trees of the forest.
 He plants firs, which the rain makes grow:
¹⁵ that which serves men as fuel,
  which they use to warm themselves
  or light fire with to bake bread,
 of that they create gods which they adore,
  from it they make idols to which they stoop.

¹⁶ Half of it they burn in the fire.
  ᵈOver it they broil a roast;ᵈ
 they eat the meat and are satisfied.
 They also warm themselves and say,
  Ah, it is warm ᵉin front ofᵉ the fire!
¹⁷ From the rest they make a god, their idol,
  to which they bow in adoration and pray,
 Save us; you are our god!

ᵈ16 Phrase transposed (compare v. 19); in text follows *eat the meat.*
ᵉ16 So 1QIsaᵃ; MT *I see.*

¹⁸ They have become unaware and insensible;
　　their eyes are glazed so they cannot see,
　　their minds are incapable of discernment.
¹⁹ They reflect not,
　　nor have the sense or comprehension to say,
　Part of this I burned in the fire;
　　I also baked bread in its embers,
　　roasted meat and ate it.
　Am I not making an abomination of what is left?
　　Do I not stoop to a mere lump of wood?
²⁰ They are followers of ashes;
　　their deluded minds have distracted them.
　They cannot liberate themselves *from them* or say,
　Surely this thing in my hand is a fraud.

²¹ Ponder these things, O Jacob, and you,*ᶠ* O Israel,
　　for you are my servant.
　I have created you to be my servant, O Israel;
　　do not disregard me.
²² I have removed your offenses like a thick fog,
　　your sins like a cloud of mist.
　Return to me; I have redeemed you.
²³ Sing, O heavens, for what the Lord has done;
　　cause it to resound, O earth beneath!
　Burst into song, O mountains,
　　forests, and all trees therein:
　the Lord has redeemed Jacob;
　　he shall be glorified in Israel.

²⁴ Thus says the Lord, your Redeemer,
　　who formed you from the womb:
　I am the Lord, the Maker of all things,
　　who alone suspends the heavens,
　　who himself gives form to the earth,
²⁵ who annuls the predictions of imposters
　　and makes fools of diviners,
　who turns wise men about
　　and makes nonsense of their knowledge,

---

*ᶠ*21　Word transposed; in text follows *created you.*

26 who fulfills the word of his servant,
    accomplishes the aims of his messengers,
  who says of Jerusalem, It shall be reinhabited,
    and of the cities of Judah, They shall be rebuilt,
    their ruins I will restore,
27 who says to the deep, Become dry;
    I am drying up your currents,
28 who says of Cyrus, He is my shepherd;
    he will do whatever I will.
  He will say of Jerusalem that it must be rebuilt,
    its temple foundations relaid.

45

Thus says the Lord to his anointed,
    to Cyrus, whom I grasp by the right hand,
  to subdue nations before him,
    to ungird the loins of rulers,
  opening doors ahead of him,
    letting no gates remain shut:
2 I will go before you and level all obstacles;
    I will break in pieces brazen doors
    and cut through iron bars.
3 I will give you hidden treasures
    and secret hoards of wealth—
  that you may know that it is I the Lord,
    the God of Israel, who calls you by name.

4 For the sake of my servant Jacob,
    and Israel my chosen, I call you by name—
    I named you when yet you knew me not.
5 I am the Lord, there is none other;
    apart from me there is no God.
    I girded you up when yet you knew me not—
6 that men from where the sun rises to where it sets
    may know that without me there is nothing,
  that I am the Lord, and that there is none other.

7 I fashion light and form darkness;
    I occasion peace and cause calamity.
    I, the Lord, do all these things.
8 Rain down from above, O heavens;
    let the skies overflow with righteousness.

Let the earth receive it and salvation "blossom;"
let righteousness spring up forthwith.
I, the Lord, create it.

⁹ Woe to those in conflict with their Maker,
mere shards of earthenware pottery!
As though the clay were to say to him who molds it,
What are you doing?
Your hands have no skill for the work!
¹⁰ Woe to those who say to their Father,
What have you begotten?
or to the Woman, What have you borne?

¹¹ Thus says the Lord,
the Holy One of Israel, their Maker:
Will you ask me*b* for signs*c* concerning my children,
or dictate to me about the deeds of my hands?
¹² It is I who made the earth
and created man upon it;
I with my hand*d* suspended the heavens,
appointing all their host.
¹³ It is I who rightfully raise him up,
who facilitate his every step;
he will rebuild my city and set free my exiles
without price or bribe, says the Lord of Hosts.

¹⁴ Thus says the Lord:
The wealth of Egypt and merchandise of Cush
*e*shall pass on to you and become yours,*e*
as shall the Sabeans, a people tall in stature.
They shall walk behind you in chains
and bow down to you, entreating you,
Surely God is in you; no other gods exist!

¹⁵ Truly thou art a God who dissembles himself,
O Savior, God of Israel.

---

*a*8   So 1QIsa*a*; LXX; MT *they bear fruit.*
*b*11   Hebrew *šĕʾālûnî, Ask me,* emended to *tišʾālûnî.*
*c*11   So 1QIsa*a*; compare 7:11. MT *ʾōtîyôt, the coming things.*
*d*12   So LXX; MT vocalization plural. Compare 48:13.
*e*14   Phrase transposed; in text follows *tall in stature.*

¹⁶ As one, the makers of inventions retired in disgrace,
  utterly dismayed and embarrassed.
¹⁷ But Israel is saved by the Lord
  with an everlasting salvation;
 you shall not be dismayed or put to shame
  worlds without end.

¹⁸ For thus says the Lord who created the heavens,
  the God who formed the earth—
 who made it secure and organized it,
  not to remain a chaotic waste,
 but designed it to be inhabited:
  I am the Lord, there is none other.
¹⁹ I speak not in secret
  from somewhere in a land of darkness;
 I do not ask Jacob's offspring
  to seek me amid chaos.
 I the Lord tell righteousness
  and am forthright of speech.

²⁰ Gather yourselves and come;
  draw near, all you fugitives of the nations.
 They who carried about their wooden idols
  and prayed to gods that could not save them
  were caught unawares.
²¹ Speak up and present your case;
  go ahead and consult one another.
 Who foretold these things of old,
  predicted them long ago?
 Did not I, the Lord,
  apart from whom there is no God?
 Did not I, the God of righteousness,
  except for whom there is no Savior?

²² Turn to me and save yourselves,
  all you ends of the earth;
 I am God, there is none other.
²³ By myself I swear it—
  righteousness has issued from my mouth,
  by a decree that cannot be revoked:
 To me every knee shall bow
  and every tongue swear *allegiance*.

²⁴ It shall be said of me,
    By the Lord alone come vindication and might.
Before him must come in shame
    all who were incensed against him.
²⁵ In the Lord shall all Israel's offspring
    justify themselves and have cause to boast.

46

Bel slumps down, Nebo is stooped over:
    their idols are *loaded* upon beasts and cattle;
the images you bore aloft
    are piled as burdens on weary animals.
² *Such gods*ᵃ altogether sag and bow down,
    unable to rescue their burden;
they themselves go into captivity.

³ Hear me, O house of Jacob,
    and all you remnant of the house of Israel,
who have been a load on me since birth,
    borne up by me from the womb:
⁴ Even to your old age, I am present;
    till you turn grey, it is I who sustain you.
It is I who made you, and I who bear you up;
    it is I who carry and rescue you.

⁵ To whom will you compare me or count me equal?
    To whom will you liken me,
    that we should appear similar?
⁶ They who squander gold from the purse
    and weigh out silver on the scales
hire a smith to make them a god
    they bow down to and worship.
⁷ They bear it aloft, carrying it on their shoulders;
    when they set it in place, there it stands,
    unable to budge from its spot.
Though they cry to it for help, it does not answer;
    it cannot save them from trouble.

⁸ Put yourselves in mind of this
    and come to your senses;
    take it to heart, you offenders.

ᵃ2   Hebrew *They*.

⁹ Review the prophecies of the events of old!
  I am God, there is none other.
  I am divine; nothing resembles me.
¹⁰ I foretell the end from the beginning,
  from ancient times things not yet done.
  I speak, and my purposes take effect;
  I accomplish all my will.

¹¹ I summon a bird of prey from the east,
  from a distant land
  the man *who performs my counsel.*
  What I have spoken, I bring to pass;
  what I have planned, I do.
¹² Hear me, you stubborn-hearted,
  who are far from righteousness:
¹³ I have brought near my righteousness;
  it is not now far off—
  my salvation shall no longer be delayed.
  I will grant deliverance in Zion,
  and to Israel my glory.

47 Get down and sit in the dust,
    O Virgin Daughter of Babylon;
  squat on the ground, dethroned,
    O Daughter of the Chaldeans.
  You shall no more be spoken of
    as delicate and refined.
² Take two grindstones and grind flour;
    unveil, disrobe, bare your legs,
    wade through streams:
³ your nakedness shall be exposed
    and your shame uncovered.
  I will take vengeance
    and not be entreated of men,
⁴ *says* our Redeemer, the Holy One of Israel,
    whose name is the Lord of Hosts.

⁵ Sit speechless; retire into obscurity,
    O Daughter of the Chaldeans.

ᵇ11 Or, *I have foreordained.*

No longer shall you be called,
    Mistress of Kingdoms.
6 I was provoked by my people,
    so I let my inheritance be defiled.
I gave them into your hand,
    and you showed them no mercy;
even the aged you weighed down heavily with your yoke.
7 You thought, I, the Eternal Mistress, exist forever!
    and did not consider these,[a]
    or remember her final destiny.

8 Now therefore hear this, O pampered lady,
    securely enthroned, thinking to herself,
I exist, and other than me there is nothing;
    I shall not be widowed or bereaved of children:
9 Bereavement and widowhood
    shall suddenly overtake you, both in one day.
They shall come upon you in full,
    notwithstanding your many magical feats
    and exceedingly strong combinations.

10 Secure in your wickedness,
    you thought, No one discerns me.
By your skill and science you were led astray,
    thinking to yourself, I exist,
    and there is none besides me!
11 Catastrophe shall overtake you,
    which you shall not know how to avert by bribes;[b]
disaster shall befall you
    from which you cannot ransom yourself:
there shall come upon you sudden ruin
    such as you have not imagined.

12 Persist, then, with your combinations
    and with your many magical feats,
    at which you have exerted yourself since your youth.
It may still be of use to you;
    perhaps you can hinder[c] it.

---

[a]7   For subject of term, see verse 6.

[b]11   Hebrew *šaḥrāh* (obscure) emended to *saḥdāh;* contrast Israel to this verse, 43:3; 45:13.

[c]12   Hebrew *taʿărôṣî, cause terror,* emended to *taʿăsorî;* compare 66:9.

¹³ But you are powerless, despite all your tactics.
　　Now let those who unravel the heavens,
　who observe the stars
　　and make predictions month by month,
　stand by you and save you!

¹⁴ See, as stubble they are burnt up in the fire,
　　unable themselves to escape the hand of the flame.
　These are no embers to warm anyone;
　　such is no fire to sit by!
¹⁵ This is what your procurers*d* have profited you—
　　those for whom you have exerted yourself
　since your youth—
　each deviates his own way;
　　none is there to save you.

48

Hear this, O house of Jacob,
　　you who are named Israel—
　though you*a* stem from the lineage*b* of Judah—
　　who take oaths in the name of the Lord
　and invoke the God of Israel,
　　though not in truth or in righteousness,
² who call yourselves of the holy city,
　　upheld by the God of Israel,
　whose name is the Lord of Hosts:
³ The prophecies of the events of the past
　I made known long beforehand;
　no sooner did they issue from my mouth,
　　than I caused them to be announced.
　Then, suddenly, I acted and they came about.

⁴ For I knew how stubborn you were—
　　your neck was an iron sinew, your brow brazen—
⁵ therefore I told you them beforehand;
　　I announced them to you before they transpired,
　lest you should say, My idols did it;
　　my graven and wrought images caused it!

---

*d*15　Or, *merchants*. Noun transposed; in text follows *exerted yourself*. Compare verse 12.
*a*1　Hebrew *they*.
*b*1　Literally, *loins*. Hebrew *mimmê, from the waters*, emended to *mimmĕ'ê;* compare the term in verse 19.

⁶ But you have heard ʿthe whole vision;ʿ
how is it you do not proclaim it?
Yet as of now, I announce to you new things,
things withheld and unknown to you,
⁷ things now coming into being, not hitherto,
things you have not heard of before,
lest you should say, Indeed I knew them!
⁸ You have not heard them,
nor have you known them;
before this your ears have not been open to them.
For I knew you would turn treacherous;
you were called a transgressor from the womb.

⁹ For my own name's sake I have bridled my wrath;
on account of my renown
I have shown restraint toward you
by not entirely destroying you.
¹⁰ See, I am refining you, though not as silver;
I am testing^d you in the crucible of affliction.
¹¹ For my own sake, on my own account, I do it,
that my name^e be not dishonored,
nor my glory, which I give to no other.

¹² Hear me, O Jacob, and Israel, my elect:
I am he who was at the first,
and I am he who is at the last.
¹³ It was my hand that founded the earth,
my right hand that stretched out the heavens;
when I call them, they arise at once.
¹⁴ All of you, assemble and hear:
Who among you^f foretold these things?
It is him the Lord loves,
who shall perform his will in Babylon;
his arm shall be against the Chaldeans.
¹⁵ I myself have spoken it, and also called him;
I have brought him, and I will prosper^g his way.

ᶜ6   Hebrew *ḥazēh kullāh, See all of it!* emended to *ḥāzût kullāh;* compare 29:11.
ᵈ10   So 1QIsaᵃ; MT *choosing.*
ᵉ11   So LXX; term not in MT.
ᶠ14   Hebrew *bāhem, among them,* emended to *bākem.*
ᵍ15   So LXX; MT *and he shall prosper.*

¹⁶ Come near me and hear this:
　I have not made predictions in secret;
　　at their coming to pass, I have been present.
　Now my Lord the Lord has sent me;
　　his Spirit *is in me.*^b

¹⁷ Thus says the Lord, the Holy One of Israel,
　　your Redeemer:
　I the Lord your God instruct you to your good,
　　guiding you in the way you should go.
¹⁸ Had you but obeyed my commandments,
　　your peace would have been as a river,
　　your righteousness like the waves of the sea;
¹⁹ your offspring would have been
　　as the sands in number,
　　your descendants as many as their grains.
　Their names would not have been cut off
　　and obliterated from my presence.

²⁰ Go forth out of Babylon, flee from Chaldea!
　　Make this announcement with resounding voice;
　broadcast it to the end of the earth.
　　Say, The Lord has redeemed his servant Jacob.
²¹ They thirsted not when he led them through arid places:
　　he caused water to flow for them from the rock;
　he cleaved the rock and water gushed out.

²² But there is no peace, says the Lord,
　　for the wicked.

49 Hear me, O isles; listen, you distant peoples:
　　The Lord called me before I was in the belly;
　before I was in my mother's womb,
　　he mentioned me by name.
² He has made my mouth like a sharp sword—
　　in the shadow^a of his hand he hid me.
　He has made me into a polished arrow—
　　in his quiver he kept me secret.

---

^b16　Compare 63:11.
^a2　Also, *guise.*

3 He said to me, You are my servant,
    Israel, in whom I will be glorified.
4 I had thought, I have labored in vain,
    I have spent my strength for nothing
    and to no purpose!
Yet my cause rested with the Lord,
    my recompense with my God.

5 For now the Lord has said—
    he who formed me from the womb
to be his servant, to restore Jacob to him,
    Israel having been gathered to him;
for I won honor in the eyes of the Lord
    when my God became my strength—
6 he said: It is too small a thing
    for you to be my servant
to raise up the tribes of Jacob
    and to restore those preserved of Israel.
I will also appoint you to be a light to the nations,*b*
    that my salvation may be to the end of the earth.

7 Thus says the Lord,
    the Redeemer and Holy One of Israel,
to him who is despised as a person,
    who is abhorred by his nation,
    a servant to those in authority:
Rulers shall rise up when they see you,
    heads of state shall prostrate themselves,
because the Lord keeps faith with you,
    because the Holy One of Israel has chosen you.

8 Thus says the Lord:
    At a favorable time I have answered you;
    in the day of salvation I have come to your aid:
I have created you and appointed you
    to be a covenant of the people,
to restore the Land and reapportion the desolate estates,
9 to say to the captives, Come forth!
    and to those in darkness, Show yourselves!

---

*b*6   Also, *Gentiles;* compare verse 22; 42:1, 6.

They shall feed along the way
    and find pasture on all barren heights;
¹⁰ they shall not hunger or thirst,
      nor be smitten by oppressive heat or by the sun:
    he who has mercy on them will guide them;
      he will lead them by springs of water.

¹¹ All my mountain ranges I will appoint as roads;
    my highways shall be on high.
¹² See these, coming from afar, these, from the northwest,
    and these, from the land of Sinim.
¹³ Shout for joy, O heavens; celebrate, O earth!
    Burst into song, O mountains!
  The Lord is comforting his people,
    showing compassion for his afflicted.

¹⁴ But Zion said, The Lord has forsaken me,
    my Lord has forgotten me.
¹⁵ Can a woman forget her suckling infant,
    or feel no compassion for the child of her womb?
  Although these shall forget, I will not forget you.
¹⁶ See, I have engraved you on my palms;
    ᶜI have sealed youᶜ to be continually before me.

¹⁷ Your sons shall hasten your ravagers away—
    those who ruined you shall depart from you.
¹⁸ Lift up your eyes and look around you;
    with one accord they gather and come to you.
  As surely as I live, says the Lord,
    you shall adorn yourself with them all as with jewels,
    bind them on you as does a bride.

¹⁹ For your ruins and ravaged places,
    and your land laid waste,
  shall now be too small for your inhabitants,
    despite the departure of your devourers.
²⁰ The children born during the time of your bereavement
    shall yet say in your ears,
  This place is too cramped for us;
    give us space in which to settle!

ᶜ16 Hebrew *ḥômōtayik, your walls*, emended to *ḥatamtîk.*

21 And you will say to yourself,
>Who bore me these while I was bereaved and barren?
I was exiled, banished;
>by whom were these reared?
When I was left to myself, where were they?

22 Thus says my Lord the Lord:
>I will lift up my hand to the nations,
>raise my ensign to the peoples;
>and they will bring your sons in their bosoms
>and carry your daughters on their shoulders.
23 Kings shall be your foster fathers,
>queens your nursing mothers.
They will bow down before you,
>their faces to the ground;
>they will lick the dust of your feet.
Then shall you know that I am the Lord,
>and that they who hope in me are not disappointed.

24 Can the warrior's spoil be taken from him,
>or the tyrant's*d* captives escape free?
25 Yet thus says the Lord: The warrior's spoil*e*
>shall indeed be taken from him,
and the tyrant's captives*f* escape free:
I myself will contend with your contenders,
>and I will deliver your children.
26 I will feed your oppressors with their own flesh;
>they shall be drunk with their own blood as with wine.
And all flesh shall know that I the Lord am your Savior,
>that your Redeemer is the Valiant One of Jacob.

50 Thus says the Lord:
>Where is your mother's bill of divorce
>with which I cast her out?
Or to which of my creditors did I sell you?
>Surely, by sinning you sold yourselves;
because of your crimes was your mother an outcast.

---

*d*24 So 1QIsa*a*; LXX. MT *ṣaddîq, the righteous one's.*

*e*25 So 1QIsa*a*; MT *captives.*

*f*25 So 1QIsa*a*; MT *spoil.*

2 Why was no one there when I came;
    why did no one answer when I called?
Was my hand too short to redeem you;
    have I no power to deliver?
By a mere rebuke I dry up the Sea;
    rivers I turn into desert—
their fish become parched*a* for lack of water
    and perish because of thirst.
3 I clothe the heavens with the blackness of mourning;
    I put up sackcloth to cover them.

4 My Lord the Lord has endowed me with a learned tongue,
    that I may know how to preach
    to those grown weary a word to wake them up.
Morning by morning he wakens my ear to hear,
    as at study;
5 my Lord the Lord has opened my ear,
    and I rebel not, nor back away:
6 I offered my back to smiters,
    my cheeks to those who plucked out the beard;
I hid not my face from insult and spitting.

7 Because my Lord the Lord helps me,
    I shall not be disgraced;
I have set my face like flint,
    knowing I shall not be confounded.
8 He who vindicates me is near me.
    Who has a dispute with me? Let us face one another!
Who will bring charges against me?
    Let him confront me with them!
9 See, my Lord the Lord sustains me.
    Who then will incriminate me?
Surely all such shall wear out like a garment;
    the moth shall consume them.

10 Who among you fears the Lord
    and heeds the voice of his servant,
who, though he walk in darkness and have no light,
    trusts in the name of the Lord and relies on his God?

---

*a*2   So 1QIsa*a*; LXX. MT *turn foul.*

¹¹ But you are lighters of fires, all of you,
who illuminate*ᵇ* with mere sparks.
Walk then by the light of your fires
and by the sparks you have kindled.
This shall you have from my hand:
you shall lie down in agony.

51 Hear me, you followers of righteousness,
seekers of the Lord:
Look to the rock from which you were cut,
to the quarry out of which you were hewn;
² look to Abraham your father,
to Sarah who bore you.
He was but one when I called him,
but I blessed him by making him many.
³ For the Lord is comforting Zion,
bringing solace to all her ruins;
he is making her wilderness like Eden,
her desert as the garden of the Lord.
Joyful rejoicing takes place there,
thanksgiving with the voice of song.

⁴ Listen to me, my people;
give heed to me, O my nation:
The law shall go forth from me;
my precepts shall be a light to the peoples.
Then, suddenly, I will act:
⁵ My righteousness shall be at hand
and my salvation proceed;
my arms shall judge the peoples—
the isles anticipate me, awaiting my arm.

⁶ Lift up your eyes to the heavens;
look on the earth beneath:
the heavens shall vanish as by smoke,
the earth wear out like a garment—
its inhabitants shall die in the manner of vermin.
But my salvation shall be everlasting;
my righteousness shall never fail.

---

*ᵇ*11 Hebrew *mĕ⁾azrê, gird up,* emended to *mĕ⁾îrê.*

⁷ Hear me, you who know righteousness,
  O people in whose heart is my law:
Do not fear the reproach of men;
  be undaunted by their ridicule.
⁸ For the moth shall consume them like a garment;
  moths shall devour them like wool.
But my righteousness shall endure forever,
  my salvation through endless generations.

⁹ Awake, arise; clothe yourself with power,
  O arm of the Lord!
Bestir yourself, as in ancient times,
  as in generations of old.
Was it not you who carved up Rahab,
  you who slew the dragon?
¹⁰ Was it not you who dried up the Sea,
  the waters of the mighty deep,
and made of ocean depths a way
  by which the redeemed might pass?
¹¹ Let the ransomed of the Lord return!
  Let them come singing to Zion,
their heads crowned with everlasting joy;
  let them obtain joy and gladness,
and sorrow and sighing flee away.

¹² I myself am your Comforter.
  Who are you that you fear mortal man,
  the children of men who shall be turned to grass?
¹³ Have you forgotten the Lord, your Maker—
  who suspends the heavens,
  who sets the earth in place—
that you go all day in constant dread
  of the oppressor's rage
as he readies himself to wreak destruction?
  What is there to the wrath of the oppressor?
¹⁴ Soon now shall he who is bowed down be set free;
  he shall not die *as those destined* for the Pit,
  neither shall he want for food.
¹⁵ It is I the Lord your God,
  whose name is the Lord of Hosts,
  who stir up the Sea so that its waves roar.

¹⁶ I will put my words in your mouth
   and shelter you in the shadow of my hand,
while I replant the heavens and set the earth in place,
   that I may say to Zion, You are my people.

¹⁷ Rouse yourself; awaken and rise up, O Jerusalem,
   you who have drunk from the Lord's hand
the cup of his wrath,
   drinking to the dregs the bowl of stupor.
¹⁸ There was none to guide her *home*
   among all the children she bore,
none to take her by the hand of all the sons she reared.

¹⁹ Twofold *calamity* has befallen you:
   desolation, ruin—and who laments you?
   famine, the sword—and who consoles*ᵃ* you?
²⁰ Your children lie in a faint at the corner of every street,
   taken in a net like bison.
They have their fill of the wrath of the Lord,
   of your God's angry rebuke.

²¹ Now therefore hear this, O wretched one,
   drunk, though not with wine.
²² Thus says the Lord, your Lord and God,
   who defends the cause of his people:
I am taking the cup of stupor from your hand;
   you shall drink no more from the bowl of my wrath.
²³ And I give it into the hand of your tormentors,
   those who said of your life,
Lie prostrate that we may go over you—
   so that you made your back as the ground,
a mere thoroughfare to passers-by.

52 Awake, arise; clothe yourself with power, O Zion!
   Put on your robes of glory, O Jerusalem, holy city.
   No more shall the uncircumcised and defiled enter you.
² Shake yourself free, rise from the dust;
   sit enthroned, O Jerusalem.
Loose yourself from the bands around your neck,
   O captive Daughter of Zion.

---

*ᵃ*19   So 1QIsaᵃ; LXX. MT *how can I console.*

3 Thus says the Lord: You were sold without price,
and you shall be redeemed without money.

4 For thus says my Lord the Lord:
At first my people went down to Egypt to sojourn there.
Then the Assyrians subjected them for nothing.
5 And now, what have I here? says the Lord.
My people are taken over without price;
those who govern them
act presumptuously, says the Lord,
and my name is constantly abused all the day.

6 Therefore shall my people come to know my name;
in that day *they shall know*
that I, who speak, am at hand.
7 *Then shall they say,*
How comely upon the mountains
are the feet of the messenger announcing peace,
who brings tidings of good,
who heralds salvation,
saying to Zion, Your God reigns!

8 Hark! Your watchmen lift up their voice;
as one they cry out for joy:
before their very eyes they see
the Lord's return to Zion.
10*b* The Lord has bared his holy arm
in the eyes of all nations,
that all ends of the earth may see
our God's salvation.
9 Break out all together into song,
you ruined places of Jerusalem:
the Lord has comforted his people;
he has redeemed Jerusalem.

11 Turn away, depart;
touch nothing defiled as you leave *Babylon.c*
Come out of her and be pure,
you who bear the Lord's vessels.

---

*a*5 Also, *mock;* so 1QIsaa. MT *wail.*
*b*10 Verse transposed; appears out of sequence in text.
*c*11 Hebrew *there.*

¹² But you shall not leave in haste or go in flight:
the Lord will go before you,
the God of Israel behind you.

¹³ My servant, being astute, shall be highly exalted;
he shall become exceedingly eminent:
¹⁴ just as he*d* appalled many—
his appearance was marred beyond human likeness,
his semblance unlike that of men—
¹⁵ So shall he yet astound*e* many nations,
rulers shutting their mouths at him—
what was not told them, they shall see;
what they had not heard, they shall consider.

53 Who has believed our revelation?
On whose account has the arm of the Lord
been revealed?

² Like a sapling he grew up in his presence,
a stalk out of arid ground.
He had no distinguished appearance,
that we should notice him;
he had no *pleasing* aspect,
that we should find him attractive.
³ He was despised and disdained by men,
a man of grief, accustomed to suffering.
As one from whom men hide their faces
he was shunned, deemed by us of no merit.

⁴ Yet he bore our sufferings, endured our griefs,
though we thought him stricken,
smitten of God, and humbled.
⁵ But he was pierced for our transgressions,
crushed because of our iniquities;
the price of our peace he incurred,
and with his wounds we are healed.
⁶ We all like sheep had gone astray,
each of us headed his own way;
the Lord brought together upon him the iniquity of us all.

---

*d*14 Hebrew *you.*

*e*15 Or, *startle;* also *purge, sprinkle.*

⁷ He was harassed, yet submissive,
    and opened not his mouth—
like a lamb led to slaughter,
    like a sheep, dumb before its shearers,
    he opened not his mouth.
⁸ By arrest and trial he was taken away.
    Who can apprise his generation
that he was cut off from the land of the living
    for the crime of my people,
    to whom the blow was due?

⁹ He was appointed among the wicked in death,^{a}
    among the rich was his burial;^{b}
yet he had done no violence,
    and deceit was not in his mouth.
¹⁰ But the Lord willed to crush him,
    causing him suffering,
that, if he^c made his life an offering for guilt,
    he might see his offspring and prolong his days,
and that the purposes of the Lord
    might prosper in his hand.

¹¹ He shall see the toil of his soul and be satisfied;
    because of his knowledge,
and by bearing their iniquities,
    shall my servant, the righteous one, vindicate many.
¹² I will assign him an inheritance among the great,
    and he shall divide the spoil with the mighty,
because he poured out his soul unto death,
    and was numbered with criminals—
he bore the sins of many,
    and made intercession for the transgressors.

54 Sing, O barren woman who did not give birth;
    break into jubilant song, you who were not in labor.
The children of the deserted wife
    shall outnumber those of the espoused, says the Lord.

---

^{a}9, ^{b}9   Terms transposed; appear reversed in text. Compare 14:20 and the lack of a burial for the wicked and violent Tyrant.
^{c}10   Hebrew *you*.

² Expand the site of your tent;
    extend the canopies of your dwellings.
  Do not hold back; lengthen your cords
    and strengthen your stakes.
³ For you shall spread abroad
    to the right and to the left;
  your offspring shall dispossess the nations
    and resettle the desolate cities.

⁴ Be not fearful, for you shall not be confounded;
    be not ashamed, for you shall not be disgraced.
  You shall forget the shame of your youth
    and remember no more
    the reproach of your widowhood.
⁵ For he who espouses you is your Maker,
    whose name is the Lord of Hosts;
  he who redeems you is the Holy One of Israel,
    who is called the God of all the earth.

⁶ The Lord calls you back
    as a spouse forsaken and forlorn,
  a wife married in youth only to be rejected,
    says your God.
⁷ I forsook you indeed momentarily,
    but with loving compassion I will gather you up.
⁸ In a fleeting surge of anger I hid my face from you,
    but with everlasting charity
  I will have compassion on you,
    says the Lord, who redeems you.

⁹ This is to me as in the days*ᵃ* of Noah,
    when I swore that the waters of Noah
    would no more flood the earth.
  So I swear to have no more anger toward you,
    never again to rebuke you.
¹⁰ For the mountains shall be removed
    and the hills collapse with shaking,
  but my charity toward you shall never be removed,
    nor my covenant of peace be shaken,
  says the Lord, who has compassion on you.

---

*ᵃ*9   So 1QIsaᵃ; MT *waters*.

¹¹ Poor wretch, tempest-tossed and disconsolate!
    I will lay antimony for your building stones
    and sapphires for your foundations;
¹² I will make your skylights of jacinth,
    your gates of carbuncle,
    and your entire boundary of precious stones.
¹³ All your children shall be taught by the Lord,
    and great shall be the peace of your posterity.
¹⁴ You shall be firmly established through righteousness;
    you will be far from oppression
    and have no cause to fear,
far from ruin, for it shall not approach you.

¹⁵ Those who gather into mobs are not of me;
    whoever masses against you shall fall because of you.
¹⁶ It is I who create the smith who fans the flaming coals,
    forging weapons to suit his purpose;
it is I who create the ravager to destroy.
¹⁷ Whatever weapon is devised against you,
    it shall not succeed;
every tongue that rises to accuse you,
    you shall refute.
This is the heritage of the servants of the Lord,
    and such is their vindication*ᵇ* by me, says the Lord.

55 Attention, all who thirst; come for water!
You who have no money,
    come and buy food, that you may eat.
Come, buy wine and milk
    with no money and at no cost.
² Why do you spend money on what is not bread,
    your labor on what does not satisfy?
Hear me well: Eat what is good,
    and your souls shall enjoy abundance.

³ Give ear and come unto me;
    pay heed, that your souls may live!
And I will make with you an everlasting covenant:
    my loving fidelity toward David.

ᵇ17 Or, *righteousness;* compare verse 14.

⁴ See, I have appointed him a witness to the nations,
 a prince and lawgiver of the peoples.
⁵ You will summon a nation that you did not know;
 a nation that did not know you will hasten to you—
because of the Lord your God,
 the Holy One of Israel, who gloriously endows you.

⁶ Inquire of the Lord while he is present;
 call upon him while he is near.
⁷ Let the wicked forsake their ways
 and sinful men their thoughts.
Let them return to the Lord,
 and he will have mercy on them;
to our God, who graciously pardons.

⁸ For my thoughts are not your thoughts,
 nor are your ways my ways, says the Lord.
⁹ But as the heavens are higher than the earth,
 so are my ways higher than your ways
 and my thoughts *higher* than your thoughts.
¹⁰ And as the rains and snows descend from the sky
 and return not to it without watering the earth,
to render it fertile and fruitful—
 providing seed for the sower and food for the eater—
¹¹ so is the word that leaves my mouth:
 it does not return to me empty;
 it accomplishes what I desire,
 achieves the purpose for which I sent it.

¹² You shall depart in joy and be led back in peace;
 the mountains and hills shall sing at your presence
 and the trees of the meadows all clap their hands.
¹³ In place of the thornbush shall come up the cypress,
 in place of nettles, the myrtle.
This shall serve as a testimony of the Lord,
 an everlasting sign that shall not be done away.

56 Thus says the Lord:
 Observe justice and perform righteousness,
for soon my salvation will come
 and my righteousness be revealed.

2 Blessed is the man who does so—
    the person who holds fast to them—
who keeps the Sabbath without profaning it,
    who stays his hand from doing any evil.

3 Let not the foreigner who adheres to the Lord say,
    The Lord will surely exclude me from his people.
And let not the eunuch say, I am but a barren tree.
4 For thus says the Lord:
    As for the eunuchs who keep my Sabbaths
and choose to do what I will—
    holding fast to my covenant—
5 to them I will give a handclasp and a name
    within the walls of my house
    that is better than sons and daughters;
· I will endow them with an everlasting name
    that shall not be cut off.

6 And the foreigners who adhere to the Lord
    to serve him,
who love the name of the Lord,
    that they may be his servants—
all who keep the Sabbath without profaning it,
    holding fast to my covenant—
7 these I will bring to my holy mountain
    and gladden in my house of prayer.
Their offerings and sacrifices
    shall be accepted on my altar,
for my house shall be known
    as a house of prayer for all nations.
8 Thus says my Lord the Lord,
    who gathers up the outcasts of Israel:
I will gather others to those already gathered.

9 All you wild beasts, you animals of the forest,
    come and devour!
10 Their watchmen are altogether blind and unaware;
    all of them are but dumb watchdogs unable to bark,
lolling seers fond of slumber.

11 Gluttonous dogs, and insatiable,
    such indeed are insensible shepherds.

They are all diverted to their own way,
   every one after his own advantage.
12 Come, *they say*, let us get wine
   and have our fill of liquor.
For tomorrow will be like today, only far better!

57

The righteous^a disappear,
   and no man gives it a thought;
the godly are gathered out,
   but no one perceives that from impending calamity
   the righteous are withdrawn.
2 They who walk uprightly shall attain to peace,
   and rest in their beds.

3 As for you, come here, you children of the sorceress,
   offspring of adulterer and harlot!
4 At whose expense do you amuse yourselves?
   At whom do you open wide the mouth
   and stick out the tongue?
Surely you are born of sin, a spurious brood,
   5 who burn with lust among the oaks,
   under every burgeoning tree,
slayers of children in the gullies
   under the crags of rocks.
6 Among the slippery stones of the ravines
   shall be your fate; they indeed are your lot.
To them you pour out libations and make offerings.
   How shall I be appeased of such things?

7 On a lofty mountain
   you have made prominent your bed,
   and there you ascend to offer sacrifices.
8 Behind doors and facades
   you have put up your emblems,
   and have exposed yourself to *others* than me:
   mounting your bed, you have laid it wide open.
And you bargain with those with whom you love to lie,
   your hand on their nakedness.^b

---

^a1 Or, *righteous one.*
^b8 Literally, *foreparts.*

⁹ You bathe*ᶜ* with oil for the king
  and increase your perfumes;
 you send your solicitors far abroad
  and debase yourself to the depths.*ᵈ*
¹⁰ Though wearied by your excessive ways,
  you have not admitted despair;
 you have found livelihood,
  and therefore have not slackened.

¹¹ Yet on whose account are you uneasy and apprehensive,
  that you pretend and do not mention me,
  nor even give me a thought?
 Is it because I have so long kept silent
  that you no longer fear me?
¹² But I will expose your fornication
  and the wantonness of your exploits.
¹³ When you cry out in distress,
  let those who flock to you save you!
 A wind shall carry all of them off;
  a vapor shall take them away.

 But they who seek refuge in me shall possess the earth
  and receive an inheritance in my holy mountain.
¹⁴ It will be said: Excavate, pave a road!
  Prepare the way;
 remove the obstacles from the path of my people!

¹⁵ Thus says he who is highly exalted,
  who abides forever, whose name is sacred:
 I dwell on high in the holy place,
  and with him who is humble and lowly in spirit—
 refreshing the spirits of the lowly,
  reviving the hearts of the humble.
¹⁶ I will not contend forever, nor always be angry;
  the spirits and souls I have made would faint before me.

¹⁷ By his sin of covetousness I was provoked;
  I struck him and hid *my face* in anger
   when he strayed by following the ways of his heart.

---

*ᶜ*9   From Hebrew root *šārâ*.
*ᵈ*9   Hebrew *Sheol*.

208

¹⁸ Yet I have seen his conduct and will recover him;
    I will guide him and amply console him
    and those who mourn for him,
¹⁹ who partake*e* of the fruit of the lips:
    Peace, well-being, to those far off
  and to those who are near,
    says the Lord who heals him.

²⁰ But the wicked are like the raging Sea,
    unable to rest,
    whose waters heave up mire and mud:
²¹ there is no peace, says my God, for the wicked.

58 Proclaim it aloud without restraint;
    raise your voice like a trumpet!
  Declare to my people their transgressions,
    to the house of Jacob their sins.
² Yet they importune me daily,
    eager to learn my ways,
  like a nation practicing righteousness
    and not forsaking the precepts of their God.

  They inquire of me concerning correct ordinances,
    desiring to draw nearer to God:
³ Why, when we fast, do you not notice?
    We afflict our bodies and you remain indifferent!
  It is because on your fast day you pursue your own ends
    and constrain all who toil for you.
⁴ You fast amid strife and contention,
    striking out savagely with the fist.
  Your present fasts are not such
    as to make your voice heard on high.

⁵ Is this the manner of fasting I have required,
    just a time for men to torment themselves?
  Is it only for bowing one's head like a reed
    and making one's bed of sackcloth and ashes?
  Do you call that a fast,
    a day of the Lord's good graces?

---

*e*19 Hebrew *bôrē⁾*, *create*, emended to *bôrê*.

⁶ Is not this the fast I require:
    To release from wrongful bondage,
    to untie the harness of the yoke,
  to set the oppressed at liberty
    and abolish all forms of subjection?
⁷ Is it not to share your food with the hungry,
    to bring home the wretchedly poor,
  and when you see men underclad to clothe them,
    and not to neglect your own kin?

⁸ Then shall your light break through like the dawn
    and your healing speedily appear;
  your righteousness will go before you,
    and the glory of the Lord will be your rear guard.

⁹ Then, should you call, the Lord will respond;
    should you cry, he will say, I am here.
  Indeed, if you will banish servitude from among you,
    and the pointing finger and offensive speech,
¹⁰ if you will give of your own to the hungry
    and satisfy the needs of the oppressed,
  then shall your light dawn amid darkness
    and your twilight become as the noonday.

¹¹ The Lord will direct you continually;
    he will satisfy your needs in the dearth
    and bring vigor to your limbs.
  And you will become like a well-watered garden,
    like a spring of unfailing waters.
¹² They who came out of you will rebuild the ancient ruins;
    you will restore the foundations of generations ago.
  You shall be called a rebuilder of fallen walls,
    a restorer of streets for resettlement.

¹³ If you will keep your feet from *trampling* the Sabbath—
    from achieving your own ends on my holy day—
  and consider the Sabbath a delight,
    the holy *day* of the Lord venerable,
  and if you will honor it
    by refraining from your everyday pursuits—
  from occupying yourselves with your own affairs
    and speaking of *business* matters—

14 then shall you delight in the Lord,
  and I will make you traverse the heights of the earth
and nourish you with the heritage of Jacob your father.
  By his mouth the Lord has spoken it.

59 Surely the Lord's hand has not become too short to save,
  nor his ear dull of hearing!
2 It is your iniquities that separate you from your God;
  your sins hide his face, so that he does not hear you.
3 For your palms are defiled with blood,
  your fingers with iniquity;
your lips speak guile, your tongue utters duplicity.
4 None calls for righteousness;
  no one sues for an honest cause.
They rely on empty words, deceitfully spoken;
  they conceive misdeeds, they beget wickedness.

5 They hatch vipers' eggs and spin spiders' webs;
  whoever eats of their eggs dies,
  and if any is smashed, there emerges a serpent.
6 Their cobwebs are useless as clothing;
  their fabrications are worthless for covering themselves.
Their works consist of wrongdoing;
  they manipulate injurious dealings.

7 Their feet rush after evil;
  they hasten to shed innocent blood.
Their thoughts are preoccupied with mischief;
  havoc and disaster follow in their wake.
8 They are unacquainted with the way of perfection;
  integrity is not within their bounds.
They have made crooked their paths;
  none who treads them knows peace.

9 Therefore redress remains far from us
  and righteousness is unable to reach us.
We look for light, but there prevails darkness;
  for a glimmer *of hope*, but we walk amid gloom.
10 We grope along the borders like the blind;
  we flounder like those without eyes.
We stumble at noon as in the dark of night;
  in the prime of life we resemble the dead.

¹¹ We grumble like bears, all of us;
  we moan incessantly like doves.
We expect justice when there is none;
  we look for salvation, but it eludes us.

¹² For our transgressions before thee have multiplied;
  our sins testify against us.
Our offenses are evident; we perceive our iniquities:
¹³ willfully denying the Lord,
  backing away from following our God,
perversely planning ways of extortion,
  conceiving in the mind and pondering
  illicit transactions.
¹⁴ And so redress is compelled to back away,
  and righteousness to stand at a distance;
truth stumbles in the public place
  and uprightness cannot enter.

¹⁵ When integrity is lacking,
  they who shun evil become a prey.
The Lord saw that there was no justice,
  and it displeased him.
¹⁶ When he saw it, he wondered
  why there was no one, not one who would intervene.

So his own arm brought about salvation for him;
  his righteousness rallied to his cause.
¹⁷ He put on righteousness as a breastplate
  and made salvation the helmet on his head;
he clothed himself with vengeance for a garment
  and wrapped himself in fury as in a robe.
¹⁸ According to what they deserve, he will repay them:
  wrath upon his adversaries,
  reprisals upon his enemies;
to the isles he will render retribution.

¹⁹ From the West men will fear the Lord Omnipotent,ᵃ
  and from the rising of the sun his glory.
For he will come *upon them* like a hostile torrent
  impelled by the Spirit of the Lord.

ᵃ19 Literally, *the name of the Lord.*

20 But he will come as Redeemer to Zion,
   to those of Jacob who repent of transgression,
says the Lord.

21 As for me, this is my covenant with them, says the Lord: My
Spirit which is upon you and my words which I have placed in your
mouth shall not depart from your mouth, nor from the mouth of
your offspring, nor from the mouth of their offspring, says the Lord,
from now on and forever.

60 Arise, shine, your light has dawned;
   the glory of the Lord has risen upon you!
2 Although darkness covers the earth,
   and a thick mist the peoples,
upon you the Lord will shine;
   over you his glory shall be visible.
3 Nations will come to your light,
   their rulers to the brightness of your dawn.
4 Lift up your eyes and look about you!
   They have all assembled to come to you:
your sons shall arrive from afar;
   your daughters shall return to your side.

5 Then, when you see it, your face will light up,
   your heart swell with awe:
the multitude of the Sea shall resort to you;
   a host of nations shall enter you.
6 A myriad of camels shall cover *your land*,*
   the dromedaries of Midian and Ephah;
all from Sheba will come,
   bearing gold and frankincense
   and heralding the praises of the Lord.
7 All Kedar's flocks will gather to you,
   the rams of Nebaioth will serve you;
they shall be accepted as offerings on my altar,
   and thus I will make glorious my house of glory.

8 Who are these, aloft like clouds,
   flying as doves to their portals?

---

*6   Hebrew *you*.

⁹ From the isles they are gathering to me,
    the ships of Tarshish in the lead,
to bring back your children from afar,
    and with them their silver and gold,
to the Lord Omnipotent,*ᵇ* your God,
    to the Holy One of Israel,
who has made you illustrious.

¹⁰ Foreigners will rebuild your walls,
    and their rulers will minister to you.
Though I struck you in anger,
    I will gladly show you mercy.
¹¹ Your gates shall always remain open;
    they shall not be shut day or night,
that a host of nations may be brought to you
    and their rulers escorted in.
¹² And the nation or kingdom
    that will not serve you shall perish;
such nations shall be utterly ruined.

¹³ The splendor of Lebanon shall become yours—
    cypresses, pines, and firs together—
to beautify the site of my sanctuary,
    to make glorious the place of my feet.
¹⁴ The sons of those who tormented you
    will come bowing before you;
all who reviled you will prostrate themselves at your feet.
    They will call you The City of the Lord,
Zion of the Holy One of Israel.

¹⁵ Although you had been forsaken and abhorred,
    with none passing through *your land*,
yet I will make you an everlasting pride,
    the joy of generation after generation.
¹⁶ You will suck the milk of the nations,
    suckling at the breasts of rulers.
Then shall you know that I, the Lord,
    am your Savior,
that your Redeemer is the Valiant One of Jacob.

---

*ᵇ*9   Literally, *the name of the Lord.*

17 In place of copper I will bring gold,
    in place of iron, silver;
  in place of wood I will bring copper,
    in place of stones, iron.
  I will make peace your rulers
    and righteousness your oppressors:
18 tyranny shall no more be heard of in your land,
    nor dispossession or disaster within your borders;
  you will regard salvation as your walls
    and homage as your gates.

19 No longer shall the sun be your light by day,
    nor the brightness of the moon
    your illumination^c at night:
  the Lord will be your everlasting light
    and your God your radiant glory.
20 Your sun shall set no more,
    nor your moon wane:
  to you the Lord shall be an endless light
    when your days of mourning are fulfilled.

21 Your entire people shall be righteous;
    they shall inherit the earth forever—
  they are the branch I have planted,
    the work of my hands, in which I am glorified.
22 The least of them shall become a clan,
    the youngest a mighty nation.
  I the Lord will hasten it in its time.

61 The Spirit of my Lord the Lord is upon me,
    for the Lord has anointed me
  to announce good tidings to the lowly;
    he has sent me to bind up the brokenhearted,
  to proclaim liberty to the captives
    and the opening of the eyes to the bound,
2 to herald the year of the Lord's favor
    and the day of vengeance of our God,
  to comfort all who mourn:

---

^{c}19 So 1QIsa^a; LXX; term not in MT.

³ to endow those who mourn in Zion,
    bestowing upon them a priestly headpiece
    in place of ashes,
  the festal anointing in place of mourning,
    a resplendent robe in place of a downcast spirit.
  They shall be called oaks of righteousness
    planted by the Lord for his glory.

⁴ They will rebuild the ancient ruins,
    raise up the old waste places;
  they will renew the desolate cities
    demolished generations ago.
⁵ Aliens will tend and pasture your flocks;
    foreigners will be your farmhands and vinedressers.

⁶ But you shall be called the priests of the Lord
    and referred to as the ministers of our God.
  You shall feed on the wealth of the nations
    and be gratified with their choicest provision.
⁷ Because their* shame was twofold,
    and shouted insults were their lot,
  therefore in their land
    shall their inheritance be twofold
  and everlasting joy be theirs.

⁸ For I the Lord love just dealings—
    but I abhor extortion in *those who* sacrifice—
  and I will appoint them a sure reward;
    I will make with them an eternal covenant.
⁹ Their offspring shall be renowned among the nations,
    their posterity in the midst of the peoples;
  all who see them will acknowledge
    that they are of the lineage the Lord has blessed.

¹⁰ I rejoice exceedingly in the Lord;
    my soul delights in my God.
  For he clothes me in garments of salvation,
    he arrays me in a robe of righteousness—
  like a bridegroom dressed in priestly attire,
    or a bride adorned with her jewels.

---

*7 Hebrew *your.*

11 For as the earth brings forth its vegetation,
     and as a garden causes what is sown to spring up in it,
   so will my Lord the Lord
     cause righteousness and praise to spring up
   in the presence of all nations.

62

For Zion's sake I will not keep silent;
     for Jerusalem's sake I will not remain still
   till her righteousness shines like a light,
     her salvation like a flaming torch.
2 The nations shall behold your righteousness
     and all their rulers your glory;
   you shall be called by a new name
     conferred by the mouth of the Lord.

3 Then shall you be a crown of glory
     in the hand of the Lord,
   a royal diadem in the palm of your God.
4 You shall no more be called the forsaken one,
     nor your land referred to as desolate;
   you shall be known as she in whom I delight
     and your land considered espoused.
   For the Lord shall delight in you,
     and your land shall be espoused.
5 As a young man weds a virgin,
     so shall your sons wed you;
   as the bridegroom rejoices over the bride,
     so shall your God rejoice over you.

6 I have appointed watchmen on your walls, O Jerusalem,
     who shall not be silent day or night.
   You who call upon the Lord, let not up
     7 nor give him respite till he reestablishes Jerusalem
   and makes it renowned in the earth.

8 The Lord has sworn by his right hand, his mighty arm:
     I will no more let your grain be food for your enemies,
   nor shall foreigners drink the new wine you have toiled for.
9 Those who harvest it shall eat it,
     giving praise to the Lord;
   those who gather it shall drink it
     within the environs of my sanctuary.

¹⁰ Pass on, go through gates;
  prepare the way for the people!
Excavate, pave a highway cleared of stones;
  raise the ensign to the nations!
¹¹ The Lord has made proclamation to the end of the earth:
  Tell the Daughter of Zion,
See, your Salvation comes,
  his reward with him, his work preceding him.
¹² They shall be called the holy people,
  the redeemed of the Lord;
and you shall be known as in demand,
  a city never deserted.

63 Who is this coming from Edom in red-stained garments?
  Who is this from Bozrah, arrayed in majesty,
  pressing forward in the strength of his power?
It is I, who am mighty to save,
  announcing righteousness!

² Why are you clothed in red, your garments
  like those who tread *grapes* in the winepress?
³ Alone I have trodden out a vatful;
  of the nations no one was with me.
I trod them down in my anger;
  in my wrath I trampled them.
Their lifeblood spattered my garments,
  and I have stained my whole attire.

⁴ For I had resolved on a day of vengeance,
  and the year of my redeemed had come.

⁵ I glanced around, but none would lend help;
  I glared, but no one would assist.
So my own arm brought about salvation for me,
  and my wrath, it assisted me.
⁶ I trod nations underfoot in my anger;
  I made them drunk by my rage
when I cast their glory to the ground.

⁷ I will recount in praise of the Lord
  the Lord's loving favors,
according to all that the Lord has done for us,

according to the great kindness
he has mercifully and most graciously
rendered the house of Israel.

8 For he thought, Surely they are my people,
sons who will not play false;
and so he became their Savior:
9 with all their troubles he troubled himself,
the angel of his presence delivering them.
In his love and compassion
he himself redeemed them;
he lifted them up and carried them
all the days of old.
10 Yet they rebelled and grieved his holy Spirit,
till he became their enemy
and himself fought against them.

11 Then his people*a* recalled the days of Moses of old:*b*
Where is he who brought them up out of the Sea
with the shepherd of his flock?
Where is he who put into him his holy Spirit,
12 who made his glorious arm proceed
at the right hand of Moses,
who divided the waters before them,
making an everlasting name for himself
13 when he led them through the deep?
Like the horse of the desert, they stumbled not;
14 like cattle descending *the slopes of* ravines,
it was the Spirit of the Lord that guided them.*c*
So thou didst lead thy people, *O Lord*,
acquiring illustrious renown.

15 O look down from heaven,
from thy holy and glorious celestial abode,
and behold!
Where now are thy zeal and thy might?
The yearnings of thy bosom and thy compassion
are withheld from us!

---

*a*11 Term transposed; in text follows *Moses.*

*b*11 Literally, *of old, of Moses.*

*c*14 So LXX; MT *gave them rest.*

¹⁶ Surely thou art our Father!
    Though Abraham does not know us
    or Israel recognize us,
  thou, O Lord, art our Father;
    Our Redeemer from Eternity is thy name.

¹⁷ Why, O Lord, hast thou made us stray from thy ways,
    hardening our hearts so that we do not fear thee?
  Relent,*d* for the sake of thy servants,
    the tribes that are thine inheritance.
¹⁸ But a little while had thy people possessed the holy place
    when our enemies trod down thy sanctuary.
¹⁹ We have become as those
    whom thou hast never ruled
  and who have not been known by thy name.

64 O that thou wouldst rend the heavens and descend,
    the mountains melting at thy presence—
² as when fire is lit for boiling water,
    which bubbles over from the heat—
  to make thyself known to thine adversaries,
    the nations trembling at thy presence—
³ as when thou didst perform awesome things
    unexpected by us: thy descent *of old*,
    when the mountains quaked before thee!
⁴ Never has it been heard or perceived by the ear,
    nor has any eye seen a God besides thee,
  who acts thus on behalf of those who wait for him.

⁵ But thou woundest those of us
    who joyfully perform righteousness,
  who remember thee by *following* thy ways—
    *ᵃ*that in them we might ever be saved.*ᵃ*
  Alas, thou wast roused to anger when we sinned,
⁶ and now we have altogether become as those defiled,
    the sum of our righteousness as a menstruous rag.
  We are decaying like leaves, all of us;
    our sins, like a wind, sweep us away.

---

*d*17 Or, *Return.*
*a*5 Phrase transposed; in text follows *sinned.*

7 Yet none calls upon thy name,
　　or rouses himself to take hold of thee.
For thou hast hidden thy face from us
　　and enfeebled*b* us at the hand of our iniquities.
8 Nevertheless, thou art our Father, O Lord;
　　we are the clay and thou art the potter,
　　and we are all alike the work of thy hands.*c*
9 Be not exceedingly angry, O Lord;
　　remember not iniquity forever.
See, consider that we are all thy people!

10 Thy holy cities have become a wilderness;
　　Zion is a desert, Jerusalem a desolation.
11 Our glorious holy temple
　　where our fathers praised thee
has been burned with fire,
　　and all places dear to us lie in ruins.
12 At all this, O Lord, wilt thou restrain thyself,
　　in silence letting us suffer so exceedingly?

65

I was available to those who did not inquire of me;*a*
　　I was accessible to those who did not seek me.
I said, Here am I; I am here,
　　to a nation that did not invoke my name.

2 I held out my hands all the day to a defiant people,
　　who walk in ways that are not good,
　　following their own imagination—
3 a people who constantly provoke me to my face,
　　sacrificing in parks, making smoke upon bricks,
4 who sit in sepulchres, spend nights in hideouts,
　　who eat swine's flesh,
　　their bowls full of polluted broth,
5 who think, Keep your distance,
　　don't come near me; I am holier than you!
Such are a smoke to my nostrils,
　　a fire smoldering all day long.

---

*b*7　Literally, *melted*.
*c*8　So 1QIsa*a*; LXX. Compare 60:21; passim. MT *hand*.
*a*1　So 1QIsa*a*; LXX; term not in MT.

⁶ See, it is written before me that I will not be still
    till I have paid back*ᵇ* into their bosom
⁷ their*ᶜ* own iniquities and their*ᶜ* fathers' alike,
    says the Lord.
  To those who kindle sacrifice in the mountains,
    who affront me on the hills, I will measure out
    in their laps the payment that has accrued.

⁸ Thus says the Lord:
    As when there is juice in a cluster of grapes
  and someone says, Don't destroy it, it is still good,
    so I will do on behalf of my servants
    by not destroying everything:
⁹ I will extract offspring out of Jacob,
    and out of Judah heirs of my mountains;
  my chosen ones shall inherit them,
    my servants shall dwell there.
¹⁰ Sharon shall become pasture for flocks,
    and the Valley of Achor a resting place
  for the herds of my people who seek me.

¹¹ As for you who forsake the Lord
    and forget my holy mountain,
  who spread tables for Luck
    and pour mixed wines for Fortune,
¹² I will destine you to the sword;
    all of you shall succumb to the slaughter.
  For when I called, you did not respond;
    when I spoke, you would not give heed.
  You did what was evil in my eyes;
    you chose to do what was not my will.

¹³ Therefore thus says my Lord the Lord:
  My servants shall eat indeed,
    while you shall hunger;
  my servants shall drink indeed,
    while you shall thirst;
  my servants shall rejoice indeed,
    while you shall be dismayed.

---

*ᵇ*6   Text adds *and paid back,* a probable duplication.
*ᶜ*7, *ᶜ*7   So LXX; MT *your.*

14 My servants shall shout indeed, for gladness of heart,
    while you shall cry out with heartbreak,
    howling from brokenness of spirit.
15 Your name shall be left
    to serve my chosen ones as a curse
    when my Lord the Lord slays you.
But his servants he will call by a different name.

16 Those of them who invoke blessings
    on themselves in the earth shall do so by the true God,
    and those of them who swear oaths in the earth
    shall do so by the God of truth.
The troubles of the past shall be forgotten
    and hidden from my eyes.

17 See, I create new heavens and a new earth;
    former events shall not be remembered
    or recalled to mind.
18 Rejoice, then, and be glad forever in what I create.
See, I create Jerusalem to be a delight
    and its people a joy.

19 I will delight in Jerusalem, rejoice in my people;
    no more shall be heard there
    the sound of weeping or the cry of distress.
20 No more shall there be infants alive but a few days,
    or the aged who do not live out their years;
    those who die young shall be a hundred years old,
    and those who fail to reach a hundred shall be accursed.

21 When men build houses, they will dwell in them;
    when they plant vineyards, they will eat their fruit.
22 They shall not build so that others may dwell,
    or plant so that others may eat.
The lifetime of my people shall be as the lifetime of a tree;
    my chosen ones shall outlast the work of their hands.

23 They shall not exert themselves in vain,
    or bear children doomed for calamity.
For they are of the lineage of those blessed by the Lord,
    and their posterity with them.
24 Before they call I will reply;
    while they are yet speaking I will respond.

²⁵ The wolf and the lamb will graze alike,
    and the lion will eat straw like the ox;
as for the serpent, dust shall be its food:
    there shall be no harm or injury done
throughout my holy mountain, says the Lord.

66

Thus says the Lord:
    The heavens are my throne
and the earth is my footstool.
What house would you build me?
    What would serve me as a place of residence?
² These are all things my hand has made,
    and thus all came into being, says the Lord.
And yet I have regard for those
    who are of a humble and contrite spirit
and who are vigilant for my word.

³ But whoever slaughters an ox
    is as one who kills a man,
and whoever sacrifices a lamb,
    as one who breaks a dog's neck;
whoever presents a grain offering
    is as one who offers swine's blood,
and whoever burns incense,
    as one who venerates idols.
Just as they have preferred to go their own ways,
    their souls delighting in their abominations,
⁴ so will I prescribe intrigues for them
    and bring upon them the thing they dread.
For when I called, no one responded;
    when I spoke, none gave heed.
They did what was evil in my eyes;
    they chose to do what was not my will.

⁵ Hear the word of the Lord,
    you who are vigilant for his word:
Your brethren who abhor you,
    and exclude you because of my name, say,
Let the Lord manifest his glory,
    that we may see cause for your joy!
But it is they who shall suffer shame.

⁶ Hark, a tumult from the city, a noise from the temple!
It is the voice of the Lord
paying his enemies what is due them.

⁷ Before she is in labor, she gives birth;
before her ordeal overtakes her, she delivers a son!
⁸ Who has heard the like,
or who has seen such things?
Can the earth labor but a day
and a nation be born at once?
For as soon as she was in labor,
Zion gave birth to her children.
⁹ Shall I bring to a crisis and not bring on birth?
says the Lord.
When it is I who cause the birth,
shall I hinder it? says your God.

¹⁰ Rejoice with Jerusalem and be glad for her,
all who love her;
join in her celebration, all who mourn for her.
¹¹ From now on nurse contentedly
at her consoling breasts;
draw at your pleasure
from the abundance of her bosom.ᵃ

¹² For thus says the Lord: See,
I will extend peace to her like a river,
the bountyᵇ of the nations like a stream in flood.
Then shall you nurse and be carried upon the hip
and dandled on the knees.
¹³ As one who is comforted by his mother
I will comfort you;
for Jerusalem you shall be comforted.

¹⁴ Your heart shall rejoice to see it,
your limbs flourish like sprouting grass,
when the hand of the Lord
shall be manifest among his servants
and his rage among his enemies.

ᵃ11 Or, *glory.*
ᵇ12 Or, *glory.*

¹⁵ See, the Lord comes with fire,
    his chariots like a whirlwind,
  to retaliate in furious anger,
    to rebuke with conflagrations of fire.
¹⁶ For with fire and with his sword shall the Lord
    execute judgment on all flesh,
  and those slain by the Lord shall be many.

¹⁷ As for the cultists who fornicate in the parks, the devotees of those who are the center *of attraction*, who eat the flesh of swine and prawn and rodents—they with [their practices and ideas]ᶜ shall be made an end of, says the Lord.

¹⁸ For I will comeᵈ to gather all nations and tongues, that they may approach and behold my glory.

¹⁹ And I will set a mark upon them, sending those of them who survive to the nations that had not heard the news concerning me, nor seen my glory—to Tarshish, Pul, and Lud (the archers), to Tubal and Javan, and to the distant isles. And they shall declare my glory among the nations ²⁰ and shall bring back all your brethren from throughout the nations to Jerusalem my holy mountain, says the Lord, as offerings to the Lord—on horses, in chariots and wagons, and on mules and dromedaries—just as the Israelites brought offerings in pure vessels to the house of the Lord. ²¹ Of them likewise I will accept men to be priests and Levites, says the Lord.

²² And as the new heavens and the new earth which I make shall endure before me, says the Lord, so shall your offspring and name endure. ²³ And New Moon after New Moon, Sabbath after Sabbath, all flesh shall come to worship before me, says the Lord. ²⁴ And they shall go out and look upon the corpses of the people who transgressed against me, whose worms do not die and whose fire shall not be extinguished. They shall be a horror to all flesh.

ᶜ17 Terms brought up from verse 18, where they follow *For I.*
ᵈ18 Hebrew *bāʾâ, come* (fem. sing.), emended to *bāʾ*.

SELECTED REFERENCE WORKS

Alcalay, Reuben. *The Complete English—Hebrew, Hebrew—English Dictionary*. Jerusalem: Massada, 1970.

Biblia Hebraica. Ed. Rudolph Kittel. Stuttgart: Württembergische Bibelanstalt, 1973.

Botterweck, G. Johannes, and Helmer Ringgren. *Theological Dictionary of the Old Testament*. Grand Rapids, Mich.: Eerdmans, 1977.

Brown, Francis, S. R. Driver, and Charles A. Briggs. *A Hebrew and English Lexicon of the Old Testament*. Oxford: Clarendon Press, 1974.

Burrows, Millar. *The Dead Sea Scrolls of St. Mark's Monastery*. Vol. 1. New Haven, Conn.: American Schools of Oriental Research, 1950.

Even-Shoshan, Avraham. *Hamilon Hehadash*. 3 vols. Jerusalem: Sivan, 1975.

Guillaume, Alfred. "Some Readings in the Dead Sea Scroll of Isaiah." *Journal of Biblical Literature* 76 (1957): 40–43.

Hulst, A. R. *Old Testament Translation Problems*. Leiden, Netherlands: Brill, 1960.

Interpreter's Bible. Vol. 5. Nashville: Abingdon, 1956.

James, Forrest D. "A Critical Examination of the Text of Isaiah." Ph.D. diss., Boston University, 1959.

Mandelkern, Solomon. *Veteris Testamenti Concordantiae*. Tel Aviv: Schocken, 1974.

Rosenbloom, Joseph R. *The Dead Sea Isaiah Scroll: A Literary Analysis*. Grand Rapids, Mich.: Eerdmans, 1970.

Septuagint Version. Grand Rapids, Mich.: Zondervan, 1970.

Young, Robert. *Analytical Concordance to the Bible*. New York: Funk and Wagnall's, 1973.

INDEX OF TERMS

229